Sixth Edition

Book

The Humanistic Tradition

The European Renaissance,
the Reformation, and Global Encounter

Book

3

Sixth Edition

The Humanistic Tradition

The European Renaissance, the Reformation, and Global Encounter

Gloria K. Fiero

Connect
Learn
Succeed™

Boston   Burr Ridge, IL   Dubuque, IA   New York   San Francisco   St. Louis
Bangkok   Bogotá   Caracas   Kuala Lumpur   Lisbon   London   Madrid   Mexico City
Milan   Montreal   New Delhi   Santiago   Seoul   Singapore   Sydney   Taipei   Toronto

THE HUMANISTIC TRADITION, BOOK 3
THE EUROPEAN RENAISSANCE, THE REFORMATION,
AND GLOBAL ENCOUNTER

Published by McGraw-Hill, an imprint of The McGraw-Hill Companies, Inc.,
1221 Avenue of the Americas, New York, NY, 10020.

This book is printed on acid-free paper.

1 2 3 4 5 6 7 8 9 0 / 0

            Library of Congress Cataloging-in-Publication Data

Fiero, Gloria K.
    The humanistic tradition / Gloria K. Fiero.– 6th ed.
        p. cm.
    Includes bibliographical references and index.
    ISBN-13: 978-0-07-352397-2 (bk. 1 : alk. paper)
    ISBN-10: 0-07-352397-6 (bk. 1 : alk. paper)
        1. Civilization, Western–History–Textbooks.
        2. Humanism–History–Textbooks.
        I. Title.

    CB245.F47 2009
    909'.09821–dc22

                                                        2009027018

Permissions Acknowledgments appear on page 149,
and on this page by reference.

Publisher: *Chris Freitag*
Director of Development: *Rhona Robbin*
Associate Sponsoring Editor: *Betty Chen*
Editorial Coordinator: *Sarah Remington*
Marketing Manager: *Pamela Cooper*
Managing Editor: *David Staloch*
Senior Production Supervisor: *Tandra Jorgensen*
Typeface: *10/12 Goudy*
Printer: *Phoenix Offset, Hong Kong*

http://www.mhhe.com

 This book was designed and produced by
Laurence King Publishing Ltd., London
www.laurenceking.com

Commissioning Editor: *Kara Hattersley-Smith*
Senior Editor: *Melissa Danny*
Production Controller: *Simon Walsh*
Picture researcher: *Emma Brown*
Designer: *Robin Farrow*

Front cover
Jan Van Eyck, *Marriage of Giovanni Arnolfini
and His Bride* (detail), 1434. Tempera and
oil on panel, 32¼ x 23½ in. National
Gallery, London.

Back cover
Queen mother head, ca. 1500–1550. Brass,
height 15½ in. © The Trustees of the British
Museum.

Frontispiece
Gentile Bellini, *Procession of the Reliquary of
the Cross in Piazza San Marco* (detail), 1496.
Oil on canvas, 12 ft. ½ in. x 24 ft. 5¼ in.
Galleria dell'Accademia, Venice. ©
Cameraphoto Arte, Venice.

Series Contents

Book 3 Contents

Preface

Each generation leaves a creative legacy, the sum of its ideas and achievements. This legacy represents the response to our effort to ensure our individual and collective survival, our need to establish ways of living in harmony with others, and our desire to understand our place in the universe. Meeting the challenges of *survival, communality,* and *self-knowledge,* we have created and transmitted the tools of science and technology, social and political institutions, religious and philosophic systems, and various forms of personal expression—the totality of which we call *culture.* Handed down from generation to generation, this legacy constitutes the humanistic tradition, the study of which is called *humanities.*

The Humanistic Tradition originated more than two decades ago out of a desire to bring a global perspective to my humanities courses. My fellow humanities teachers and I recognized that a western-only perspective was no longer adequate to understanding the cultural foundations of our global world, yet none of the existing texts addressed our needs. At the time, the challenge was daunting—covering the history of western poetry and prose, art, music, and dance was already an ambitious undertaking for a survey course; how could we broaden the scope to include Asia, Africa, and the Americas without over-packing the course? What evolved was a thematic approach to humanities, not as a collection of disciplines, but as a discipline in itself. This thematic approach considers the interrelatedness of various forms of expression as they work to create, define, and reflect the unique culture of a given time and place. It offers a conceptual framework for students to begin a study of the humanistic tradition that will serve them throughout their lives. I am gratified that others have found this approach to be highly workable for their courses, so much so that *The Humanistic Tradition* has become a widely adopted book for the humanities course.

The Humanistic Tradition pioneered a flexible six-book format in recognition of the varying chronological range of humanities courses. Each slim volume was also convenient for students to bring to classes, the library, and other study areas. The sixth edition continues to be available in this six-book format, as well as in a two-volume set for the most common two-term course configuration.

The Sixth Edition of
The Humanistic Tradition

While the sixth edition of *The Humanistic Tradition* contains a number of new topics, images, and selections, it remains true to my original goal of offering a manageable and memorable introduction to global cultures. At the same time, I have worked to develop new features that are specifically designed to help students master the material and critically engage with the text's primary source readings, art

reproductions, and music recordings. The integration of literary, visual, and aural primary sources is a hallmark of the text, and every effort has been made to provide the most engaging translations, the clearest color images, and the liveliest recorded performances, as well as the most representative selections for every period. The book and companion supplements are designed to offer all of the resources a student and teacher will need for the course.

New Features that Promote Critical Thinking

New to the sixth edition are special features that emphasize connections between time periods, styles, and cultures, and specific issues of universal significance. These have been added to encourage critical thinking and classroom discussion.

- **Exploring Issues** focuses on controversial ideas and current debates, such as the battle over the ownership of antiquities, the role of the non-canonical Christian gospels, the use of optical devices in Renaissance art, the dating of African wood sculptures, and creationism versus evolution.
- **Making Connections** brings attention to contrasts and continuities between past and present ideas, values, and styles. Examples include feudalism East and West, Classical antiquities as models for Renaissance artists, and African culture as inspiration for African-American artists.

New Features that Facilitate Learning and Understanding

The sixth edition provides chapter introductions and summaries that enhance the student's grasp of the materials, and a number of features designed to make the materials more accessible to students:

- **Looking Ahead** offers a brief, preliminary overview that introduces students to the main theme of the chapter.
- **Looking Back** closes each chapter with summary study points that encourage students to review key ideas.
- **Iconographic "keys"** to the meaning of images have been inset alongside selected artworks.
- **Extended captions** to illustrations throughout the text provide additional information about artworks and artists.
- **Chronology boxes** in individual chapters place the arts and ideas in historical background.
- **Before We Begin** precedes the Introduction with a useful guide to understanding and studying humanities.

Organizational Improvements and Updated Content

The sixth edition responds to teachers' requests that the coverage of Mesopotamia precede Egypt and other ancient African cultures in the opening chapters. The global coverage has been refined with revised coverage of the early Americas, new content on archeological discoveries in ancient Peru, a segment on the role of the West in the Islamic Middle East, and a discussion of China's global ascendance. Chapters 36 through 38 have been updated and reorganized: Ethnicity and ethnic identity have been moved to chapter 38 (Globalism and the Contemporary World), which brings emphasis to recent developments in digital technology, environmentalism, and global terrorism. Other revisions throughout the text also respond to teacher feedback; for example, a description of the *bel canto* style in music has been added; Jan van Eyck's paintings appear in both chapters 17 and 19 (in different contexts); and T. S. Eliot's works are discussed in both chapters 32 and 35.

Among the notable writers added to the sixth edition are William Blake, Jorge Luis Borges, Seamus Heaney, and John Ashbury. New additions to the art program include works by Benozzo Gozzoli, Buckminster Fuller, Kara Walker, Jeff Wall, Damien Hirst, El Anatsui, and Norman Foster.

Beyond *The Humanistic Tradition*

Connect Humanities

Connect Humanities is a learning and assessment tool designed and developed to improve students' performance by making the learning process more efficient and more focused through the use of engaging, assignable content, which is text-specific and mapped to learning objectives, and integrated tools. Using this platform, instructors can deliver assignments easily online, and save time through an intuitive and easy to use interface and through modifiable pre-built assignments.

Connect provides instructors with the Image Bank, a way to easily browse and search for images and to download them for use in class presentations.

Visit mcgrawhillconnect.com

Traditions: Humanities Readings through the Ages

Traditions is a new database conceived as both a stand-alone product as well as a companion source to McGraw-Hill's humanities titles. The collection is broad in nature, containing both western and non-western readings from ancient and contemporary eras, hand-picked from such disciplines as literature, philosophy, and science. The flexibility of Primis Online's database allows the readings to be arranged both chronologically and by author.

Visit www.primisonline.com/traditions

Music Listening Compact Discs

Two audio compact discs have been designed exclusively for use with *The Humanistic Tradition*. CD One corresponds to the music listening selections discussed in Books 1–3 (Volume I), and CD Two contains the music in Books 4–6 (Volume II). Music logos (right) that appear in the margins of the text refer to the Music Listening Selections found on the audio compact discs. The compact discs can be packaged with any or all of the six books or two-volume versions of the text.

Online Learning Center

A complete set of web-based resources for *The Humanistic Tradition* can be found at

www.mhhe.com/fierotht6e

Materials for students include an audio pronunciation guide, a timeline, research and writing tools, links to select readings, and suggested readings and Web sites. The instructor side of the Online Learning Center includes discussion and lecture suggestions, music listening guides, key themes and topics, and study questions for student discussion and review and written assignments.

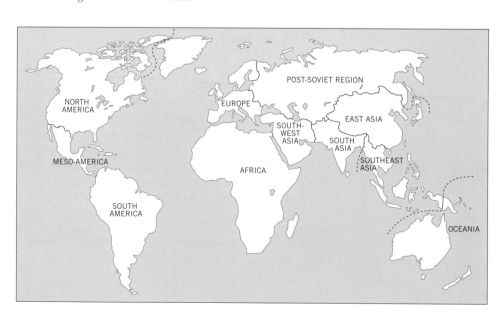

Key map indicating areas shown as white highlights on the locator maps

Acknowledgments

Personal thanks go to my discerning editor, Betty Chen (McGraw-Hill), and to the editorial and production staff of Laurence King Publishing. As with former editions, my colleague and husband, James H. Dormon, read all parts of the manuscript and made substantive editorial suggestions. This edition is dedicated to him. I am also grateful to Eric C. Shiner (curator and art historian) for his assistance in contemporary Asian art.

In the preparation of the sixth edition, I have benefited from the suggestions and comments generously offered by Donald F. Andrews (Chattanooga State Technical Community College), Samuel Barnett (University of Maryland), Bobbie Bell (Seminole Community College), Marjorie Berman (Red Rocks Community College), Terri Birch (Harper College), Pat Bivin (International Academy of Design and Technology), Casey Blanton (Daytona Beach Community College), Diane Boze (Northeastern State University), Nellie Brannan (Brevard Community College), Diane S. Brown (Valencia Community College, Osceola), Joyce Caldwell Smith (University of Tennessee at Chattanooga), Cynthia Clegg (Pepperdine University), Harry S. Coverston (University of Central Florida), Julie deGraffenried (Baylor University), Ann Dunn (University of North Carolina, Asheville), Renae Edge (Norwalk Community College), Monika Fleming (Edgecombe Community College), A. Flowers (College of Alameda), Rod Freeman (Estrella Mountain College), Arby L. Frost (Roanoke College), Samuel Garren (North Carolina A&T University), Caryl Gibbs (Rose State College), Robin Hardee (Santa Fe College), Melissa T. Hause (Belhaven College), Barbara A. Hergianto (South Florida Community College), Dale Hoover (Edison College), Ron Israel (San Diego Mesa College), Marian Jacobson (Albany College of Pharmacy), Theresa James (South Florida Community College), Judith Jamieson (Providence College), Keith W. Jensen (William Rainey Harper College), Jerry Jerman (University of Oklahoma), Patrick Kiley (Marian College), Donald Koke (Butler County College), Jayson Larremore (Oral Roberts University), Bonnie Loss (Glendale Community College), Diana Lurz (Rogers State University), Eldonna Loraine May (Wayne State University), Barbara J. Mayo (Northeast Lakeview College), Susan McClung (Hillsborough Community College), Trudy McNair (Valencia Community College), Richard Middleton-Kaplan (Harper College), Yvonne J. Milspaw (Harrisburg Area Community College), Maureen Moore (Cosumnes River College), Sean P. Murphy (College of Lake County), Judy Navas (Sonoma State University), Jack L. Nawrocik (St. Philip's College), James Norwood (University of Minnesota), Craig Payne (Indian Hills College), Randall M. Payne (South Florida Community College), Laurel S. Peterson (Norwalk Community College), Richard W. Peyton (Florida Agricultural and Mechanical University), Anne L. Pierce (Hampton University), William H. Porterfield (West Virginia State Community & Technical College), Judith Poxon (Sacramento City College), Robin Poynor (University of Florida), Verbie Lovorn Prevost (University of Tennessee at Chattanooga), Andreas W. Reif (Southern New Hampshire University), Denise M. Rogers (University of Louisiana at Lafayette), Karen Rumbley (Valencia Community College), Maria Rybakova (San Diego State University), John Scolaro (Valencia Community College), Vanessa Sheldon (College of the Desert), Mary Slater (Missouri Valley College), Linda Spain (Linn-Benton Community College), Hartley S. Spatt (SUNY Maritime College), Lisa Stokes (Seminole Community College), Alice Taylor (West Los Angeles College), Andreia Thaxton (Florida Community College at Jacksonville), Randall K. Van Schepen (Roger Williams University), Andrew Vassar (Northeastern State University), John Michael Vohlidka (Gannon University), Laura Wadenpfuhl (New Jersey City College), John R. Webb (Highland Community College), Jason Whitmarsh (Florida State College at Jacksonville), and Linda Woodward (Lone Star Montgomery College).

—Gloria K. Fiero

BEFORE WE BEGIN

Studying humanities engages us in a dialogue with *primary sources*: works original to the age in which they were produced. Whether literary, visual, or aural, a primary source is a text; the time, place, and circumstances in which it was created constitute the context; and its various underlying meanings provide the subtext. Studying humanities from the perspective of text, context, and subtext helps us understand our cultural legacy and our place in the larger world.

Text

The *text* of a primary source refers to its medium (that is, what it is made of), its form (its outward shape), and its content (the subject it describes).

Literature: Literary form varies according to the manner in which words are arranged. So, *poetry*, which shares rhythmic organization with music and dance, is distinguished from *prose*, which normally lacks regular rhythmic patterns. Poetry, by its freedom from conventional grammar, provides unique opportunities for the expression of intense emotions. Prose usually functions to convey information, to narrate, and to describe.

Philosophy, (the search for truth through reasoned analysis), and *history* (the record of the past) make use of prose to analyze and communicate ideas and information.

In literature, as in most forms of expression, content and form are usually interrelated. The subject matter or form of a literary work determines its *genre*. For instance, a long narrative poem recounting the adventures of a hero constitutes an *epic*, while a formal, dignified speech in praise of a person or thing constitutes a *eulogy*.

The Visual Arts: The visual arts employ a wide variety of media, ranging from the traditional colored pigments used in painting, to wood, clay, marble, and (more recently) plastic and neon used in sculpture, to a wide variety of digital media, including photography and film. The form or outward shape of a work of art depends on the manner in which the artist manipulates the elements of color, line, texture, and space. Unlike words, these formal elements lack denotative meaning.

The visual arts are dominantly spatial, that is, they operate and are apprehended in space. Artists manipulate form to describe or interpret the visible world (as in the genres of portraiture and landscape), or to create worlds of fantasy and imagination. They may also fabricate texts that are non-representational, that is, without identifiable subject matter.

Music and Dance: The medium of music is sound. Like literature, music is durational: it unfolds over the period of time in which it occurs. The major elements of music are melody, rhythm, harmony, and tone color—formal elements that also characterize the oral life of literature.

However, while literary and visual texts are usually descriptive, music is almost always nonrepresentational: it rarely has meaning beyond sound itself. For that reason, music is the most difficult of the arts to describe in words.

Dance, the artform that makes the human body itself the medium of expression, resembles music in that it is temporal and performance-oriented. Like music, dance exploits rhythm as a formal tool, and like painting and sculpture, it unfolds in space as well as in time.

Studying the text, we discover the ways in which the artist manipulates medium and form to achieve a characteristic manner of execution or expression that we call *style*. Comparing the styles of various texts from a single era, we discover that they usually share certain defining features and characteristics. Similarities between, for instance, ancient Greek temples and Greek tragedies, or between Chinese lyric poems and landscape paintings, reveal the unifying moral and aesthetic values of their respective cultures.

Context

The *context* describes the historical and cultural environment of a text. Understanding the relationship between text and context is one of the principal concerns of any inquiry into the humanistic tradition. To determine the context, we ask: In what time and place did our primary source originate? How did it function within the society in which it was created? Was it primarily decorative, didactic, magical, or propagandistic? Did it serve the religious or political needs of the community? Sometimes our answers to these questions are mere guesses. For instance, the paintings on the walls of Paleolithic caves were probably not "artworks" in the modern sense of the term, but, rather, magical signs associated with religious rituals performed in the interest of communal survival.

Determining the function of the text often serves to clarify the nature of its form, and vice-versa. For instance, in that the Hebrew Bible, the *Song of Roland*, and many other early literary works were spoken or sung, rather than read, such literature tends to feature repetition and rhyme, devices that facilitate memorization and oral delivery.

Subtext

The *subtext* of a primary source refers to its secondary or implied meanings. The subtext discloses conceptual messages embedded in or implied by the text. The epic poems of the ancient Greeks, for instance, which glorify prowess and physical courage, suggest an exclusively male perception of virtue. The state portraits of the seventeenth-century French king Louis XIV bear the subtext of unassailable and absolute power. In our own time, Andy Warhol's serial adaptations of Coca-Cola bottles offer wry commentary on the commercial mentality of American society. Examining the implicit message of the text helps us determine the values of the age in which it was produced, and offers insights into our own.

Chapter
15

Adversity and Challenge: The Fourteenth-Century Transition

ca. 1300–1400

"So many bodies were brought to the churches every day that the consecrated ground did not suffice to hold them . . ."
Boccaccio

Figure 15.1 GIOTTO, *Lamentation*, 1305–1306. Fresco, 7 ft. 7 in. × 7 ft. 9 in. In one of the most moving frescoes from the Arena Chapel, Giotto has transformed a traditional episode from the Passion of Christ into a theatrical drama. His staging of the event reflects the trend toward realistic representation that marks the fourteenth century.

LOOKING AHEAD

The fourteenth century brought Western Europe out of the Middle Ages and into the early Modern Era. Three cataclysmic events wrenched medieval customs and practices out of their steady, dependable rhythms, radically altering all aspects of life and cultural expression: a long and debilitating war between England and France, the Avignon Papacy and Great Schism, and the ensuing decline of the Roman Catholic Church, and the persistent struggle for survival against the onslaught of the bubonic plague. In economic life, manorialism slowly gave way to entrepreneurial capitalism. In political life, the feudal hierarchy was replaced by centralized forms of government among rising nation-states. In the arts, there were distinct signs of a revitalized self-consciousness, increasing fidelity to nature, and a growing attention to gender and class. The cultural developments of this transitional century would come to shape a modern world-system dominated by the West.

Europe in Transition

The Hundred Years' War

The feudal histories of France and England provided the context for a war (more accurately a series of wars) that would last for more than 100 years (1337–1453). Larger and more protracted than any medieval conflict, the Hundred Years' War was the result of the long-standing English claim to continental lands held by the Norman rulers of England, whose ancestors were vassals of the French king. French efforts to wrest these feudal territories from English hands ignited decades of hostility and chronic resentment between the two burgeoning nation-states. But the immediate cause of the war was the English claim to the French throne, occasioned by the death of Charles IV (1294–1328), the last of the male heirs in a long line of French kings that had begun with Hugh Capet in 987.

The war that began in 1337 was marked by intermittent battles, in many of which the French outnumbered the English by three or four to one. Nevertheless, the English won most of the early battles of the war, owing to their use of three new "secret" weapons: the foot soldier, the longbow, and gunpowder—the invisible enemy that would ultimately eliminate the personal element in military combat. Along with the traditional cavalry, the English army depended heavily on foot soldiers armed with longbows (Figure 15.2). The thin, steel-tipped arrows of the 6-foot longbow could be fired more quickly and at a longer range than those of the traditional crossbow. Because the thin arrows of the longbow easily pierced the finest French chain mail, plate mail soon came to replace chain mail. However, within the next few centuries, even plate mail

Science and Technology

1300	eyeglasses come into use in Europe
1310	mechanical clocks appear in Europe
1346	gunpowder and longbows are utilized by the English army at the Battle of Crécy
1370	the steel crossbow is adopted as a weapon of war
1377	the first quarantine station for plague victims is established in Ragusa (modern-day Dubrovnik)

became obsolete, since it proved useless against artillery that employed gunpowder.

Introduced into Europe by the Muslims, who acquired it from the Chinese, gunpowder was first used in Western combat during the Hundred Years' War. In the first battle of the war, however, the incendiary substance proved too potent for the poorly cast English cannons, which issued little more than terrifying noise. Still, gunpowder, which could lay waste a city, constituted an extraordinary advance in military technology.

Throughout the Hundred Years' War the English repeatedly devastated the French armies; nevertheless, the financial and physical burdens of garrisoning French lands ultimately proved too great for the English. Facing a revitalized army under the charismatic leadership of Joan of Arc, England finally withdrew from France in 1450. Of peasant background, the sixteen-year-old Joan begged the French king to allow her to obey the voices of the Christian saints who had directed her to expel the English (Figure 15.3). Donning armor and riding a white horse, she led the French into battle. Her success forced the English to withdraw from Orléans, but initiated her martyrdom. Betrayed by her supporters in 1431, she was condemned as a heretic and burned at the stake.

The Hundred Years' War dealt a major blow to feudalism. The use of gunpowder and the longbow, which put physical distance between combatants, worked to outmode hand-to-hand combat, thus rendering obsolete the medieval code of chivalry. Further, because the French were greatly outnumbered by the English, they resorted to ambush, a tactic that violated the "rules" of feudal warfare. While contemporary literary accounts of the war glorified the performance of chivalric deeds, the new military tactics clearly inaugurated the impersonal style of combat that has come to dominate modern warfare.

By the mid-fifteenth century, the French nobility was badly depleted, and those knights who survived the war found themselves "outdated." In France, feudal allegiances were soon superseded by systems of national conscription. The English Parliament, which had met frequently during the war in order to raise taxes for repeated military campaigns, used the opportunity this provided to bargain for greater power, including the right to initiate legislation. By the end of the fourteenth century, the English had laid the groundwork for a constitutional monarchy that

Figure 15.2 *The End of the Siege of Ribodane: English Soldiers Take a French Town*, late fifteenth century. Manuscript illumination. Wooden siege machines like that on the left, cannons, and longbows gave the English great advantages in attacking French towns. The miniature also shows the heavy plate mail worn by buth the French and the English.

Figure 15.3 Joan of Arc, from **ANTOINE DUFOUR'S** *Lives of Famous Women*, 1504. French manuscript. Almost immediately after her death, the so-called Maid of Orléans became the national heroine of France. She was declared a martyr in 1455. While she has become a semilegendary figure, numerous transcripts of her trial (recovered in the nineteenth century) attest to her strong personality

bridged the gap between medieval feudalism and modern democracy. In the decades following the war, England and France were ready to move in separate directions, politically and culturally.

The Decline of the Church

The growth of the European nation-states contributed to the weakening of the Christian commonwealth, especially where Church and state competed for influence and authority. The two events that proved most damaging to the prestige of the Catholic Church were the Avignon Papacy (1309–1377) and the Great Schism (1378–1417). The term "Avignon Papacy" describes the relocation of the papacy from Rome to the city of Avignon in southern France (see Map 16.1) in response to political pressure from the French king Philip IV ("the Fair"). Attempting to compete in prestige and political influence with the secular rulers of Europe, the Avignon popes established a luxurious and powerful court, using stringent (and occasionally corrupt) means to accomplish their purpose. The increasing need for church revenue led some of the Avignon popes to sell church offices (a practice known as **simony**), to levy additional taxes upon clergymen, to elect members of their own families to ecclesiastical office, and to step up the sale of **indulgences** (pardons from temporal penalties for sins committed by lay Christians). From the twelfth century on, the Church had sold these certificates of grace—drawn from the "surplus" of good works left by the saints—to lay Christians who bought them as a means of speeding their own progress to Heaven or to benefit their relatives and friends in Purgatory. While the seven popes who ruled from Avignon were able administrators, their unsavory efforts at financial and political aggrandizement damaged the reputation of the Church.

The return of the papacy to Rome in 1377 was followed by one of the most devastating events in church history: a rift between French and Italian factions of the College of Cardinals led to the election of two popes, one who ruled from Avignon, the other from Rome. This schism produced two conflicting claims to universal sovereignty and violent controversy within the Church. As each pope excommunicated the other, lay people questioned whether any Christian soul might enter Heaven. The Great Schism proved even more detrimental to church prestige than the Avignon Papacy, for while the latter had prompted strong anticlerical feelings—even shock—in Christians who regarded Rome as the traditional home of the papacy, the schism violated the very sanctity of the Holy Office. The ecumenical council at Pisa in 1409 tried to remedy matters by deposing both popes and electing another (the "Pisan pope"), but, when the popes at Rome and Avignon refused to step down, the Church was rent by *three* claims to the throne of Christ, a disgraceful situation that lasted for almost a decade.

Anticlericalism and the Rise of Devotional Piety

In 1417, the Council of Constance healed the schism, authorizing Pope Martin V to rule from Rome, but ecclesiastical discord continued. Fifteenth-century popes refused to acknowledge limits to papal power, thus hampering the efforts of church councils to exercise authority over the papacy. The Avignon Papacy and the Great Schism drew criticism from uneducated Christians and intellectuals alike. Two of the most vocal church critics were the Oxford scholar John Wycliffe (ca. 1330–1384) and the Czech preacher Jan Hus (ca. 1373–1415). Wycliffe and Hus attacked papal power and wealth. They called for the abolition of pilgrimages and relic worship, insisting that Christian belief and practice must rest solidly in the Scriptures, which they sought to translate into the vernacular. The Church vigorously condemned Wycliffe and his bands of followers, who were called Lollards. Hus stood trial for heresy and was burned at the stake in 1415. Disenchanted with the institutional Church, lay Christians increasingly turned to private forms of devotional piety and to mysticism—the effort to know God directly and intuitively.

Popular mysticism challenged the authority of the institutional Church and threatened its corporate hold over Catholicism. Throughout the Middle Ages, mystics—many of whom came from the cloister—had voiced their passionate commitment to Christ. The twelfth-century mystic Hildegard of Bingen (see chapter 12), whose visionary interpretations of Scripture were intensely personal, received the approval of the institutional Church. By the thirteenth century, however, as churchmen sought to centralize authority in the hands of male ecclesiastics, visionary literature was looked upon with some suspicion. The Church condemned

the lyrical descriptions of divine love penned by the thirteenth-century mystic Marguerite of Porete, for instance, and Marguerite herself was burned at the stake in 1310. Nonetheless, during the fourteenth century a flood of mystical and devotional literature engulfed Europe. The writings of the great fourteenth-century German mystics Johannes Eckhart (ca. 1260– 1327) and Heinrich Suso, of the English Julian of Norwich (1342–ca. 1416), and of the Swedish Saint Bridget (ca. 1303–1373) describe—in language that is at once intimate and ecstatic—the heightened personal experience of God. Such writings—the expression of pious individualism—mark an important shift from the Scholastic reliance on religious authority to modern assertions of faith based on inner conviction.

The Black Death

While warfare, religious turmoil, and peasant unrest brought havoc to fourteenth century Europe, their effects were compounded by a devastating natural catastrophe: the bubonic plague struck Europe in 1347, destroying 50 percent of its population within less than a century. Originating in Asia and spread by the Mongol tribes that dominated that vast area, the disease devastated China and the Middle East, interrupting long-distance trade and cross-cultural encounters that had flourished for two centuries. The plague was carried into Europe by flea-bearing black rats infesting the commercial vessels that brought goods to Mediterranean ports. Within two years of its arrival it ravaged much of the Western world. In its early stages, it was transmitted by the bite of either the infected flea or the host rat; in its more severe stages, it was passed on by those infected with the disease. The symptoms of the malady were terrifying: buboes (or abscesses) that began in the lymph glands of the groin or armpits of the afflicted slowly filled with pus, turning the body a deathly black, hence the popular label "the Black Death." Once the boils and accompanying fever appeared, death usually followed within two to three days. Traditional treatments, such as the bleeding of victims and fumigation with vapors of vinegar, proved useless. No connection was perceived between the ubiquitous rats and the plague itself, and in the absence of a clinical understanding of bacterial infection, the medical profession of the day was helpless. (The bacillus of the bubonic plague was not isolated until 1894.)

The plague hit hardest in the towns, where the concentration of population and the lack of sanitation made the infestation all the more difficult to contain. Four waves of bubonic plague spread throughout Europe between 1347 and 1375, attacking some European cities several times and nearly wiping out their entire populations (Figure **15.4**). The virulence of the plague and the mood of mounting despair horrified the Florentine writer Giovanni Boccaccio (1313–1375). In his preface to the *Decameron*, a collection of tales told by ten young people who abandoned plague-ridden Florence for the safety of a country estate, Boccaccio described the physical conditions of the pestilence, as well as its psychological consequences. He recorded with somber precision how

Figure 15.4 *The Black Death*, miniature from a rhymed Latin chronicle of the events of 1349–1352 by Egidius, abbot of Saint Martin's, Tournai, France, ca. 1355. Manuscript illumination.

widespread death had forced Florentine citizens to abandon the traditional forms of grieving and forego the age-old rituals associated with death and burial. Boccaccio's stirring vernacular prose captured the mood of dread that prevailed in Florence, as people fled their cities, homes, and even their families.

READING 15.1 From Boccaccio's Introduction to the *Decameron* (1351)

In the year of Our Lord 1348 the deadly plague broke 1
out in the great city of Florence, most beautiful of Italian
cities. Whether through the operation of the heavenly
bodies or because of our own iniquities which the just
wrath of God sought to correct, the plague had arisen in
the East some years before, causing the death of
countless human beings. It spread without stop from one
place to another, until, unfortunately, it swept over the
West. Neither knowledge nor human foresight availed
against it, though the city was cleansed of much filth by 10
chosen officers in charge and sick persons were forbidden
to enter it, while advice was broadcast for the
preservation of health. Nor did humble supplications
serve. Not once but many times they were ordained in the
form of processions and other ways for the propitiation of
God by the faithful, but, in spite of everything, toward the
spring of the year the plague began to show its ravages in
a way short of miraculous.

It did not manifest itself as in the East, where if a man
bled at the nose he had certain warning of inevitable 20
death. At the onset of the disease both men and women
were afflicted by a sort of swelling in the groin or under
the armpits which sometimes attained the size of a
common apple or egg. Some of these swellings were
larger and some smaller, and all were commonly called
boils. From these two starting points the boils began in a
little while to spread and appear generally all over the
body. Afterwards, the manifestation of the disease
changed into black or livid spots on the arms, thighs and
the whole person. In many these blotches were large and 30
far apart, in others small and closely clustered. Like the
boils, which had been and continued to be a certain
indication of coming death, these blotches had the same
meaning for everyone on whom they appeared.

Neither the advice of physicians nor the virtue of any
medicine seemed to help or avail in the cure of these
diseases. Indeed, whether the nature of the malady did
not suffer it, or whether the ignorance of the physicians
could not determine the source and therefore could take
no preventive measures against it, the fact was that not 40
only did few recover, but on the contrary almost everyone
died within three days of the appearance of the signs—
some sooner, some later, and the majority without fever or
other ill. Moreover, besides the qualified medical men, a
vast number of quacks, both men and women, who had
never studied medicine, joined the ranks and practiced
cures. The virulence of the plague was all the greater in
that it was communicated by the sick to the well by
contact, not unlike fire when dry or fatty things are
brought near it. But the evil was still worse. Not only did 50
conversation and familiarity with the diseased spread the
malady and even cause death, but the mere touch of the

clothes or any other object the sick had touched or used, seemed to spread the pestilence. . . .

Because of such happenings and many others of a like sort, various fears and superstitions arose among the survivors, almost all of which tended toward one end—to flee from the sick and whatever had belonged to them. In this way each man thought to be safeguarding his own health. Some among them were of the opinion that by living temperately and guarding against excess of all kinds, they could do much toward avoiding the danger; and forming a band they lived away from the rest of the world. Gathering in those houses where no one had been ill and living was more comfortable, they shut themselves in. They ate moderately of the best that could be had and drank excellent wines, avoiding all luxuriousness. With music and whatever other delights they could have, they lived together in this fashion, allowing no one to speak to them and avoiding news either of death or sickness from the outer world.

Others, arriving at a contrary conclusion, held that plenty of drinking and enjoyment, singing and free living and the gratification of the appetite in every possible way, letting the devil take the hindmost, was the best preventative of such a malady; and as far as they could, they suited the action to the word. Day and night they went from one tavern to another drinking and carousing unrestrainedly. At the least inkling of something that suited them, they ran wild in other people's houses, and there was no one to prevent them, for everyone had abandoned all responsibility for his belongings as well as for himself, considering his days numbered. Consequently most of the houses had become common property and strangers would make use of them at will whenever they came upon them even as the rightful owners might have done. Following this uncharitable way of thinking, they did their best to run away from the infected.

Meanwhile, in the midst of the affliction and misery that had befallen the city, even the reverend authority of divine and human law had almost crumbled and fallen into decay, for its ministers and executors, like other men, had either died or sickened, or had been left so entirely without assistants that they were unable to attend to their duties. As a result everyone had leave to do as he saw fit.

[Others, in an effort to escape the plague, abandoned the city, their houses, their possessions, and their relatives.] The calamity had instilled such horror into the hearts of men and women that brother abandoned brother, uncles, sisters and wives left their dear ones to perish, and, what is more serious and almost incredible, parents avoided visiting or nursing their very children, as though these were not their own flesh. . . . So great was the multitude of those who died in the city night and day, what with lack of proper care and the virulence of the plague, that it was terrible to hear of, and worse still to see. Out of sheer necessity, therefore, quite different customs arose among the survivors from the original laws of the townspeople.

It used to be common, as it is still, for women, friends and neighbors of a dead man, to gather in his house and mourn there with his people, while his men friends and many other citizens collected with his nearest of kin outside the door. Then came the clergy, according to the standing of the departed, and with funereal pomp of tapers and singing he was carried on the shoulders of his peers to the church he had elected before death. Now, as the plague gained in violence, these customs were either modified or laid aside altogether, and new ones were instituted in their place, so that, far from dying among a crowd of women mourners, many passed away without the benefit of a single witness. Indeed, few were those who received the piteous wails and bitter tears of friends and relatives, for often, instead of mourning, laughter, jest and carousal accompanied the dead—usages which even naturally compassionate women had learned to perfection for their health's sake. It was a rare occurrence for a corpse to be followed to church by more than ten or twelve mourners—not the usual respectable citizens, but a class of vulgar grave-diggers who called themselves "sextons" and did these services for a price. They crept under the bier and shouldered it, and then with hasty steps rushed it, not to the church the deceased had designated before death, but oftener than not to the nearest one. . . .

More wretched still were the circumstances of the common people and, for a great part, of the middle class, for, confined to their homes either by hope of safety or by poverty, and restricted to their own sections, they fell sick daily by thousands. There, devoid of help or care, they died almost without redemption. A great many breathed their last in the public streets, day and night; a large number perished in their homes, and it was only by the stench of their decaying bodies that they proclaimed their death to their neighbors. Everywhere the city was teeming with corpses. A general course was now adopted by the people, more out of fear of contagion than of any charity they felt toward the dead. Alone, or with the assistance of whatever bearers they could muster, they would drag the corpses out of their homes and pile them in front of the doors, where often, of a morning, countless bodies might be seen. Biers were sent for. When none was to be had, the dead were laid upon ordinary boards, two or three at once. It was not infrequent to see a single bier carrying husband and wife, two or three brothers, father and son, and others besides. . . .

So many bodies were brought to the churches every day that the consecrated ground did not suffice to hold them, particularly according to the ancient custom of giving each corpse its individual place. Huge trenches were dug in the crowded churchyards and the new dead were piled in them, layer upon layer, like merchandise in the hold of a ship. A little earth covered the corpses of each row, and the procedure continued until the trench was filled to the top.

Q **What aspects of Boccaccio's Introduction to the _Decameron_ reflect a shift to Realism in prose literature?**

Q **Are there any modern analogies to the pandemic that Boccaccio describes?**

The Effects of the Black Death

Those who survived the plague tried to fathom its meaning and purpose. Some viewed it as the manifestation of God's displeasure with the growing worldliness of contemporary society, while others saw it as a divine warning to all Christians, but especially to the clergy, whose profligacy and moral laxity were commonly acknowledged facts. Those who perceived the plague as God's scourge urged a return to religious orthodoxy; some endorsed fanatic kinds of atonement. Groups of flagellants, for instance, wandered the countryside lashing their bodies with whips in frenzies of self-mortification. At the other extreme, there were many who resolved to "eat, drink, and be merry" in what might be the last hours of their lives. Still others, in a spirit of doubt and inquiry, questioned the very existence of a god who could work such evils on humankind.

The abandonment of the church-directed rituals of funeral and burial described by Boccaccio threatened tradition and shook the confidence of medieval Christians. Inevitably, the old medieval regard for death as a welcome release from earthly existence began to give way to a gnawing sense of anxiety and a new self-consciousness. Some of these changes are mirrored in the abundance of death-related pictorial images, including purgatorial visions and gruesome depictions of death and burial. Of all the plague-related themes depicted in the arts, the most popular was the "Dance of Death," or *danse macabre*. Set forth in both poetry and the visual arts, the Dance of Death portrayed death as a grinning skeleton or cadaver shepherding a procession of his victims to the grave (Figure **15.5**).

In the medieval morality play *Everyman* (see chapter 12), Death is a powerful antagonist. But in visual representations, he assumes subtle guises—ruler, predator, and seducer—and is a sly and cajoling figure who mocks the worldly pursuits of his unsuspecting victims. The procession (which might have originated in conjunction with popular dances) included men, women, and children from all walks of life and social classes: peasants and kings, schoolmasters and merchants, priests and nuns—all succumb to Death's ravishment. The Dance of Death objectified the new regard for death as "the Great Equalizer," that is, as an impartial phenomenon threaten-ing every individual, regardless of status or wealth. The sense of vulnerability is a prevailing motif in fourteenth- and fifteenth-century verse. Note, for example, these lines written by François Villon (1431–ca. 1463), the greatest French poet of his time.

> I know this well, that rich and poor
> Fools, sages, laymen, friars in cowl,
> Large-hearted lords and each mean boor,[1]
> Little and great and fair and foul,
> Ladies in lace, who smile or scowl,
> From whatever stock they stem,
> Hatted or hooded, prone to prowl,
> Death seizes every one of them.

If the psychological impact of the Black Death was traumatic, its economic effects were equally devastating. Widespread death among the poor caused a shortage of labor, which in turn created a greater demand for workers. The bargaining power of those who survived the plague was thus improved. In many parts of Europe, workers pressed to raise their status and income. Peasants took advantage of opportunities to become tenant farmers on lands leased by lords in need of laborers. Others fled their rural manors for cities where jobs were readily available. This exodus from the countryside spurred urban growth and contributed to the slow disintegration of manorialism.

All of Europe, however, was disadvantaged by the climatic disasters that caused frequent crop failure and famine, and by the continuing demands of financially threatened feudal overlords. Violent working-class revolts—the first examples of labor rebellion in Western history—broke out in France and England in the mid-fourteenth century. In 1358, French peasants (known as *jacques*) staged an angry protest (the *Jacquerie*) that took the lives of hundreds of noblemen before it was suppressed by the French king. In England, the desperation of the poor was manifested in the Peasants' Revolt of 1381, led by Wat Tyler and described in the *Chronicles* of the French historian Jean Froissart (1338–1410). Despite their ultimate failure, these revolts left their imprint on the social history of the West. They frightened landowners everywhere and lent an instability to class relationships that hastened the demise of the old feudal order.

Literature in Transition

The Social Realism of Boccaccio

Fourteenth-century Europeans manifested an unprecedented preoccupation with differences in class, gender, and personality. Both in literature and in art, there emerged a new fidelity to nature and to personal experience in the everyday world. This close, objective attention to human society and social interaction may be described as "Social Realism." The New Realism is evident in the many woodcuts of the Dance of Death (see Figure 15.5), where class differences are clearly drawn, and

Figure 15.5 HANS HOLBEIN THE YOUNGER,
Dance of Death, ca. 1490. Woodcut.

---

[1] Peasant; a rude and illiterate person.

in the 100 lively vernacular tales that make up Boccaccio's *Decameron* (part of the preface to which appeared earlier in this chapter). The context for this frame tale is, of course, the plague-ravaged city of Florence: eager to escape the contagion, seven young women and three young men retreat to a villa in the suburbs of Florence, where, to pass the time, each tells a story on each of ten days. The stories, designed as distractions from the horrors of the pandemic, are, in effect, amusing secular entertainments. They provide insight, however, into the social concerns and values of both the fictional narrators and Boccaccio's reading public.

Boccaccio borrowed many stories in the *Decameron* from popular fables, *fabliaux* (humorous narrative tales), and contemporary incidents. His characters resemble neither the allegorical figures of *Everyman* nor the courtly stereotypes of *Lancelot*. Rather, they are realistically conceived, high-spirited individuals who prize cleverness, good humor, and the world of the flesh over the classic medieval virtues of chivalry, piety, and humility. A case in point is the "Tale of Filippa," a delightful story that recounts how a woman from the Italian town of Prato shrewdly escapes legal punishment for committing adultery. The heroine, Madame Filippa, candidly confesses that she has a lover; however, she bitterly protests the city ordinance that serves a double standard of justice: one law for men, another for women. Filippa's proposal that women should not waste the passions unclaimed by their husbands but, rather, be allowed to enjoy the "surplus" with others—a view that might enlist the support of modern-day feminists—rings with good-humored defiance. Boccaccio's Filippa strikes a sharp note of contrast with the clinging heroines of the medieval romance. While Guinevere, for instance, wallows in longing for Lancelot (see Reading 11.3), Filippa boldly defends her right to sexual independence. Like many a male protagonist, she fearlessly challenges and exploits fortusne to serve her own designs.

The *Decameron* must have had special appeal for men and women who saw themselves as the heroes and heroines of precarious and rapidly changing times. Toward the end of his life, Boccaccio repented writing what he himself called his "immoral tales"; nevertheless, his stories, as the following example illustrates, remain a lasting tribute to the varieties of human affection and desire.

READING 15.2 From Boccaccio's "Tale of Filippa" from the *Decameron* (1351)

Once upon a time, in the town of Prato, there used to be a law in force—as pernicious, indeed, as it was cruel, to the effect that any woman caught by her husband in the act of adultery with a lover, was to be burned alive, like any vulgar harlot who sold herself for money.

While this statute prevailed, a beautiful lady called Filippa, a devout worshiper of Cupid, was surprised in her bedroom one night by her husband, Rinaldo de' Pugliesi, in the arms of Lazzarino de' Guazzagliotri, a

Chronology

1309–1377	Avignon Papacy
1337–1453	Hundred Years' War
1347–1375	Black Death
1358	*Jacquerie* (peasant uprising)
1378–1417	Great Schism

high-born Adonis of a youth of that city, whom she loved as the apple of her eye.

Burning with rage at the discovery, Rinaldo could scarcely forbear running upon them, and slaying them on the spot. Were it not for the misgivings he had for his own safety, if he gave vent to his wrath, he would have followed his impulse. However, he controlled his evil intent, but could not abandon his desire to demand of the town's statute, what it was unlawful for him to bring about—in other words, the death of his wife.

As he had no lack of evidence to prove Filippa's guilt, he brought charges against her, early in the morning, at daybreak, and without further deliberation, had her summoned before the court.

Now Filippa was a high-spirited woman, as all women are who truly love, and though many of her friends and relatives advised her against going, she resolved to appear before the magistrate, preferring a courageous death, by confessing the truth, to a shameful life of exile, by a cowardly flight that would have proved her unworthy of the lover in whose arms she had lain that night.

Accordingly, she presented herself before the provost, with a large following of men and women who urged her to deny the charges. She asked him firmly and without moving a muscle what he desired of her. The provost, seeing her so beautiful, courteous and so brave—as her words demonstrated—felt a certain pity stirring in his heart at the thought that she might confess a crime for which he would be obliged to sentence her to death to save his honor. But then, seeing he could not avoid cross-questioning her on the charge proffered against her, he said:

"Madam, here as you see, is Rinaldo, your husband, who is suing you on the grounds of finding you in the act of adultery with another man, and who therefore demands that I sentence you to death for it, as the law, which is in force, requires. I cannot pass sentence if you do not confess your guilt with your own lips. Be careful of your answers, then, and tell me if what your husband charges you with is true."

Filippa, not at all daunted, replied in a very agreeable voice: "Your honor, it is true that Rinaldo is my husband, and that last night he found me in the arms of Lazzarino, where I had lain many another time, out of the great and true love I bear him. Far be it from me ever to deny it.

"As you are doubtless aware, laws should be equal for all, and should be made with the consent of those whom they affect. Such is not the case with this particular statute, which is stringent only with us poor women, who, after all, have it in our power to give pleasure to many more people than men ever could. Moreover, when this law was drawn up, not a single woman gave her consent or was so much as invited to give it. For all these reasons, it surely deserves to be considered reprehensible. If you insist upon enforcing it, not at the risk of my body, but of your immortal soul, you are at liberty to do so; but before you proceed to pass judgment, I beg you to grant me a small request. Simply ask my husband whether I have ever failed to yield myself to him entirely, whenever he chose, and as often as he pleased." 60

Without waiting for the magistrate to question him, Rinaldo immediately answered that there was no doubt Filippa had always granted him the joy of her body, at each and every request of his. 70

"That being the case, your honor," she went on, directly, "I'd like to ask him, since he has always had all he wanted of me and to his heart's content, what was I to do with all that was left over? Indeed, what am I to do with it? Throw it to the dogs? Isn't it far better to let it give enjoyment to some gentleman who loves me more than his life, than to let it go to waste or ruin?" 80

As it happened, the whole town had turned out to attend the sensational trial that involved a lady of such beauty and fame, and when the people heard her roguish question, they burst into a roar of laughter, shouting to a man that she was right and had spoken well.

That day, before court was adjourned, that harsh statute was modified at the magistrate's suggestion to hold only for such women as made cuckolds of their husbands for love of money.

As for Rinaldo, he went away crest-fallen at his mad venture, while Filippa returned home victorious, feeling in her joy that she had, in a sense, been delivered from the flames. 90

Q How does Boccaccio's tale illustrate new attitudes toward women in Italian society?

The Feminism of Christine de Pisan

Just decades after Boccaccio took the woman's view in the "Tale of Filippa," the world's first feminist writer, Christine de Pisan (1364–1430?), came on the scene. The daughter of an Italian physician, Christine wedded a French nobleman when she was fifteen—medieval women usually married in their mid to late teens. Ten years later, when her husband died, Christine was left to support three children, a challenge she met by becoming the first female professional writer. Christine attacked the long antifemale tradition that had demeaned women and denied them the right to a university education. She criticized her literary contemporaries for creating negative stereotypes that slandered the female image. Her feminism is all the more significant because it occurred in a time in which men were making systematic efforts to restrict female inheritance of land and female membership in the guilds. In an early poem, the "Epistle to the God of Love" (1399), Christine protested the persistent antifemale bias of churchmen and scholars with these spirited words:

> Some say that many women are deceitful,
> Wily, false, of little worth;
> Others that too many are liars,
> Fickle, flighty, and inconstant;
> Still others accuse them of great vices,
> Blaming them much, excusing them nothing,
> Thus do clerics, night and day,
> First in French verse, then in Latin,
> Based on who knows what books
> That tell more lies than drunkards do.

Christine was keenly aware of the fact that Western literary tradition did not offer a representative picture of women's importance to society. Eager to correct this inequity, she became a spokesperson for women, both Christian and pagan. Her chauvinistic poem celebrating Joan of Arc emphasizes the heroism of a sixteen-year-old girl ("stronger and more resolute than Achilles or Hector") whose leadership brought France to victory when thousands of men had failed to do so. In her *Book of the City of Ladies*, Christine attacks male misogyny and exalts the accomplishments of famous women throughout the ages. Patterned as an allegorical debate, *The City of Ladies* pictures Christine herself "interviewing" three goddesses—Lady Reason, Lady Rectitude, and Lady Justice (Figure **15.6**). She seeks moral guidance on matters such as whether women can and should be educated in the same manner as men (I.27) and why men claim it is not good for women to be educated at all (II.36). Excerpts from these two portions of Christine's landmark feminist work follow.

READING 15.3 From Christine de Pisan's *Book of the City of Ladies* (1405)

Book I. 27 Christine Asks Reason Whether God Has Ever Wished to Ennoble the Mind of Woman With the Loftiness of the Sciences; and Reason's Answer.

... please enlighten me again, whether it has ever pleased this God, who has bestowed so many favors on women, to honor the feminine sex with the privilege of the virtue of high understanding and great learning, and whether women ever have a clever enough mind for this. I wish very much to know this because men maintain that the mind of women can learn only a little." 1

She answered, "My daughter, since I told you before, you know quite well that the opposite of their opinion is true, and to show you this even more clearly, I will give you proof through examples. I tell you again—and don't doubt the contrary—if it were customary to send daughters to school like sons, and if they were then taught the natural sciences, they would learn as thoroughly and understand the subtleties of all the arts and sciences as well as sons. And by chance there happen to be such women, for, as I touched on before, just as women have 10

Figure 15.6 Anonymous, *La Cité des Dames de Christine de Pizan*, ca. 1410. Illumination on parchment. In this miniature, Christine is pictured in conversation with the allegorical figures of Reason, Rectitude, and Justice. On the right, she assists in building the City of Ladies.

more delicate bodies than men, weaker and less able to perform many tasks, so do they have minds that are freer and sharper whenever they apply themselves." 20

"My lady, what are you saying? With all due respect, could you dwell longer on this point, please. Certainly men would never admit this answer is true, unless it is explained more plainly, for they believe that one normally sees that men know more than women do."

She answered, "Do you know why women know less?"

"Not unless you tell me, my lady."

"Without the slightest doubt, it is because they are not involved in many different things, but stay at home, where it is enough for them to run the household, and 30 there is nothing which so instructs a reasonable creature as the exercise and experience of many different things."

"My lady, since they have minds skilled in conceptualizing and learning, just like men, why don't women learn more?"

She replied, "Because, my daughter, the public does not require them to get involved in the affairs which men are commissioned to execute, just as I told you before. It is enough for women to perform the usual duties to which they are ordained. As for judging from experience, since 40 one sees that women usually know less than men, that therefore their capacity for understanding is less, look at men who farm the flatlands or who live in the mountains. You will find that in many countries they seem completely savage because they are so simple-minded. All the same, there is no doubt that Nature provided them with the qualities of body and mind found in the wisest and most learned men. All of this stems from a failure to learn,

though, just as I told you, among men and women, some possess better minds than others. . . . 50

Book II. 36 Against Those Men Who Claim It Is Not Good for Women to Be Educated.

Following these remarks, I, Christine, spoke, "My lady, I realize that women have accomplished many good things and that even if evil women have done evil, it seems to me, nevertheless, that the benefits accrued and still accruing because of good women—particularly the wise and literary ones and those educated in the natural science whom I mentioned above—outweigh the evil. Therefore, I am amazed by the opinion of some men who claim that they do not want their daughters, wives, or kinswomen to be educated because their mores[1] would be ruined as a result." 60

She responded, "Here you can clearly see that not all opinions of men are based on reason and that these men are wrong. For it must not be presumed that mores necessarily grow worse from knowing the moral sciences, which teach the virtues, indeed, there is not the slightest doubt that moral education amends and ennobles them. How could anyone think or believe that whoever follows good teaching or doctrine is the worse for it? Such an opinion cannot be expressed or maintained. I do not mean that it would be good for a man or a woman to 70 study the art of divination or those fields of learning which are forbidden—for the holy Church did not remove them from common use without good reason—but it

---

[1] Customs.

should not be believed that women are the worse for knowing what is good.

"Quintus Hortensius,[2] a great rhetorician and consummately skilled orator in Rome, did not share this opinion. He had a daughter, named Hortensia, whom he greatly loved for the subtlety of her wit. He had her learn letters and study the science of rhetoric, which she mastered so thoroughly that she resembled her father Hortensius not only in wit and lively memory but also in her excellent delivery and order of speech—in fact, he surpassed her in nothing. As for the subject discussed above, concerning the good which comes about through women, the benefits realized by this woman and her learning were, among others, exceptionally remarkable. That is, during the time when Rome was governed by three men, this Hortensia began to support the cause of women and to undertake what no man dared to undertake. There was a question whether certain taxes should be levied on women and on their jewelry during a needy period in Rome. This woman's eloquence was so compelling that she was listened to, no less readily than her father would have been, and she won her case.

"Similarly, to speak of more recent times, without searching for examples in ancient history, Giovanni Andrea, a solemn law professor in Bologna not quite sixty years ago, was not of the opinion that it was bad for women to be educated. He had a fair and good daughter, named Novella, who was educated in the law to such an advanced degree that when he was occupied by some task and not at leisure to present his lectures to his students, he would send Novella, his daughter, in his place to lecture to the students from his chair. And to prevent her beauty from distracting the concentration of her audience, she had a little curtain drawn in front of her. In this manner she could on occasion supplement and lighten her father's occupation. He loved her so much that, to commemorate her name, he wrote a book of remarkable lectures on the law which he entitled *Novella super Decretalium*, after his daughter's name.

"Thus, not all men (and especially the wisest) share the opinion that it is bad for women to be educated. But it is very true that many foolish men have claimed this because it displeased them that women knew more than they did. Your father, who was a great scientist and philosopher, did not believe that women were worth less by knowing science; rather, as you know, he took great pleasure from seeing your inclination to learning. The feminine opinion of your mother, however, who wished to keep you busy with spinning and silly girlishness, following the common custom of women, was the major obstacle to your being more involved in the sciences. But just as the proverb already mentioned above says, 'No one can take away what Nature has given,' your mother could not hinder in you the feeling for the sciences which you, through natural inclination, had nevertheless gathered together in little droplets. I am sure that, on

80

90

100

110

120

---

[2] Quintus Hortensius (114–50 B.C.E.).

account of these things, you do not think you are worth less but rather that you consider it a great treasure for yourself; and you doubtless have reason to."

And I, Christine, replied to all of this, "Indeed, my lady, what you say is as true as the Lord's Prayer."

130

Q With what arguments does Lady Reason defend the intelligence of women?

Q What role does education play in matters of gender equality?

The Social Realism of Chaucer

The master of fourteenth-century English vernacular literature, Geoffrey Chaucer (1340–1400), was a contemporary of Boccaccio and Christine de Pisan. A middle-class civil servant and diplomat, soldier in the Hundred Years' War, and a citizen of the bustling city of London, Chaucer left an indelible image of his time in a group of stories known as the *Canterbury Tales*. Modeled broadly on Boccaccio's *Decameron*, this versified frame tale recounts the stories told by a group of pilgrims to entertain each other while traveling from London to the shrine of Saint Thomas à Becket in Canterbury. Chaucer's twenty-nine pilgrims, who include a miller, a monk, a plowman, a knight, a priest, a scholar, and a prioress, provide a literary cross-section of late medieval society. Although they are type characters, representative of the nobility, the clergy, the merchant, and the commoner, they are also individual personalities. The effeminate Pardoner, the lusty Wife of Bath, and the belligerent Miller are creatures of flesh and blood, whose interaction throughout the journey contributes to our perception of them as participants in Chaucer's human comedy. Chaucer characterizes each pilgrim by descriptive detail, by their lively and humorous conversations, and by the twenty stories they tell, which range from moral tales and beast fables to *fabliaux* of the most risqué and bawdy sort.

Like his medieval predecessors, Chaucer tended to moralize, reserving special scorn for clerical abuse and human hypocrisy. But unlike his forebears, whose stories were often peopled by literary stereotypes, Chaucer brought his characters to life by means of vivid detail. His talent in this direction is best realized through a brief comparison. In a twelfth-century verse narrative called *Equitan*, written by Marie de France, a notable poet in the Norman court of England, we find the following description of the heroine:

> Very desirable was the lady; passing tender of body and sweet of vesture, coiffed and fretted with gold. Her eyes were blue, her face warmly colored, with a fragrant mouth, and a dainty nose. Certainly she had no peer in all the realm.

Compare Chaucer's descriptions of the Wife of Bath and the Miller (from the "Prologue"). Then, in direct comparison with the lines from *Equitan*, consider Chaucer's evocation of Alison (the Miller's wife) in "The Miller's Tale" which, though too long to reproduce here, is recommended to all who might enjoy a spicy yarn.

READING 15.4 From Chaucer's "Prologue" and "The Miller's Tale" in the *Canterbury Tales* (ca. 1390)

Here begins the Book of the Tales of Canterbury: When   1
April with its gentle showers has pierced the March
drought to the root and bathed every plant in the moisture
which will hasten the flowering; when Zephyrus with his
sweet breath has stirred the new shoots in every wood and
field, and the young sun has run its half-course in the Ram,
and small birds sing melodiously, so touched in their hearts
by Nature that they sleep all night with open eyes—then
folks long to go on pilgrimages, and palmers to visit foreign
shores and distant shrines, known in various lands; and   10
especially from every shire's end of England they travel to
Canterbury, to seek the holy blessed martyr who helped
them when they were sick.

One day in that season when I stopped at the Tabard in
Southwark, ready to go on my pilgrimage to Canterbury
with a truly devout heart, it happened that a group of
twenty-nine people came into that inn in the evening. They
were people of various ranks who had come together by
chance, and they were all pilgrims who planned to ride to
Canterbury. The rooms and stables were large enough for   20
each of us to be well lodged, and, shortly after the sun had
gone down, I had talked with each of these pilgrims and
had soon made myself one of their group. We made our
plans to get up early in order to start our trip, which I am
going to tell you about. But, nevertheless, while I have time
and space, before I go farther in this account, it seems
reasonable to tell you all about each of the pilgrims, as
they appeared to me; who they were, and of what rank,
and also what sort of clothes they wore.

. . . .

There was a good Wife from near Bath, but she was   30
somewhat deaf, which was a shame. She had such skill in
clothmaking that she surpassed the weavers of Ypres and
Ghent. In all her parish there was no woman who could go
before her to the offertory; and if someone did, the Wife
of Bath was certainly so angry that she lost all charitable
feeling. Her kerchiefs were of fine texture; those she wore
upon her head on Sunday weighed, I swear, ten pounds.
Her fine scarlet hose were carefully tied, and her shoes
were uncracked and new. Her face was bold and fair and
red. All of her life she had been an estimable woman: she   40
had had five husbands, not to mention other company in
her youth—but of that we need not speak now. And three
times she had been to Jerusalem; she had crossed many
a foreign river; she had been to Rome, to Bologna, to St.
James' shrine in Galicia, and to Cologne. About journeying
through the country she knew a great deal. To tell the truth
she was gap-toothed. She sat her gentle horse easily, and
wore a fine headdress with a hat as broad as a buckler or
a shield, a riding skirt about her large hips, and a pair of
sharp spurs on her heels. She knew how to laugh and joke   50
in company, and all the remedies of love, for her skill was
great in that old game.

. . . .

The Miller was a very husky fellow, tremendous in bone
and in brawn which he used well to get the best of all
comers; in wrestling he always won the prize. He was
stocky, broad, and thickset. There was no door which he
could not pull off its hinges or break by ramming it with his
head. His beard was as red as any sow or fox, and as
broad as a spade. At the right on top of his nose he had a
wart, from which there grew a tuft of hairs red as the   60
bristles of a sow's ears, and his nostrils were wide and
black. A sword and a shield hung at his side. His mouth
was as huge as a large furnace, and he was a jokester and
a ribald clown, most of whose jests were of sin and
scurrility. He knew quite well how to steal grain and charge
thrice over, but yet he really remained reasonably honest. The
coat he wore was white and the hood blue. He could play the
bagpipe well and led us out of town to its music.

. . . .

The young wife was pretty, with a body as neat and graceful
as a weasel. She wore a checked silk belt, and around her   70
loins a flounced apron as white as fresh milk. Her smock
was white also, embroidered in front and in back, inside and
outside and around the collar, with coal-black silk. The
strings of her white hood were of the same material as her
collar; her hair was bound with a wide ribbon of silk set
high on her head. And, truly, she had a wanton eye. Her
eyebrows were plucked thin and were arched and black as
any sloe.[1] She was even more delightful to look at than a
young, early-ripe pear tree, and she was softer than lamb's
wool. A leather purse, with a silk tassel and metal   80
ornaments, hung from her belt. In all the world there is no
man so wise that, though he looked far and near, he could
imagine so gay a darling or such a wench. Her coloring was
brighter than that of a coin newly forged in the Tower, and
her singing was as loud and lively as a swallow's sitting on
a barn. In addition, she could skip about and play like any
kid or calf following its mother. Her mouth was as sweet as
honey or mead, or a pile of apples laid up in hay or heather.
She was as skittish as a young colt, and tall and straight as
a mast or wand. On her low collar she wore a brooch as   90
broad as the boss on a shield. Her shoes were laced high on
her legs. She was a primrose, a trillium,[2] fit to grace the bed of
any lord or to marry any good yeoman.

Q **Which of Chaucer's descriptive devices are most effective in evoking character and personality?**

Chaucer uses sprightly similes ("graceful as a weasel," "as sweet as honey") and vivid details ("a checked silk belt," "high laced" shoes) to bring alive the personality and physical presence of the Miller's wife. (He also hints at the contradiction between her chaste exterior and her sensual nature, a major feature in the development of the story in which she figures.) By comparison, Marie de France's portrait is a pallid and stereotypical adaptation of the standard

---

[1] A small, dark berry.
[2] A lily.

medieval female image: the courtly lady, the Virgin Mary, and the female saint. Chaucer's humanizing techniques bring zesty realism to both his pilgrim-narrators and the characters featured in their tales. Writing in the everyday language of his time (Middle English, as distinguished from the more Germanic Old English that preceded it), Chaucer shaped the development of English literature, much as Dante, a century earlier, had influenced the course of Italian poetry.

Art and Music in Transition

Giotto's New Realism

The shift to Realism evidenced in the works of Boccaccio and Chaucer was anticipated in painting by the Florentine artist Giotto (1266–1337). The follower of Cimabue, Giotto was hailed by his contemporaries as the leader of a new direction in visual representation.

MAKING CONNECTIONS

Figure 15.7 CIMABUE, *Madonna Enthroned*, ca. 1280–1290. Tempera on wood, 12 ft. 7½ in. × 7 ft. 4 in.

A comparison of Cimabue's *Madonna Enthroned*, completed around 1290 (Figure **15.7**) with Giotto's rendering of the same subject some twenty years later (Figure **15.8**), provides evidence of the shift to Realism that accompanied the transition from the medieval to the Modern Era. Both are huge, iconic images, well over 10 feet in height. Like Cimabue, Giotto shows an oversized Virgin on a Gothic throne set against an airless gold background. But Giotto renounces the graceful Gothic line and flat, decorative stylization reminiscent of the Byzantine icons that inspired Cimabue's late medieval painting. Instead, he models the form by way of gradations of light and shade, a technique known as **_chiaroscuro_** that gives the Madonna an imposing three-dimensional presence. (Note the forward projection of her knees, which provide support for the baby Jesus—here more childlike than Cimabue's toga-clad infant.) Rather than placing the angels one above another on either side of the throne, Giotto arranges them in positions that suggest their presence in three-dimensional space. The kneeling angels at the foot of the throne, like those on the sides, bring dramatic attention to the central figures. In contrast with Cimabue's idealized Madonna, Giotto has created a robust and lifelike image that anticipates the pictorial Realism of Italian Renaissance art (see chapter 17).

Figure 15.8 GIOTTO, *Madonna Enthroned*, ca. 1310. Tempera on panel, 10 ft. 8 in. × 6 ft. 8 in.

Giotto brought an equally dramatic naturalism to his frescoes. In 1303, the wealthy banker and money-lender Enrico Scrovegni commissioned him to paint a series of frescoes for the family chapel in Padua. On the walls of the Arena Chapel, Giotto illustrated familiar episodes from the narrative cycle that recounts the lives of the Virgin and Christ (Figure **15.9**). While wholly traditional in subject matter, the enterprise constituted an innovative approach that transformed the tiny barrel-vaulted chamber into a theater in which the individual scenes, lit from the west and viewed from the center, appear to take place in real space.

In the *Lamentation* (see Figure 15.1), the figures appear in a shallow but carefully defined space delimited by craggy rocks and a single barren tree. Two foreground mourners viewed from behind enhance the illusion of spatial depth and call attention to the poignant expression of the Mother of God. Dramatic expression is also heightened by gestures of lament that vary from the tender remorse of Mary Magdalene, who embraces the feet of Jesus, to the impassioned dismay of John the Evangelist, who flings back his arms in astonished grief, a sentiment echoed among the

weeping angels that flutter above the scene. Giotto gives weight, volume, and emotional resonance to figures whose gravity and dignity call to mind Classical sculpture. Like the characters in Boccaccio's *Decameron* and Chaucer's *Canterbury Tales*, those in Giotto's paintings are convincingly human: while they are not individualized to the point of portraiture, neither are they stereotypes. Giotto advanced the trend toward Realism already evident in Late Gothic art. At the same time, he gave substance to the spirit of lay piety and individualism that marked the fourteenth century.

Devotional Realism and Portraiture

In religious art, Realism enhanced the devotional mood of the age. Traditional scenes of the lives of Christ and the Virgin became at once more pictorial and detailed, a reflection of the new concern with Christ's human nature and his suffering. Images of the Crucifixion and the *Pietà* (the Virgin holding the dead Jesus), which had been a popular object of veneration since the tenth century, were now depicted with a new expressive intensity. One anonymous German artist of the mid-fourteenth century rendered the *Pietà* (the word means both "pity" and "piety") as a traumatic moment between a despairing Mother and her Son, whose broken torso and elongated arms are as rigid as the wood from which they were carved (Figure **15.10**). This votive sculpture captures the torment of Christ's martyrdom with fierce energy.

In the domain of fourteenth-century monumental sculpture the most notable personality was the Dutch artist Claus Sluter (ca. 1350–1406). Sluter's *Well of Moses*, executed between 1395 and 1406 for the Carthusian monastery at Champmol just outside of Dijon, France, was originally part of a 25-foot-tall stone fountain designed to celebrate the sacraments of Eucharist and baptism. The Crucifixion group that made up the superstructure is lost, but the pedestal

Figure 15.9 GIOTTO, Arena Chapel (Cappella Scrovegni), Padua, interior looking toward the choir. Height 42 ft., width 27 ft. 10 in., length 96 ft. Unlike the artists of ancient Egyptian frescoes, who applied paint to a dry surface, Giotto made use of the technique known as **buon fresco** ("true fresco"), in which the artist applied earth pigments onto the wet lime or gypsum plaster surface.

of the fountain with its six Old Testament prophets—Moses, David, Jeremiah, Zachariah, Daniel, and Isaiah—survives in its entirety (Figure **15.11**). Carrying scrolls engraved with their messianic texts, the life-sized prophets are swathed in deeply cut, voluminous draperies. Facial features are individualized so as to render each prophet with a distinctive personality. As in Giotto's *Lamentation*, mourning angels (at the corners of the pedestal above the heads of the prophets) cover their faces or wring their hands in gestures of anguish and despair. So intensely theatrical is the Realism of the Champmol ensemble that scholars suspect Sluter might have been inspired by contemporary mystery plays, where Old Testament characters regularly took the stage between the acts to "prophesy" New Testament events.

Devotional Realism is equally apparent in illuminated manuscripts, and especially in the popular prayer book known as the Book of Hours. This guide to private prayer featured traditional recitations for the canonical hours—the sets of prayers recited daily at three-hour intervals: matins, lauds, prime, terce, sext, none, vespers, and compline—as well as prayers to the Virgin and the saints. As manuals for personal piety and alternatives

Figure 15.10
Anonymous,
The Röttgen Pietà,
ca. 1370. Height 89 cm.

Figure 15.11 CLAUS SLUTER, figure of Moses on the *Well of Moses*, 1395–1406. Painted stone, height approx. 6 ft. Moses is seen here in the center with King David on his left. Time has robbed this piece of the brightly colored paint and metal accessories—the scholarly Jeremiah (far left) bore a pair of copper spectacles—that once gave it a startling lifelike presence.

to daily church ritual, Books of Hours were in great demand, especially among prosperous Christians. In the miniatures of these prayer books, scenes from sacred history are filled with realistic and homely details drawn from everyday life. Even miraculous events are made more believable as they are presented in lifelike settings and given new dramatic fervor. Such is the case with the animated **grisaille** (gray-toned) miniatures found in a prayer book executed around 1325 for Jeanne d'Evreux, queen of France, by the French court painter Jean Pucelle (Figure **15.12**). In contrast with the stylized treatment of the

Figure 15.12 JEAN PUCELLE, *Betrayal* and *Annunciation* from the *Book of Hours of Jeanne d'Evreux, Queen of France*, 1325–1328. Miniature on vellum, each folio 3½ × 2⁷⁄₁₆ in.

Betrayal of Christ in the thirteenth century *Psalter of Saint Swithin* (see Figure 13.13), Pucelle's figures are accurately proportioned and, modeled in subtle *chiaroscuro*, substantial in form. In the Annunciation, pictured on the *recto* (right) folio, the artist engaged receding diagonal lines to create the illusion of a "doll's house" that holds an over-sized Madonna.

Pucelle's experiments in empirical perspective and his lively renderings of traditional subjects were carried further by the three brothers Jean, Pol, and Herman Limbourg, who flourished between 1385 and 1415. Their generous patron Jean, Duke of Berry and brother of the king of France, commissioned from them a remarkable series of Books of Hours illustrated with religious and secular subjects. For the calendar pages of the *Très Riches Heures* (*Very Precious Hours*), the Limbourgs painted scenes illustrating the mundane activities and labors peculiar to each month of the year. In the scene for the month of February—the first snowscape in Western art—three peasants warm themselves by the fire, while others hurry to complete their chores (Figure **15.13**).The Limbourgs show a new fascination with natural details: dovecote and beehives covered with new-fallen snow, sheep that huddle together in a thatched pen, smoke curling from a chimney, and even the genitalia of two of the laborers who warm themselves by the fire.

Devotional Realism also overtook the popular subject of the Madonna and Child: the new image of the Virgin as a

humble matron tenderly nurturing the Infant Jesus (Figure **15.14**) replaced earlier, more hieratic representations of Mary Enthroned (see Figures 13.29 and 13.35). In paintings of the Virgin as "Nursing Madonna," the Infant is shown as a lively baby, not as the miniature adult of earlier renderings. Fourteenth-century artists frequently introduced descriptive details from mystery plays and from the writings of mystics like Saint Bridget of Sweden. Indeed, the interchange of imagery between devotional literature, medieval drama, and the visual arts was commonplace.

In light of the growing interest in the human personality—so clearly revealed in the literature of Boccaccio and Chaucer—it is no surprise that fourteenth-century artists produced the first portrait paintings since Classical antiquity. Most such portraits appear in manuscripts. In panel painting, the anonymous portrait of John the Good, king of France (Figure **15.15**), documents the new consciousness of the particular as opposed to the generalized image of humankind.

The *Ars Nova* in Music

The cultural transformation that characterizes the fourteenth century is apparent in its music, which composers of that era perceptively called the ***ars nova*** ("new art"). The *ars nova* is a musical style that, in its aural expressiveness, parallels the richly detailed Realism apparent in fourteenth-century literature and the visual arts. The new art

Figure 15.13 JEAN, POL, AND HERMAN LIMBOURG, *February*, plate 3 from the *Très Riches Heures (Very Precious Hours) du Duc de Berry*, ca. 1413–1416. Illumination, 8¾ × 5⅚ in.

features a distinctive rhythmic complexity, achieved in part by **isorhythm** (literally "same rhythm"): the close repetition of identical rhythmic patterns in different portions of a composition. Isorhythm, an expression of the growing interest in the manipulation of pitches and rhythms, gave unprecedented unity to musical compositions.

In France, the leading proponent of the *ars nova* was the French poet, priest, and composer Guillaume de Machaut (1300–1377). In his day, Machaut was more widely known and acclaimed than Chaucer and Boccaccio. Like the Limbourg brothers, Machaut held commissions from the French aristocracy, including the Duke of Berry. Machaut penned hundreds of poems, including a verse drama interspersed with songs, but his most important musical achievement was his *Messe de Notre Dame (Mass of Our Lady)*. Departing from the medieval tradition of treating the Mass as five separate compositions (based on Gregorian chant), he unified the parts into a single polyphonic composition, adding a sixth movement, the "Ite missa est." Distinctive to our listening selection of the "Ite missa est" is the diversity of rhythmic style, the appearance of **syncopation**, and the use of instruments, either doubling

Figure 15.14 AMBROGIO LORENZETTI, *Madonna del Latte* (*Nursing Madonna*), ca. 1340. Fresco.

Outside France, polyphonic music flourished. The blind Italian composer Francesco Landini (ca. 1325–1397) produced graceful instrumental compositions and eloquent two- and three-part songs. Landini's 150 works constitute more than one-third of the surviving music of the fourteenth century—evidence of his enormous popularity. Italian composers favored florid polyphonic works that featured a close relationship between musical parts. The *caccia* (Italian for "chase"), for instance, which dealt with such everyday subjects as fishing and hunting, was set to lively music in which one voice part "chased" another. Another popular polyphonic composition, the **round**, featured several voices that enter one after another, each repeating the same words and music (as in "Row, Row, Row Your Boat"). The Middle English round "Sumer is icumen in" is an example of polyphony at its freshest and most buoyant.

Although fourteenth-century polyphony involved both voices and instruments, manuscripts of the period did not usually specify whether a given part of a piece was instrumental or vocal. Custom probably dictated the performance style, not only for vocal and instrumental ensembles, but for dance as well.

Figure 15.15 *King John the Good*, ca. 1356–1359(?). Canvas on panel, 21⅛ × 13⅜ in. Following the tradition of Classical and medieval coins and medals, the earliest portraits in Western painting feature the human profile.

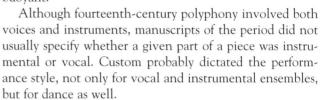

or playing the lower parts of the four-voice setting. Machaut's effort at coherence of design is clear evidence that composers had begun to rank musical effect as equal to liturgical function. This new treatment of the Catholic liturgy set a precedent for many composers, including the sixteenth-century Palestrina and the Baroque master Johann Sebastian Bach (see chapter 23).

Machaut's sacred compositions represent only a small part of his total musical output. His secular works include 142 polyphonic **ballades** that look back to the vernacular songs of the *trouvères*; but their attention to expressive detail is unique. They introduce new warmth and lyricism, as well as vivid poetic imagery—features that parallel the humanizing currents in fourteenth-century art and literature. "One who does not compose according to feelings," wrote Machaut, "falsifies his work and his song."

See Music Listening Selections at end of chapter.

LOOKING BACK

Europe in Transition

- The fourteenth century witnessed the transition from medieval to early modern culture in the West. During this era, violence uprooted tradition, corruption bred cynicism, and widespread death generated insecurity and fear.
- The two great catalysts of the age—the Hundred Years' War and the Black Death—brought about a collapse of the medieval order, along with political, military, and economic unrest. A new kind of warfare, featuring the use of gunpowder, outmoded older methods of combat. By the end of the century, the population of Western Europe had declined by approximately 50 percent.
- The relocation of the papacy to Avignon, and the Great Schism, which divided the papacy and produced two conflicting claims to universal sovereignty, led to controversy within the Church and widespread popular criticism.

Literature in Transition

- In Italy, Boccaccio penned vernacular tales to entertain urban audiences. Rejecting literary stereotypes, allegorical intent, and religious purpose, he brought to life the personalities of self-motivated men and women.
- In France, Christine de Pisan attacked the antifemale tradition in life and letters, and ushered in the birth of feminism in Western literature.
- Geoffrey Chaucer, an English middle-class civil servant and soldier, left an indelible image of his time in the *Canterbury Tales*. This versified human comedy was framed in the setting of a pilgrimage whose participants tell stories to entertain each other while traveling to Canterbury.

Art and Music in Transition

- Giotto pioneered the new direction in realistic representation. His robust, lifelike figures, posed in three-dimensional space, anticipated the art of the Italian Renaissance.
- The New Realism was also evident in the rise of portraiture and in a more humanized approach to traditional religious subjects.
- In the sculpture of Claus Sluter and in manuscript illumination, as in panel and fresco painting, true-to-life detail and emotional expressiveness came to replace Gothic abstraction and stylization.
- Promoted by Guillaume de Machaut, the *ars nova* brought warmth and lyricism to secular and religious music that featured increased rhythmic complexity and aural expressiveness.

Music Listening Selections

CD One Selection 15 Machaut, *Messe de Notre Dame* (Mass of Our Lady), "Ite missa est, Deo gratias," 1364.
CD One Selection 16 Anonymous, English round, "Sumer is icumen in," fourteenth century.

Glossary

ars nova (Latin, "new art") a term used for the music of fourteenth-century Europe to distinguish it from that of the old art (*ars antiqua*); it featured new rhythms, new harmonies, and more complicated methods of musical notation

ballade a secular song that tells a story in simple verse, usually repeating the same music for each stanza

buon fresco (Italian "true fresco") the technique of applying earth pigments onto a wet lime or gypsum plaster surface

caccia (Italian, "chase") a lively fourteenth-century Italian musical form that deals with everyday subjects, such as hunting and fishing

chiaroscuro (Italian, "light–dark") in drawing and painting, the technique of modeling form in gradations of light and shade to produce the illusion of three-dimensionality

grisaille (French, "gray-toned") the use of exclusively gray tones in painting or drawing

indulgence a church pardon from the temporal penalties for sins; the remission of purgatorial punishment

isorhythm the close repetition of identical rhythmic patterns in different sections of a musical composition

round a type of polyphonic composition that features successive voices that enter one after another, each repeating exactly the same melody and text

simony the buying or selling of church office or preferment (see Simon Magus, Acts of the Apostles 8:9–24)

syncopation a musical effect of uneven rhythm resulting from changing the normal pattern of accents and beats

Chapter

16

Classical Humanism in the Age of the Renaissance

ca. 1300–1600

". . . man is, with complete justice, considered and called a great miracle and a being worthy of all admiration."
Pico della Mirandola

Figure 16.1 BENOZZO GOZZOLI, *Procession of the Magi*, 1459. Fresco. East wall of the Medici Chapel, Medici Palace, Florence. In the upper left corner is a self-portrait of the artist who identifies himself with an inscription on the headband of his red hat. Some scholars see the faces of the six-year-old Giuliano de' Medici and the ten-year-old Lorenzo de' Medici in the figures just below the artist.

LOOKING AHEAD

Classical humanism, the movement to recover and revive Greco-Roman culture, was the phenomenon that gave the Renaissance (the word literally means "rebirth") its distinctive, secular stamp. Classical humanists were the cultural archeologists of their age. They uncovered lost evidence of the splendor of Greco-Roman antiquity and avidly consumed the fruits of the Classical legacy. Unattached to any single school or university, this new breed of humanists pursued what the ancient Romans had called *studia humanitatis*, a program of study that embraced grammar, rhetoric, history, poetry, and moral philosophy. These branches of learning fostered training in the moral and aesthetic areas of human knowledge—the very areas of experience with which this textbook is concerned. While such an educational curriculum was assuredly not antireligious—indeed, most Renaissance humanists were devout Catholics—its focus was secular rather than religious. For the humanists, life on earth was not a vale of tears but, rather, an extended occasion during which human beings might cultivate their unique talents and abilities. Classical humanists saw no conflict between humanism and religious belief. They viewed their intellectual mission as both pleasing to God and advantageous to society in general. Humanism, then, grounded in a reevaluation of Classical literature and art, represented a shift in emphasis rather than an entirely new pursuit; it involved a turning away from exclusively otherworldly preoccupations to a robust, this-worldly point of view.

Italy: Birthplace of the Renaissance

The Renaissance designates that period in European history between roughly 1300 and 1600, during which time the revival of Classical humanism spread from its birthplace in Florence, Italy, throughout Western Europe. Italy was the homeland of Roman antiquity, the splendid ruins of which stood as reminders of the greatness of Classical civilization. The least feudalized part of the medieval world and Europe's foremost commercial and financial center, Italy had traded with Southwest Asian cities even in the darkest days of the Middle Ages. It had also maintained cultural contacts with Byzantium, the heir to Greek culture. The cities of Italy, especially Venice and Genoa (Map **16.1**), had profited financially from the Crusades (see chapter 11) and—despite the ravages of the plague—continued to enjoy a high level of commercial prosperity. In fourteenth-century Florence, shopkeepers devised a practical system (based on Arab models) of tracking debits and credits: double-entry bookkeeping helped merchants to maintain systematic records of transactions in what was the soundest currency in the West, the Florentine gold florin. Fifteenth-century handbooks on arithmetic, foreign currency, and even good penmanship encouraged the commercial activities of traders and bankers.

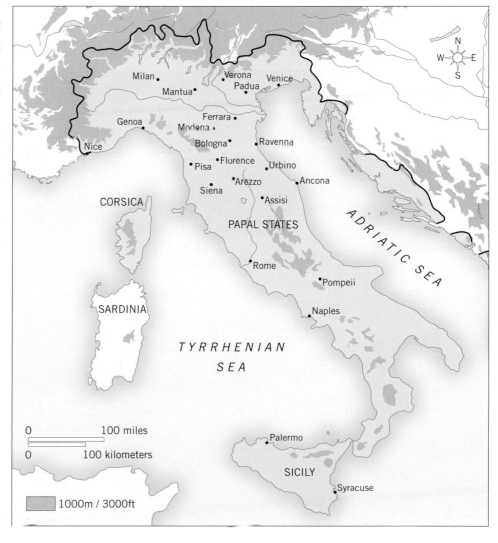

Map 16.1 Renaissance Italy, 1300–1600.

The pursuit of money and leisure, rather than a preoccupation with feudal and chivalric obligations, marked the lifestyle of merchants and artisans who lived in the bustling city-states of Italy. In a panoramic cityscape commissioned for the Palazzo Pubblico (Town Hall) of Siena, Ambrogio Lorenzetti (whom we met in chapter 15) celebrated the positive effects of good government on urban life (Figure 16.2), while a matching fresco illustrated the evil effects of bad government. Throughout Italy, the Avignon Papacy and the Great Schism had produced a climate of anticlericalism and intellectual skepticism. Middle-class men and women challenged canonical sources of authority that frowned upon profit-making and the accumulation of wealth. In this materialistic and often only superficially religious society, the old medieval values no longer made sense, while those of pre-Christian antiquity seemed more compatible with the secular interests and ambitions of the rising merchant class. The ancient Greeks and Romans were indeed ideal historical models for the enterprising citizens of the Italian city-states.

Politically, Renaissance Italy had much in common with ancient Greece. Independent and disunited, the city-states of Italy, like those of ancient Greece, were fiercely competitive. As in Golden Age Greece, commercial rivalry among the Italian city-states led to frequent civil wars. In Italy, however, such wars were not always fought by citizens (who,

as merchants, were generally ill prepared for combat), but by *condottieri* (professional soldiers) whose loyalties, along with their services, were bought for a price. The papacy, a potential source of political leadership, made little effort to unify the rival Italian communes. Rather, as temporal governors of the Papal States (the lands located in central Italy), Renaissance popes joined in the game of power politics, often allying with one group of city-states against another.

The Medici

Italian Renaissance cities were ruled either by members of the petty nobility, by mercenary generals, or—as in the case of Florence and Venice—by wealthy middle-class families. In Florence, a city of approximately 50,000, some 100 families dominated political life. The most notable of these was the Medici, a wealthy banking family that rose to power during the fourteenth century and gradually assumed the reins of state. Partly because the commercial ingenuity of the Medici enhanced the material status of the Florentine citizens, and partly because strong, uninterrupted leadership guaranteed local economic stability, the Medici ruled Florence for four generations. The Medici merchant-princes, Cosimo (1389–1464), Piero (1416–1468), and Lorenzo, known as "the Magnificent" (1449–1492) (Figure 16.3), supported scholarship and patronized the arts.

Figure 16.2 AMBROGIO LORENZETTI, *Effects of Good Government in the City and the Country*, from *The Allegory of Good Government*, 1338–1339. Peace and prosperity are the themes of this urban landscape, a view of Siena's bustling commune: merchants sell their wares at storefronts, classes are in progress in a schoolroom, revelers dance in the street, and builders work on rooftop construction.

Figure 16.3 ANDREA DEL VERROCCHIO, *Lorenzo de' Medici*, ca. 1478. Terracotta, 25⅞ × 23¼ × 12⅞ in. The patron of Ficino, Botticelli, and Michelangelo, Lorenzo followed in the footsteps of his grandfather Cosimo, the first of the great Medici humanists. Personally engaged in humanist studies, he also wrote vernacular poems and songs that were performed in the popular street pageants of Florence.

The Medici, like many wealthy Florentines, embellished their city with a private stone palace. Designed by Michelozzo di Bartolomeo (1396–1472) to resemble both a fortress and a private home, it attracted foreign ambassadors, artists, and notable humanists. Roughly cut masonry appears on the ground floor and windows are located high up for purposes of security. The upper stories, topped by a Classically inspired cornice, are lighter and more elegant, their windows divided by Corinthian colonettes (Figure 16.4). For the walls of the Medici Chapel, Cosimo commissioned

Figure 16.4 MICHELOZZO, exterior of the Medici Palace, 1444–1460. The Medici coat of arms, consisting of seven balls, is seen at the corner of the second course of the palace. The meaning of the balls is variously interpreted: most likely, they represent the coins signifying the Medici as bankers and pawnbrokers.

an elaborate set of frescoes that united sacred and secular themes. *The Procession of the Magi*, painted by Benozzo Gozzoli (ca. 1420–1497), cleverly casts members of the Medici family and their allies as characters in a traditional Christian scene (see Figure 16.1). Dressed in dark blue, Cosimo sits on a donkey (a sign of Christlike humility) bearing the Medici insignia; on his left, seated on a white horse and wearing a richly brocaded doublet, is his son Piero. Tradition holds that the sumptuously dressed figure who leads the procession is an idealized portrait of Lorenzo, who would have been only ten years old at the time the fresco was painted.

Affluence coupled with intellectual discernment and refined taste inspired the Medici to commission works from some of the greatest artists of the Renaissance: Brunelleschi, Botticelli, Verrocchio, and Michelangelo. For almost two centuries, scholars, poets, painters, and civic leaders shared common interests, acknowledging one another as leaders of a vigorous cultural revival.

Classical Humanism

Classical culture did not disappear altogether with the fall of Rome in 476 C.E. It was preserved by countless Christian and Muslim scholars, revived by Charlemagne in the Early Middle Ages, and championed by such medieval intellectuals as Aquinas (who took Aristotle as his master) and Dante (who chose Virgil as his guide). But the Classical humanists of the Renaissance generated a deeper and more all-embracing appreciation of Greco-Roman antiquity than any of their predecessors. They advocated the recovery and uncensored study of the entire body of Greek and Latin manuscripts and the self-conscious imitation of Classical art and architecture. They regarded Classical authority not exclusively as a means of clarifying Christian truths, but as the basis for a new appraisal of the role of the individual in the world order. Thus, although Renaissance humanists still prized the Liberal Arts as the basis for intellectual advancement, they approached the Classics from a different point of view than that of their Scholastic predecessors. Whereas the Scholastics had studied the Greco-Roman legacy as the foundation for Christian dogma and faith, Renaissance humanists discovered in the Greek and Latin Classics a rational guide to the fulfillment of the human potential. Moreover, the Renaissance revival of humanism differed from earlier revivals because it attracted the interest of a broad base of the population and not a mere handful of theologians, as was the case, for instance, in Carolingian or later medieval times.

Petrarch: "Father of Humanism"

The most famous of the early Florentine humanists was the poet and scholar Francesco Petrarch (1304–1374). Often called the "father of humanism," Petrarch devoted his life to the recovery, copying, and editing of Latin manuscripts. In quest of these ancient sources of wisdom, he traveled all over Europe, hand-copying manuscripts he could not beg or buy from monastic libraries, borrowing others from friends, and gradually amassing a private library of more than 200 volumes. Petrarch was a tireless popularizer of Classical studies. Reviving the epistolary (letter-writing) tradition that had practically disappeared since Roman times, he wrote hundreds of letters describing his admiration for antiquity and his enthusiasm for the Classics, especially the writings of the Roman statesman Cicero (see chapter 6). In his letters, Petrarch eulogized and imitated Cicero's polished prose style, which stood in refined contrast to the corrupt Latin of his own time.

The intensity of Petrarch's passion for antiquity and his eagerness to rescue it from neglect come across powerfully in a letter addressed to his friend Lapo da Castiglionchio. Here, he laments the scarcity and incompetence of copyists, bemoans the fact that books that are difficult to understand have "sunk into utter neglect," and defends his ambition to preserve them, despite the inordinate amount of time it takes to copy them. (Such fervor, shared by his successors, surely motivated the invention of print technology within a hundred years of his death.) In the letter to Lapo, part of which is reproduced below, Petrarch vows to sacrifice the precious hours of his old age to the pleasures of copying Cicero (whom he calls fondly by his middle name, Tullius).

READING 16.1 From Petrarch's Letter to Lapo da Castiglionchio (ca. 1351)

Your Cicero has been in my possession four years and   1
more. There is a good reason, though, for so long a delay;
namely, the great scarcity of copyists who understand
such work. It is a state of affairs that has resulted in an
incredible loss to scholarship. Books that by their nature
are a little hard to understand are no longer multiplied,
and have ceased to be generally intelligible, and so have
sunk into utter neglect, and in the end have perished.
This age of ours consequently has let fall, bit by bit, some
of the richest and sweetest fruits that the tree of   10
knowledge has yielded; has thrown away the results of the
vigils and labors of the most illustrious men of genius,
things of more value, I am almost tempted to say, than
anything else in the whole world. . . .

But I must return to your Cicero. I could not do without
it, and the incompetence of the copyists would not let me
possess it. What was left for me but to rely upon my own
resources, and press these weary fingers and this worn
and ragged pen into service? The plan that I followed was

this. I want you to know it, in case you should ever have   20
to grapple with a similar task. Not a single word did I read
except as I wrote. But how is that, I hear someone say;
did you write without knowing what it was that you were
writing? Ah! but from the very first it was enough for me to
know that it was a work of Tullius, and an extremely rare
one too. And then as soon as I was fairly started I found
at every step so much sweetness and charm, and felt so
strong a desire to advance, that the only difficulty which I
experienced in reading and writing at the same time came
from the fact that my pen could not cover the ground so   30
rapidly as I wanted it to, whereas my expectation had
been rather that it would outstrip my eyes, and that my
ardor for writing would be chilled by the slowness of my
reading. So the pen held back the eye, and the eye drove
on the pen, and I covered page after page, delighting in
my task, and committing many and many a passage to
memory as I wrote. For just in proportion as the writing is
slower than the reading does the passage make a deep
impression and cling to the mind.

And yet I must confess that I did finally reach a point   40
in my copying where I was overcome by weariness; not
mental, for how unlikely that would be where Cicero was
concerned, but the sort of fatigue that springs from
excessive manual labor. I began to feel doubtful about this
plan that I was following, and to regret having undertaken
a task for which I had not been trained; when suddenly I
came across a place where Cicero tells how he himself
copied the orations of—someone or other; just who it was I
do not know, but certainly no Tullius, for there is but one
such man, one such voice, one such mind. These are his   50
words: "You say that you have been in the habit of reading
the orations of Cassius[1] in your idle moments. But I," he
jestingly adds, with his customary disregard of his
adversary's feelings, "have made a practice of *copying*
them, so that I might *have* no idle moments." As I read this
passage I grew hot with shame, like a modest young soldier
who hears the voice of his beloved leader rebuking him. I
said to myself, "So Cicero copied orations that another
wrote, and you are not ready to copy his? What ardor! What
scholarly devotion! what reverence for a man of godlike   60
genius!" These thoughts were a spur to me, and I pushed
on, with all my doubts dispelled. If ever from my darkness
there shall come a single ray that can enhance the splendor
of the reputation which his heavenly eloquence has won
for him, it will proceed in no slight measure from the fact
that I was so captivated by his ineffable sweetness that I
did a thing in itself most irksome with such delight and
eagerness that I scarcely knew I was doing it at all.

So then at last your Cicero has the happiness of
returning to you, bearing you my thanks. And yet he also   70
stays, very willingly, with me; a dear friend, to whom I give
the credit of being almost the only man of letters for whose
sake I would go to the length of spending my time, when

---

[1] More probably Lucius Licenius Crassus (140–91 B.C.E.), one of the great Roman orators and a principal figure in Cicero's treatise *On Oratory*.

the difficulties of life are pressing on me so sharply and inexorably and the cares pertaining to my literary labors make the longest life seem far too short, in transcribing compositions not my own. I may have done such things in former days, when I thought myself rich in time, and had not learned how stealthily it slips away: but I now know that this is of all our riches the most uncertain and **80** fleeting; the years are closing in upon me now, and there is no longer any room for deviation from the beaten path. I am forced to practice strict economy; I only hope that I have not begun too late. But Cicero! he assuredly is worthy of a part of even the little that I have left. Farewell.

Q In what ways does Petrarch's letter exemplify the aims and passions of the Renaissance humanist?

Nothing in the letter to Lapo suggests that Petrarch was a devout Christian; yet, in fact, Petrarch's affection for Cicero was matched only by his devotion to Saint Augustine and his writings. Indeed, in their introspective tone and their expression of intimate feelings and desires, Petrarch's letters reveal the profound influence of Augustine's *Confessions*, a work that Petrarch deeply admired. Torn between Christian piety and his passion for Classical antiquity, Petrarch experienced recurrent psychic conflict. In his writings there is a gnawing and unresolved dissonance between the dual imperatives of his heritage: the Judeo-Christian will to believe and the Classical will to reason. Such self-torment—evident in Petrarch's poems, over 300 examples of which make up the *Canzoniere* (*Songbook*)—implies that Petrarch remained, in part, a medieval man. Yet it did not prevent him from pursuing worldly fame. At Rome in 1341, he proudly received the laurel crown for outstanding literary achievement. The tradition, which looks back to the ancient Greek practice of honoring victors in the athletic games with wreaths made from the foliage of the laurel tree, survives in our modern honorary title "poet *laureate*."

The object of Petrarch's affection and the inspiration for the *Canzoniere* was a married Florentine woman named Laura de Sade. Petrarch dedicated hundreds of love lyrics to Laura, many of which were written after she died of bubonic plague in 1348. While Petrarch used Latin, the language of learning, for his letters and essays, he wrote his poems and songs in vernacular Italian. His favorite poetic form was the **sonnet**, a fourteen-line lyric poem. The sonnet form originated among the poets of Sicily, but it was Petrarch who brought it to perfection. He favored a rhyme scheme (difficult to replicate in English translation) of abab/abab for the octave (the first eight lines) and cde/cde for the sestet (the last six lines). Influenced by the "sweet style" of his Italian forebears and, more generally, by *troubadour* songs and Islamic lyric verse, Petrarch's sonnets are a record of his struggle between the flesh and the spirit. In their self-reflective and even self-indulgent tone, they are strikingly modern, especially where they explore Petrarch's love for Laura—and for love itself. In the first of the two sonnets below, Petrarch explores the conflicting emotional

states evoked by his unfulfilled desire. These are phrased intriguingly in contrasting sets: peace/war, burn/freeze, grief/laughter, and so on. In the second sonnet, Petrarch employs vivid imagery—"a field without flowers," "[a] ring without gem"—to picture the void left by Laura's death.

READING 16.2 From Petrarch's *Canzoniere*
(ca. 1350)

Sonnet 134

I find no peace, yet I am not at war;	**1**
I fear and hope, I burn and freeze;	
I rise to heaven, and fall to earth's floor	
Grasping at nothing, the world I seize.	
She imprisons me, who neither jails nor frees,	**5**
Nor keeps me for her self, nor slips the noose;	
Love does not kill, nor set me free,	
Love takes my life, but will not set me loose.	
I have no eyes yet see, no tongue yet scream;	
I long to perish, and seek release;	**10**
I hate myself, and love another.	
I feed on grief, and in my laughter weep;	
Both death and life displease me;	
Lady, because of you, I suffer.	

Sonnet 338

Death, you have left the world without its sun,	**1**
Gloomy and cold, Love blind and without arms,	
Loveliness bare, and sick all beauty's charms,	
Myself distressed and by this load undone,	
Courtesy banished, honesty pretext:	**5**
I alone mourn, though not alone I should;	
For you uprooted a clear shoot of good.	
Torn the first valour, which will be the next?	
They ought to weep, the earth, the sea, the air,	
The human lineage that without her is	**10**
Like a field without flowers, ring without gem.	
They did not know her while she was with them;	
I did, who am left here and weep for this,	
And the sky did, that with my grief grows fair.	

Q What are the main features of the Petrarchan sonnet?

Q Which of these two English translations preserves the Petrachan rhyme scheme?

In his own time, Petrarch was acclaimed as the finest practitioner of the sonnet form. His sonnets were translated by Chaucer and set to music by Landini (see chapter 15). During the sixteenth century, Michelangelo Buonarroti in Italy and the English poets Thomas Wyatt, Edmund Spenser, and William Shakespeare (see chapter 19) wrote sonnets modeled on those of Petrarch. Petrarch's influence as a Classical humanist was equally significant. He established the standards for the study of the Latin classics, and, by insisting on the union of ethics and eloquence, he pioneered the modern ideal of the educated individual. Although Petrarch never learned to read Greek, he encouraged his contemporaries and friends (including Boccaccio) to master the language of the first philosophers. Petrarch's passion for Classical learning initiated something of a cult, which at its worst became an infatuation with everything antique, but which at its best called forth a diligent examination of the Classical heritage.

Civic Humanism

The effort to recover, copy, and produce accurate editions of Classical writings dominated the early history of the Renaissance in Italy. By the middle of the fifteenth century, almost all of the major Greek and Latin manuscripts of antiquity were available to scholars. Throughout Italy, the small study retreat, or *studiolo*, filled with manuscripts, musical instruments, and the artifacts of scientific inquiry, came to be considered essential to the advancement of intellectual life. Wealthy patrons like Federico da Montefeltro, Duke of Urbino and his wife Battista Sforza (Figures **16.5** and **16.6**) encouraged humanistic education, commissioning private studies for their villas and for the ducal palace itself (Figure **16.7**). Among the humanists of Italy, Classical writings kindled new attitudes concerning the importance of active participation in civic life. Aristotle's view of human beings as "political animals" (see chapter 4) and Cicero's glorification of duty to the state (see chapter 6) encouraged humanists to perceive that the exercise of civic responsibility was the hallmark of the cultivated individual. Such civic humanists as Leonardo Bruni and Coluccio Salutati, who served Florence as chancellors and historians during the Renaissance, defended the precept that one's highest good was activity in the public interest.

Alberti and Renaissance *Virtù*

A formative figure of the Early Renaissance was the multi-talented Florentine humanist Leon Battista Alberti (1404–1474) (Figure **16.8**). A mathematician, architect, engineer, musician, and playwright, Alberti's most original literary contribution (and that for which he was best known in his own time) was his treatise *On the Family*. Published in 1443, *On the Family* is the first sociological inquiry into the structure, function, and responsibilities of the family. It is also a moralizing treatise that defends the importance of a Classical education and hard work as prerequisites for worldly success. In Alberti's view, skill, talent, fortitude, ingenuity, and the ability to determine one's destiny—qualities summed up in the single Italian word *virtù*—are essential to human enterprise. *Virtù*, Alberti observes, is not inherited; rather, it must be cultivated. Not to be confused with the English word "virtue," *virtù* describes the self-confident vitality of the self-made individual.

In *On the Family*, Alberti warns that idleness is the enemy of human achievement, while the performance of "manly tasks" and the pursuit of "fine studies" are sure means to worldly fame and material fortune. Pointing to the success of his own family, he defends the acquisition of wealth as the reward of free-spirited *virtù*. The buoyant optimism so characteristic of the age of the Renaissance is epitomized in Alberti's statement that "man can do anything he wants." Alberti himself—architect, mathematician, and scholar—was living proof of that viewpoint.

READING 16.3 From Alberti's *On the Family* (1443)

Let Fathers . . . see to it that their sons pursue the study of letters assiduously and let them teach them to understand and write correctly. Let them not think they have taught them if they do not see that their sons have learned to read and write perfectly, for in this it is almost the same to know badly as not to know at all. Then let the children learn arithmetic and gain a sufficient knowledge of geometry, for these are enjoyable sciences suitable to young minds and of great use to all regardless of age or social status. Then let them turn once more to   10
the poets, orators, and philosophers. Above all, one must try to have good teachers from whom the children may learn excellent customs as well as letters. I should want my sons to become accustomed to good authors. I should want them to learn grammar from Priscian and Servius and to become familiar, not with collections of sayings and extracts, but with the works of Cicero, Livy, and Sallust above all, so that they might learn the perfection and splendid eloquence of the elegant Latin tongue from the very beginning. They say that the same   20
thing happens to the mind as to a bottle: if at first one puts bad wine in it, its taste will never disappear. One must, therefore, avoid all crude and inelegant writers and study those who are polished and elegant, keeping their works at hand, reading them continuously, reciting them often, and memorizing them. . . .

Think for a moment: can you find a man—or even imagine one—who fears infamy, though he may have no strong desire for glory, and yet does not hate idleness and sloth? Who can ever think it possible to achieve   30
honors and dignity without the loving study of excellent arts, without assiduous work, without striving in difficult manly tasks? If one wishes to gain praise and fame, he must abhor idleness and laziness and oppose them as deadly foes. There is nothing that gives rise to dishonor and infamy as much as idleness. Idleness has always been the breeding-place of vice. . . .

Therefore, idleness which is the cause of so many evils must be hated by all good men. Even if idleness were not a deadly enemy of good customs and the cause of every   40
vice, as everyone knows it is, what man, though inept, could wish to spend his life without using his mind, his limbs, his every faculty? Does an idle man differ from a tree trunk, a statue, or a putrid corpse? As for me, one who does not care for honor or fear shame and does not act with prudence and intelligence does not live well. But one who lies buried in idleness and sloth and completely neglects good deeds and fine studies is

Figure 16.5 and **16.6 PIERO DELLA FRANCESCA**, (above) *Battista Sforza, Duchess of Urbino* and *Federico da Montefeltro, Duke of Urbino*, after 1475. Oil and tempera on panel, each 18½ x 13 in. The two profile portraits made up a diptych that commemorated the marital union of the two rulers. Federico became wealthy as a *condottiere* and diplomat. Battista, who died at the age of twenty-six, bore eight daughters and one son. The two are shown against an expansive landscape designating the lands they ruled in central Italy.

Figure 16.7 (below) The *studiolo* of Federico da Montefeltro in the Palazzo Ducale, Urbino, Italy, 1476. In the panels that line the walls of the study, the illusion of real books, scientific devices, musical instruments, and military equipment—objects related to Federico's intellectual and civic accomplishments—was created by way of **intarsia** (inlaid wood), a technique perfected in Renaissance Florence. The half-length portraits (above) represent Christian notables, and Classical and Renaissance humanists.

Figure 16.8 LEON BATTISTA ALBERTI, *Self-Portrait*, ca. 1435. Bronze, 7²⁹⁄₃₂ × 5¹¹⁄₃₂ in. This bronze self-portrait of Alberti revives the tradition of the Roman medals that commemorated the achievements of notable rulers. The artist includes his personal emblem, a winged eye that resembles an Egyptian hieroglyth.

altogether dead. One who does not give himself body and soul to the quest for praise and virtue is to be deemed unworthy of life. . . . 50

[Man] comes into this world in order to enjoy all things, be virtuous, and make himself happy. For he who may be called happy will be useful to other men, and he who is now useful to others cannot but please God. He who uses things improperly harms other men and incurs God's displeasure, and he who displeases God is a fool if he thinks he is happy. We may, therefore, state that man is created by Nature to use, and reap the benefits of, all things, and that he is born to be happy. . . . 60

I believe it will not be excessively difficult for a man to acquire the highest honors and glory, if he perseveres in his studies as much as is necessary, toiling, sweating, and striving to surpass all others by far. It is said that man can do anything he wants. If you will strive with all your strength and skill, as I have said, I have no doubt you will reach the highest degree of perfection and fame in any profession. . . .

To those of noble and liberal spirit, no occupations seem less brilliant than those whose purpose is to make money. If you think a moment and try to remember which are the occupations for making money, you will see that they consist of buying and selling, lending and collecting. I believe that these occupations whose purpose is gain may seem vile and worthless to you, for you are of noble and lofty spirit. In fact, selling is a mercenary trade; you serve the buyer's needs, pay yourself for your work, and make a profit by charging others more than you yourself have paid. You are not selling goods, therefore, but your labors; you are reimbursed for the cost of your goods, and for your labor you receive a profit. Lending would be a laudable generosity if you did not seek interest, but then it would not be a profitable business. Some say that these occupations, which we shall call pecuniary, always entail dishonesty and numerous lies and often entail dishonest agreements and fraudulent contracts. They say, therefore, that those of liberal spirit must completely avoid them as dishonest and mercenary. But I believe that those who judge all pecuniary occupations in this manner are wrong. Granted that acquiring wealth is not a glorious enterprise to be likened to the most noble professions. We must not, however, scorn a man who is not naturally endowed for noble deeds if he turns to these other occupations in which he knows he is not inept and which, everyone admits, are of great use to the family and to the state. Riches are useful for gaining friends and praise, for with them we can help those in need. With wealth we can gain fame and prestige if we use it munificently for great and noble projects. 100

70

80

90

Q **What is Alberti's opinion of the business of money-making? What, according to him, is the value of wealth?**

Ficino: The Platonic Academy

After the fall of Constantinople to the Ottoman Turks in 1453, Greek manuscripts and Byzantine scholars poured into Italy, contributing to the efflorescence of what the humanist philosopher Marsilio Ficino (1433–1499) called "a golden age." Encouraged by the availability of Greek resources and supported by his patron Cosimo de' Medici, Ficino translated the entire corpus of Plato's writings from Greek into Latin, making them available to Western scholars for the first time since antiquity. Ficino's translations and the founding of the Platonic Academy in Florence (financed by Cosimo) launched a reappraisal of Plato and the Neoplatonists that had major consequences in the domains of art and literature. Plato's writings—especially the *Symposium*, in which love is exalted as a divine force—advanced the idea, popularized by Ficino, that "platonic" (or spiritual) love attracted the soul to God. Platonic love became a major theme among Renaissance poets and painters, who held that spiritual love was inspired by physical beauty.

Pico della Mirandola

While Ficino was engaged in popularizing Plato, one of his most learned contemporaries, Giovanni Pico della Mirandola (1463–1494), undertook the translation of various ancient literary works in Hebrew, Arabic, Latin, and Greek. Humanist, poet, and theologian, Pico sought not only to bring to light the entire history of human thought, but to prove that all intellectual expression shared the same divine purpose and design. This effort to discover a "unity of truth" in all philosophic thought—similar to but more comprehensive than the medieval quest for synthesis and so dramatically different from our own modern pluralistic outlook—came to dominate the arts and ideas of the High Renaissance.

Pico's program to recover the past and his reverence for the power of human knowledge continued a tradition that looked back to Petrarch; at the same time, his monumental efforts typified the activist spirit of Renaissance *individualism*—the affirmation of the unique, self-fashioning potential of the human being. In Rome, at the age of twenty-four, Pico boldly challenged the Church to debate some 900 theological propositions that challenged the institutional Church in a variety of theological and philosophical matters. The young scholar did not get the opportunity to debate his theses; indeed, he was persecuted for heresy and forced to flee Italy. As an introduction to the disputation, Pico had prepared the Latin introduction that has come to be called the *Oration on the Dignity of Man*. In this "manifesto of humanism," Pico drew on a wide range of literary sources to build an argument for free will and the perfectibility of the individual. Describing the individual's position as only "a little lower than the angels," he stressed man's capacity to determine his own destiny on the hierarchical "chain of being" that linked the divine and brute realms. Although Pico's *Oration* was not circulated until after his death, its assertion of free will and its acclamation of the unlimited potential of the individual came to symbolize the collective ideals of the Renaissance humanists. The Renaissance view that the self-made individual occupies the center of a rational universe is nowhere better described than in the following excerpt.

READING 16.4 From Pico's *Oration on the Dignity of Man* (1486)

Most esteemed Fathers,[1] I have read in the ancient writings 1
of the Arabians that Abdala the Saracen[2] on being asked
what, on this stage, so to say, of the world, seemed to him
most evocative of wonder, replied that there was nothing to
be seen more marvelous than man. And that celebrated
exclamation of Hermes Trismegistus,[3] "What a great miracle
is man, Asclepius"[4] confirms this opinion.

And still, as I reflected upon the basis assigned for these
estimations, I was not fully persuaded by the diverse
reasons advanced by a variety o persons for the 10
preeminence of human nature; for example: that man is the
intermediary between creatures, that he is the familiar

of the gods above him as he is lord of the beings beneath
him; that, by the acuteness of his senses, the inquiry of his
reason and the light of his intelligence, he is the interpreter
of nature, set midway between the timeless unchanging and
the flux of time; the living union (as the Persians say), the
very marriage hymn of the world, and, by David's testimony[5]
but little lower than the angels. These reasons are all,
without question, of great weight; nevertheless, they do 20
not touch the principal reasons, those, that is to say, which
justify man's unique right to such unbounded admiration.
Why, I asked, should we not admire the angels themselves
and the beatific choirs more?

At long last, however, I feel that I have come to some
understanding of why man is the most fortunate of living
things and, consequently, deserving of all admiration; of
what may be the condition in the hierarchy of beings
assigned to him, which draws upon him the envy, not of
the brutes alone, but of the astral beings and of the very 30
intelligences which dwell beyond the confines of the
world. A thing surpassing belief and smiting the soul with
wonder. Still, how could it be otherwise? For it is on this
ground that man is, with complete justice, considered and
called a great miracle and a being worthy of all admiration.

Hear then, oh Fathers, precisely what this condition of
man is; and in the name of your humanity, grant me your
benign audition as I pursue this theme.

God the Father, the Mightiest Architect, had already
raised, according to the precepts of His hidden wisdom, 40
this world we see, the cosmic dwelling of divinity, a temple
most august. He had already adorned the supercelestial
region with Intelligences, infused the heavenly globes with
the life of immortal souls and set the fermenting dung-
heap of the inferior world teeming with every form of
animal life. But when this work was done, the Divine
Artificer still longed for some creature which might
comprehend the meaning of so vast an achievement, which
might be moved with love at its beauty and smitten with
awe at its grandeur. When, consequently, all else had been 50
completed, . . . in the very last place, He bethought Himself
of bringing forth man. Truth was, however, that there
remained no archetype according to which He might
fashion a new offspring, nor in His treasure-houses the
wherewithal to endow a new son with a fitting
inheritance, nor any place, among the seats of the
universe, where this new creature might dispose himself to
contemplate the world. All space was already filled; all
things had been distributed in the highest, the middle and
the lowest orders. Still, it was not in the nature of the 60

---

[1] The assembly of clergymen to whom the oration was to be addressed.
[2] The Arabic philosopher and translator Abd-Allah Ibn al Muqaffa (718–775).
[3] The Greek name (Hermes Thrice-Great) for the Egyptian god Thoth, the presumed author of a body of occult philosophy that mingled Neoplatonism, alchemy, and mystical interpretations of the Scriptures.
[4] The Greek god of healing and medicine.
[5] In Psalms 8.6.

power of the Father to fail in this last creative élan; nor was it in the nature of that supreme Wisdom to hesitate through lack of counsel in so crucial a matter; nor, finally, in the nature of His beneficent love to compel the creature destined to praise the divine generosity in all other things to find it wanting in himself.

At last, the Supreme Maker decreed that this creature, to whom He could give nothing wholly his own, should have a share in the particular endowment of every other creature. Taking man, therefore, this creature of indeterminate image, **70** He set him in the middle of the world and thus spoke to him:

"We have given you, Oh Adam, no visage proper to yourself, nor any endowment properly your own, in order that whatever place, whatever form, whatever gifts you may, with premeditation, select, these same you may have and possess through your own judgment and decision. The nature of all other creatures is defined and restricted within laws which We have laid down; you, by contrast, impeded by no such restrictions, may, by your own free will, to whose custody We have assigned you, trace for yourself the lineaments of your **80** own nature. I have placed you at the very center of the world, so that from that vantage point you may with greater ease glance round about you on all that the world contains. We have made you a creature neither of heaven nor of earth, neither mortal nor immortal, in order that you may, as the free and proud shaper of your own being, fashion yourself in the form you may prefer. It will be in your power to descend to the lower, brutish forms of life; [or] you will be able, through your own decision, to rise again to the superior orders whose life is divine." **90**

Oh unsurpassed generosity of God the Father, Oh wondrous and unsurpassable felicity of man, to whom it is granted to have what he chooses, to be what he wills to be! The brutes, from the moment of their birth, bring with them, as Lucilius[6] says, "from their mother's womb" all that they will ever possess. The highest spiritual beings were, from the very moment of creation, or soon thereafter, fixed in the mode of being which would be theirs through measureless eternities. But upon man, at the moment of his creation, God bestowed seeds pregnant with all possibilities, the germs of every **100** form of life. Whichever of these a man shall cultivate, the same will mature and bear fruit in him. If vegetative, he will become a plant; if sensual, he will become brutish; if rational, he will reveal himself a heavenly being; if intellectual, he will be an angel and the son of God. And if, dissatisfied with the lot of all creatures, he should recollect himself into the center of his own unity, he will there, become one spirit with God, in the solitary darkness of the Father, Who is set above all things, himself transcend all creatures.

Who then will not look with awe upon this our chameleon, **110** or who, at least, will look with greater admiration on any other being? This creature, man, whom Asclepius the Athenian, by reason of this very mutability, this nature capable of transforming itself, quite rightly said was symbolized in the mysteries by the figure of Proteus. This is the source of those metamorphoses, or transformations, so

celebrated among the Hebrews and among the Pythagoreans;[7] . . . . while the Pythagoreans transform men guilty of crimes into brutes or even, if we are to believe Empedocles,[8] into plants; and Mohamet,[9] imitating them, was known **120** frequently to say that the man who deserts the divine law becomes a brute. And he was right; for it is not the bark that makes the tree, but its insensitive and unresponsive nature; nor the hide which makes the beast of burden, but its brute and sensual soul; nor the orbicular form which makes the heavens, but their harmonious order. Finally, it is not freedom from a body, but its spiritual intelligence, which makes the angel. If you see a man dedicated to his stomach, crawling on the ground, you see a plant and not a man; or if you see a man bedazzled by the empty forms of the imagination, as **130** by the wiles of Calypso,[10] and through their alluring solicitations made a slave to his own senses, you see a brute and not a man. If, however, you see a philosopher, judging and distinguishing all things according to the rule of reason, him shall you hold in veneration, for he is a creature of heaven and not of earth; if, finally, a pure contemplator, unmindful of the body, wholly withdrawn into the inner chambers of the mind, here indeed is neither a creature of earth nor a heavenly creature, but some higher divinity, clothed with human flesh.

Q In what ways, according to Pico, is man "a great miracle" (line 6)?

Q Why does he call man "our chameleon" (line 110)?

Castiglione: The Well-Rounded Person

By far the most provocative analysis of Renaissance individualism is that found in *The Book of the Courtier*, a treatise written between 1513 and 1518 by the Italian diplomat and man of letters Baldassare Castiglione (1478–1529) (Figure **16.9**). Castiglione's *Courtier* was inspired by a series of conversations that had taken place among a group of sixteenth-century aristocrats at the court of Urbino, a mecca for humanist studies located in central Italy. The subject of these conversations, which Castiglione probably recorded from memory, concerns the qualifications of the ideal Renaissance man and woman. Debating this subject at length, the members of the court arrive at a consensus that affords the image of *l'uomo universale*: the well-rounded person. Castiglione reports that the ideal man should master all the skills of the medieval warrior and display the physical proficiency of a champion athlete. But he also must possess the refinements of a humanistic education. He must know Latin and Greek (as well as his own native language), be familiar with the

---

[7] Followers of the Greek philosopher and mathematician Pythagoras (fl. 530 B.C.E.); see chapter 5.

[8] A Greek philosopher and poet (495–435 B.C.E.).

[9] The prophet Muhammad (570–632); see chapter 10.

[10] In Greek mythology, a sea nymph who lured Odysseus to remain with her for seven years.

Figure 16.9 RAPHAEL, *Portrait of Baldassare Castiglione*, ca. 1515. Oil on canvas, approx. 30¼ × 26½ in.

Classics, speak and write well, and be able to compose verse, draw, and play a musical instrument. Moreover, all that the Renaissance gentleman does, he should do with an air of nonchalance and grace, a quality summed up in the Italian word *sprezzatura*. This unique combination of breeding and education would produce a cultured individual to serve a very special end: the perfection of the state. For, as Book Four of *The Courtier* explains, the primary duty of the well-rounded person is to influence the ruler to govern wisely.

Although, according to Castiglione, the goal of the ideal gentleman was to cultivate his full potential as a human being, such was not the case with the Renaissance gentlewoman. The Renaissance woman should have a knowledge of letters, music, and art—that is, like the gentleman, she should be privileged with a humanistic education—but in no way should she violate that "soft and delicate tenderness that is her defining quality." Castiglione's peers agreed that "in her ways, manners, words, gestures, and bearing, a woman ought to be very unlike a man." Just as the success of the courtier depends on his ability to influence those who rule, the success of the lady rests with her skills in entertaining the male members of the court.

Castiglione's handbook of Renaissance etiquette was based on the views of a narrow, aristocratic segment of society. But despite its selective viewpoint, it was immensely popular: in 1527, the Aldine Press in Venice printed *The Courtier* in an edition of more than 1000 copies. It was translated into five languages and went through fifty-seven editions before the year 1600. Historically, *The Book of the Courtier* is an index to cultural changes that were taking place between medieval and early modern times. It departs from exclusively feudal and Christian educational ideals and formulates a program for the cultivation of both mind *and* body that has become fundamental to modern Western education. Representative also of the shift from medieval to modern values is Castiglione's preoccupation with manners rather than morals; that is, with *how* individuals act and how their actions may impress their peers, rather than with the intrinsic moral value of those actions.

READING 16.5 From Castiglione's *The Book of the Courtier* (1518)

[Count Ludovico de Canossa says:] "I am of opinion that   1
the principal and true profession of the Courtier ought to
be that of arms; which I would have him follow actively
above all else, and be known among others as bold and
strong, and loyal to whomsoever he serves. And he will
win a reputation for these good qualities by exercising
them at all times and in all places, since one may never
fail in this without severest censure. And just as among
women, their fair fame once sullied never recovers its
first lustre, so the reputation of a gentleman who bears   10
arms, if once it be in the least tarnished with cowardice
or other disgrace, remains forever infamous before the
world and full of ignominy.[1] Therefore the more our
Courtier excels in this art, the more he will be worthy of
praise. . . .

"Then coming to the bodily frame, I say it is enough if
this be neither extremely short nor tall, for both of these
conditions excite a certain contemptuous surprise, and
men of either sort are gazed upon in much the same way
that we gaze on monsters. Yet if we must offend in one   20
of the two extremes, it is preferable to fall a little short
of the just measure of height than to exceed it, for
besides often being dull of intellect, men thus huge of
body are also unfit for every exercise of agility, which
thing I should much wish in the Courtier. And so I would
have him well built and shapely of limb, and would have
him show strength and lightness and suppleness, and
know all bodily exercises that befit a man of war;
whereof I think the first should be to handle every sort of
weapon well on foot and on horse, to understand the   30
advantages of each, and especially to be familiar with
those weapons that are ordinarily used among
gentlemen; for besides the use of them in war, where
such subtlety in contrivance is perhaps not needful,
there frequently arise differences between one
gentleman and another, which afterwards result in duels
often fought with such weapons as happen at the
moment to be within reach; thus knowledge of this kind
is a very safe thing. Nor am I one of those who say that
skill is forgotten in the hour of need; for he whose skill   40
forsakes him at such a time, indeed gives token that he

---

[1] Shame, dishonor.

has already lost heart and head through fear.

"Moreover I deem it very important to know how to wrestle, for it is a great help in the use of all kinds of weapons on foot. Then, both for his own sake and for that of his friends, he must understand the quarrels and differences that may arise, and must be quick to seize an advantage, always showing courage and prudence in all things. Nor should he be too ready to fight except when honor demands it. . . .

"There are also many other exercises, which although not immediately dependent upon arms, yet are closely connected therewith, and greatly foster manly sturdiness; and one of the chief among these seems to me to be the chase [hunting], because it bears a certain likeness to war: and truly it is an amusement for great lords and befitting a man at court, and furthermore it is seen to have been much cultivated among the ancients. It is fitting also to know how to swim, to leap, to run, to throw stones, for besides the use that may be made of this in war, a man often has occasion to show what he can do in such matters; whence good esteem is to be won, especially with the multitude, who must be taken into account withal. Another admirable exercise, and one very befitting a man at court, is the game of tennis, in which are well shown the disposition of the body, the quickness and suppleness of every member, and all those qualities that are seen in nearly every other exercise. Nor less highly do I esteem vaulting on horse, which although it be fatiguing and difficult, makes a man very light and dexterous more than any other thing; and besides its utility, if this lightness is accompanied by grace, it is to my thinking a finer show than any of the others.

"Our Courtier having once become more than fairly expert in these exercises, I think he should leave the others on one side: such as turning somersaults, rope-walking, and the like, which savor of the mountebank and little befit a gentleman.

"But since one cannot devote himself to such fatiguing exercises continually, and since repetition becomes very tiresome and abates the admiration felt for what is rare, we must always diversify our life with various occupations. For this reason I would have our Courtier sometimes descend to quieter and more tranquil exercises, and in order to escape envy and to entertain himself agreeably with everyone, let him do whatever others do, yet never departing from praiseworthy deeds, and governing himself with that good judgment which will keep him from all folly; but let him laugh, jest, banter, frolic and dance, yet in such fashion that he shall always appear genial and discreet, and that everything he may do or say shall be stamped with grace."

[Cesare Gonzaga says:] "But having before now often considered whence this grace springs, laying aside those men who have it by nature, I find one universal rule concerning it, which seems to me worth more in this matter than any other in all things human that are done or said: and that is to avoid affectation to the uttermost and as it were a very sharp and dangerous rock; and, to

use possibly a new word, to practice in everything a certain nonchalance that shall conceal design and show that what is done and said is done without effort and almost without thought[2]. . . ."

[Count Ludovico says:] "I think that what is chiefly important and necessary for the Courtier, in order to speak and write well, is knowledge; for he who is ignorant and has nothing in his mind that merits being heard, can neither say it nor write it.

"Next he must arrange in good order what he has to say or write; then express it well in words, which (if I do not err) ought to be precise, choice, rich and rightly formed, but above all, in use even among the masses; because such words as these make the grandeur and pomp of speech, if the speaker has good sense and carefulness, and knows how to choose the words most expressive of his meaning, and to exalt them, to mould position and order that they shall at a glance show and make known their dignity and splendor, like pictures placed in good and proper light.

"And this I say as well of writing as of speaking: in which however some things are required that are not needful in writing—such as a good voice, not too thin and soft like a woman's, nor yet so stern and rough as to smack of the rustic's—but sonorous, clear, sweet and well sounding, with distinct enunciation, and with proper bearing and gestures; which I think consist in certain movements of the whole body, not affected or violent, but tempered by a calm face and with a play of the eyes that shall give an effect of grace, accord with the words, and as far as possible express also, together with the gestures, the speaker's intent and feeling.

"But all these things would be vain and of small moment, if the thoughts expressed by the words were not beautiful, ingenious, acute, elegant and grave— according to the need.

"I would have him more than passably accomplished in letters, at least in those studies that are called the humanities, and conversant not only with the Latin language but with the Greek, for the sake of the many different things that have been admirably written therein. Let him be well versed in the poets, and not less in the orators and historians, and also proficient in writing verse and prose, especially in this vulgar[3] tongue of ours; for besides the enjoyment he will find in it, he will by this means never lack agreeable entertainment with ladies, who are usually fond of such things. And if other occupations or want of study prevent his reaching such perfection as to render his writings worthy of great praise, let him be careful to suppress them so that others may not laugh at him. . . .

"My lords, you must know that I am not content with the Courtier unless he be also a musician and unless, besides understanding and being able to read notes, he

---

[2] That is, with nonchalance (in Italian, *sprezzatura*).
[3] Common speech; that is, Italian.
[4] Various.

can play upon divers[4] instruments. For if we consider rightly, there is to be found no rest from toil or medicine for the troubled spirit more becoming and praiseworthy in time of leisure, than this; and especially in courts, where besides the relief from tedium that music affords us all, many things are done to please the ladies, whose tender and gentle spirit is easily penetrated by harmony and filled with sweetness. Thus it is no marvel that in both ancient and modern times they have always been inclined to favor musicians, and have found refreshing spiritual food in music. . . .

"I wish to discuss another matter, which I deem of great importance and therefore think our Courtier ought by no means to omit: and this is to know how to draw and to have acquaintance with the very art of painting.

"And do not marvel that I desire this art, which to-day may seem to savor of the artisan and little to befit a gentleman; for I remember having read that the ancients, especially throughout Greece, had their boys of gentle birth study painting in school as an honorable and necessary thing, and it was admitted to the first rank of liberal arts; while by public edict they forbade that it be taught to slaves. Among the Romans too, it was held in highest honor. . . ."

[The discussion turns to defining the court lady. Giuliano de' Medici addresses the company of ladies and gentlemen:] ". . . although my lord Gaspar has said that the same rules which are set the Courtier serve also for the Lady, I am of another mind; for while some qualities are common to both and as necessary to man as to woman, there are nevertheless some others that befit woman more than man, and some are befitting man to which she ought to be wholly a stranger. The same I say of bodily exercises; but above all, methinks that in her ways, manners, words, gestures and bearing a woman ought to be very unlike a man; for just as it befits him to show a certain stout and sturdy manliness, so it is becoming in a woman to have a soft and dainty tenderness with an air of womanly sweetness in her every movement. . . .

"Now, if this precept be added to the rules that these gentlemen have taught the Courtier, I certainly think she ought to be able to profit by many of them, and to adorn herself with admirable accomplishments, as my lord Gaspar says. For I believe that many faculties of the mind are as necessary to woman as to man; likewise gentle birth, to avoid affectation, to be naturally graceful in all her doings, to be mannerly, clever, prudent, not arrogant, not envious, not slanderous, not vain, not quarrelsome, not silly, to know how to win and keep the favor of her mistress and of all others, to practice well and gracefully the exercises that befit women. I am quite of the opinion, too, that beauty is more necessary to her than to the Courtier, for in truth that woman lacks much who lacks beauty. . . .

[The Court Lady:] "must have not only the good sense to discern the quality of him with whom she is speaking, but knowledge of many things, in order to entertain him

graciously; and in her talk she should know how to choose those things that are adapted to the quality of him with whom she is speaking, and should be cautious lest occasionally, without intending it, she utter words that may offend him. Let her guard against wearying him by praising herself indiscreetly or by being too prolix. Let her not go about mingling serious matters with her playful or humorous discourse, or jests and jokes with her serious discourse. Let her not stupidly pretend to know that which she does not know, but modestly seek to do herself credit in that which she does know—in all things avoiding affectation, as has been said. In this way she will be adorned with good manners, and will perform with perfect grace the bodily exercises proper to women; her discourse will be rich and full of prudence, virtue and pleasantness; and thus she will be not only loved but revered by everyone, and perhaps worthy to be placed side by side with this great Courtier as well in qualities of the mind as in those of the body. . . .

"Since I may fashion this Lady as I wish, not only am I unwilling to have her practice such vigorous and rugged manly exercises, but I would have her practice even those that are becoming to women, circumspectly and with that gentle daintiness which we have said befits her; and thus in dancing I would not see her use too active and violent movements, nor in singing or playing those abrupt and oft-repeated diminutions[5] which show more skill than sweetness; likewise the musical instruments that she uses ought, in my opinion, to be appropriate to this intent. Imagine how unlovely it would be to see a woman play drums, fifes or trumpets, or other like instruments; and this because their harshness hides and destroys that mild gentleness which so much adorns every act a woman does. Therefore when she starts to dance or make music of any kind, she ought to bring herself to it by letting herself be urged a little, and with a touch of shyness which shall show that noble shame which is the opposite of effrontery. . . .

"And to repeat in a few words part of what has been already said, I wish this Lady to have knowledge of letters, music, painting, and to know how to dance and make merry; accompanying the other precepts that have been taught the Courtier with discreet modesty and with the giving of a good impression of herself. And thus, in her talk, her laughter, her play, her jesting, in short, in everything, she will be very graceful, and will entertain appropriately, and with witticisms and pleasantries befitting her, everyone who shall come before her. . . ."

Q **What are the primary characteristics of Castiglione's courtier? What are those of his court lady?**

Q **How do Castiglione's views of the well-rounded individual compare with your own?**

---

[5] Rapid ornamentation or variation of a line of music, here implying excessive virtuosity.

Renaissance Women

As *The Book of the Courtier* suggests, the Renaissance provided greater opportunities for education among upper-class women than were available to their medieval counterparts. The Renaissance woman might have access to a family library and, if it pleased her parents, to a humanistic education. The Bolognese painter Lavinia Fontana (1552–1614), a product of family tutelage in painting and the arts, continued her career well after her marriage to a fellow artist, who gave up his own career and helped to rear their eleven children. Noted for her skillful portraits, Fontana received numerous commissions for works that commemorated the luxurious weddings of the nobility. Her *Portrait of a Noblewoman* depicts a lavishly dressed young bride (whose identity is unknown) adorned with gold earrings, headdress, belt and pectoral chains, all of which are encrusted with pearls and rubies (Figure 16.10). A bodice of shimmering satin ribbons and a red velvet dress enhance the image of wealth, loyalty (symbolized by the dog), and

Figure 16.10 LAVINIA FONTANA, *Portrait of a Noblewoman*, ca. 1580. Oil on canvas, 3 ft. 9¼ in. × 35¼ in.

gentility—virtues that (along with her dowry) the young woman would likely bring to the marriage. Once married, Renaissance women's roles and rights were carefully limited by men, most of whom considered women their social and intellectual inferiors. Even such enlightened humanists as Alberti perpetuated old prejudices that found women "almost universally timid by nature, soft, and slow." Indeed, according to Alberti, nature had decreed "that men should bring things home and women care for them." Although Renaissance women were held in high esteem as housekeepers and mothers, they were not generally regarded as respectable models for male children, who, Alberti explained, should be "steered away from womanly customs and ways." Married (usually between the ages of thirteen and sixteen) to men considerably older than themselves, women often inherited large fortunes and lucrative businesses; and, as they came into such positions, they enjoyed a new sense of independence that often discouraged them from remarrying.

Renaissance women's occupations remained limited to service tasks, such as midwifery and innkeeping, but there is ample evidence that by the sixteenth century they reaped the advantages of an increasingly commercialized economy in which they might compete successfully with men. If, for centuries, women had dominated the areas of textiles, food preparation, and healthcare, many also rose to prominence in positions of political power. Elizabeth, queen of England, and Caterina Sforza of Milan are but two of the more spectacular examples of women whose strong will and political ingenuity shaped history. The seeds of feminism planted by Christine de Pisan (see chapter 15) flowered among increasing numbers of women writers and patrons. Battista Sforza, niece of Francesco Sforza, the powerful ruler of Milan, shared the efforts of her husband Duke Federico da Montefeltro in making Urbino a cultural and intellectual center. The Duchess of Urbino (see Figure 16.5) was admired for her knowledge of Greek and Latin and for her role as patron of the arts.

Women Humanists

Women humanists, a small but visible group of wealthy aristocrats, often had to choose between marriage, the convent, and the pursuit of a Liberal Arts education. The Humanist study of Greek and Latin and (in particular) intellectual inquiry into the moral philosophy of Plato, Aristotle, and Cicero, attracted a small group of women, mostly from northern Italy. To her patrons and friends throughout Europe, the Venetian humanist Cassandra Fedele (1465–1558) penned elegant Latin letters in the tradition of Petrarch (see Reading 16.1). The Roman humanist Vittoria Colonna (1490–1547) wrote religious verse and vernacular poems mourning the loss of her husband. Her passionate admirer, Michelangelo, compared her to "a block of marble whose talent was hidden deep within." Most female humanists, however, had to contend with the criticisms of their male peers. In their writings they repeatedly defend their own efforts by citing the achievements of famous women who preceded them—a theme

that earlier appeared in the writings of Boccaccio and Christine de Pisan (see Reading 15.3). Such was the case with Laura Cereta (1468–1499), the daughter of a Brescian aristocrat, who married at the age of fifteen and continued her studies even after the death of her husband (some eighteen months later). In her letters, she denounces the frivolous attention to outward forms of luxury among the women of her time. She also describes the difficulties encountered by intelligent women.

The letter known as the *Defense of Liberal Instruction of Women* (1488) is Cereta's bitter counterattack against a critic who had praised her as a prodigy, implicitly condemning her female humanist contemporaries. "With just cause," objects Cereta, "I am moved to demonstrate how great a reputation for learning and virtue women have won by their inborn excellence." To the conventional list of famous women—Babylonian sibyls, biblical heroines, ancient goddesses, and notable Greek and Roman writers and orators—Cereta adds the female humanists of her own time. Finally, she tries to explain why outstanding women are so few in number:

> The explanation is clear: women have been able by nature to be exceptional, but have chosen lesser goals. For some women are concerned with parting their hair correctly, adorning themselves with lovely dresses, or decorating their fingers with pearls and other gems. Others delight in mouthing carefully composed phrases, indulging in dancing, or managing spoiled puppies. Still others wish to gaze at lavish banquet tables, to rest in sleep, or, standing at mirrors, to smear their lovely faces. But those in whom a deeper integrity yearns for virtue, restrain from the start their youthful souls, reflect on higher things, harden the body with sobriety and trials, and curb their tongues, open their ears, compose their thoughts in wakeful hours, their minds in contemplation, to letters bonded to righteousness. For knowledge is not given as a gift, but [is gained] with diligence. The free mind, not shirking effort, always soars zealously toward the good, and the desire to know grows ever more wide and deep. It is because of no special holiness, therefore, that we [women] are rewarded by God the Giver with the gift of exceptional talent. Nature has generously lavished its gifts upon all people, opening to all the doors of choice through which reason sends envoys to the will, from which they learn and convey its desires. The will must choose to exercise the gift of reason.
>
> [But] where we [women] should be forceful we are [too often] devious; where we should be confident we are insecure.

Lucretia Marinella

The most extraordinary of sixteenth-century female humanists, the Venetian writer Lucretia Marinella (1571–1653), was neither devious nor insecure. The daughter and the wife of physicians, Marinella published a great many works, including religious verse, madrigals, a pastoral drama, a life of the Virgin, and an epic poem that celebrated the role of Venice in the Fourth Crusade (see chapter 11). However, the work that marks Marinella's dual importance as humanist and feminist was her treatise *The Nobility and Excellence of Women and the Defects and Vices of Men*. This formal polemic (the first of its kind written by a woman) was a direct response to a contemporary diatribe on the defects of women—an attack that rehearsed the traditional misogynistic litany that found woman vain, jealous, lustful, fickle, idle, and inherently flawed. The first part of Marinella's treatise observes the standard model for dispute and debate (employed by Christine de Pisan, Laura Cereta, and others) in which womankind is defended by a series of examples of illustrious women drawn from history. More remarkable—indeed, unique to its time—is Marinella's attack on what she perceived as the defects and vices of men. Using the very techniques that prevailed in humanist polemics, Marinella presents each defect—brutality, obstinacy, ingratitude, discourtesy, inconstancy, vanity—and proceeds to illustrate each by the evidence of illustrious men from Classical and biblical antiquity. Moreover, and in a manner worthy of modern feminists, she attempts to analyze the psychological basis for misogyny, contending that certain flaws—specifically anger, envy, and self-love—drive even the wisest and most learned men to attack women. The excerpts below suggest that while humanism was an enterprise dominated by men, it provided women with the tools by which they might advance their intellectual status and voice their own complaints.

READING 16.6 From Marinella's *The Nobility and Excellence of Women and the Defects and Vices of Men* (1600)

A reply to the flippant and vain reasoning adopted by men in their own favor

It seems to me that I have clearly shown that women are **1** far nobler and more excellent than men. Now it remains for me to reply to the false objections of our slanderers. These are of two sorts, some founded on specious reasonings and others solely on authorities and their opinions. Commencing with the latter, I maintain that I am not obliged to reply to them at all. If I should affirm that the element of air does not exist, I would not be obliged to reply to the authority of Aristotle or of other writers who say that it does.

I do not, however, wish to wrong famous men in denying **10** their conclusions, since certain obstinate people would regard this as being unjust. I say, therefore, that various reasons drove certain wise and learned men to reprove and vituperate women. They included anger, self-love, envy, and insufficient intelligence. It can be stated therefore that when Aristotle or some other man reproved women, the reason for it was either anger, envy, or too much self-love.

It is clear to everyone that anger is the origin of indecent accusations against women. When a man wishes to fulfill his unbridled desires and is unable to because of the **20** temperance and continence of a woman, he immediately becomes angry and disdainful and in his rage says every bad thing he can think of, as if the woman were something evil and hateful. The same can be said of the envious man, who when he sees someone worthy of praise can only look at them with a distorted view. And thus when a man sees that a woman is superior to him, both in virtue and in beauty, and that she is justly honored and loved even by him, he tortures himself and is consumed with envy. Not being able to give vent to his emotions in any other way, he **30** resorts with sharp and biting tongue to false and specious vituperation and reproof. The same occurs as a result of the too great love that men bear for themselves, which causes them to believe that they are more outstanding in wit and intelligence and by nature superior to women—an exaggerated arrogance and over-inflated and haughty pride. But if with a subtle intelligence they should consider their own imperfections, oh how humble and low they would become! Perhaps one day, God willing, they will perceive it.

All these reasons therefore induced the good Aristotle to **40** blame women—the principal among them, I believe, being the envy he bore them. For three years, as Diogenes Laertius[1] relates, he had been in love with a lady concubine of Hermias[2] who, knowing of his great and mad love for her, gave her to him as his wife. He, arrogant with joy, made sacrifices in honor of his new lady and goddess—as it was the custom in those times to make to Ceres of Eleusis[3]—and also to Hermias who had given her to him. Pondering then on all those worthy and memorable matters, he became envious of his wife and jealous of her **50** state, since, not being worshiped like a god by anyone, he could not equal it. Thus he turned to reviling women even though he knew they were worthy of every praise.

It can also be added that, like a man of small intelligence (pardon me you Aristotelians who are reading this . . .) he attributed the reasons for his long error to Hermias's lady, and not to his own unwise intellect, and proceeded to utter shameful and dishonorable words in order to cover up the error he had committed and to lower the female sex, which was an unreasonable thing to do. **60**

To these two motives can also be added self-love, since he judged himself to be a miracle of nature and grew so excessively conceited that he reputed every other person in the world to be unworthy of his love. Therefore, whenever he remembered the time when he had been subservient to women and was secretly ashamed of it, he sought to cover up his failing by speaking badly of them.

The fact that it was disdain against certain women that induced him to injure the female sex is something that must of necessity be believed. He had been a lover, and as I have **70** shown above, an unbridled lover. These were the reasons that induced poor Aristotle to say that women were more

---

[1] The third-century C.E. author of *Lives and Opinions of Eminent Philosophers*.
[2] The ruler of Atarneus whom Aristotle was said to have tutored.
[3] A nature deity whose cult was celebrated annually in Greece.

dishonest and given to gossiping than men, and more envious and slanderous. He did not see that in calling them slanderous, he too was joining the ranks of the slanderers.

In *History of Animals*, book IX, and in other places, he says that women are composed of matter, imperfect, weak, deficient and poor-spirited—things we have discussed. It could also be thoughtlessness that caused him to deceive himself about the nature and essence of women. Perhaps a 80 mature consideration of their nobility and excellence would have proved too great a burden for his shoulders. As we know, there are many people who believe that the earth moves and the sky remains still,[4] others that there are infinite worlds,[5] still others that there is only one, and some that the fly is nobler than the heavens. Each and every person defends his or her opinion obstinately and with infinite arguments, and these are the replies that we give to those who vituperate the female sex.

There have also been some men who, on discovering a 90 woman who was not very good, have bitingly and slanderously stated that all women are bad and wicked. They have made the grave error of basing a universal criticism on one particular case. It is true, however, that, having realized their error, they have then astutely praised good women. One reply is sufficient for the moral philosophers and poets who, when they criticize women are merely criticizing the worst ones. . . .

Of men who are ornate, polished, painted, and bleached

For men born to politics and civil life it is becoming, to a certain extent, to be elegant and polished. Everyone knows 100 this, and it has been verified by Della Casa, Guazzo, Sabba, and *The Book of the Courtier*.[6] If, according to these authors' reasoning, this is right for men, we must believe that it is even more right for women, since beauty shines brighter among the rich and elegantly dressed than among the poor and rude. Tasso[7] demonstrates this in *Torrismondo*, by means of the Queen's speech to Rosmonda:

Why do you not adorn your pleasing limbs and with pleasing clothes augment that beauty which heaven has given you courteously and generously? Unadorned beauty 110 in humble guise is like a rough, badly polished gem, which in a humble setting shines dully.

Since beauty is woman's special gift from the Supreme Hand, should she not seek to guard it with all diligence? And when she is endowed with but a small amount of that excellent quality, should she not seek to embellish it by

every means possible, provided it is not ignoble? I certainly believe that it is so. When man has some special gift such as physical strength, which enables him to perform as a gladiator or swagger around, as is the common usage, does 120 he not seek to conserve it? If he were born courageous, would he not seek to augment his natural courage with the art of defense? But if he were born with little courage would he not practice the martial arts and cover himself with plate and mail and constantly seek out duels and fights in order to demonstrate his courage rather than reveal his true timidity and cowardice?

I have used this example because of the impossibility of finding a man who does not swagger and play the daredevil. If there is such a one people call him effeminate, 130 which is why we always see men dressed up like soldiers with weapons at their belts, bearded and menacing, and walking in a way that they think will frighten everyone. Often they wear gloves of mail and contrive for their weapons to clink under their clothing so people realize they are armed and ready for combat and feel intimidated by them.

What are all these things but artifice and tinsel? Under these trappings of courage and valor hide the cowardly souls of rabbits or hunted hares, and it is the same with all 140 their other artifices. Since men behave in this way, why should not those women who are born less beautiful than the rest hide their less fortunate attributes and seek to augment the little beauty they possess through artifice, provided it is not offensive?

Why should it be a sin if a woman born with considerable beauty washes her delicate face with lemon juice and the water of beanflowers and privets[8] in order to remove her freckles and keep her skin soft and clean? Or if with columbine, white bread, lemon juice, and pearls she creates 150 some other potion to keep her face clean and soft? I believe it to be merely a small one. If roses do not flame within the lily pallor of her face, could she not, with some art, create a similar effect? Certainly she could, without fear of being reproved, because those who possess beauty must conserve it and those who lack it must make themselves as perfect as possible, removing every obstacle that obscures its splendor and grace. And if writers and poets, both ancient and modern, say that her golden hair enhances her beauty, why should she not color it blonde and make ringlets and curls in it so 160 as to embellish it still further?. . . .

But what should we say of men who are not born beautiful and who yet make great efforts to appear handsome and appealing, not only by putting on clothes made of silk and cloth of gold as many do, spending all their money on an item of clothing, but by wearing intricately worked neckbands? What should we say of the medallions they wear in their caps, the gold buttons, the pearls, the pennants and plumes and the great number of liveries[9] that bring ruin on their houses? They go around with their hair waved, greased, and 170 perfumed so that many of them smell like walking

---

[4] A reference to the heliocentric theory defended by Copernicus in his treatise *On the Revolution of the Heavenly Spheres* published in 1543 (see chapter 23).

[5] A reference to the claim made by Giordano Bruno (1548–1600) that the universe was infinite and might contain many solar systems. Bruno was burned at the stake in Rome the year that Marinella's treatise was published.

[6] A reference to four famous sixteenth-century handbooks on manners.

[7] The Italian poet Torquato Tasso (1495–1544), whose tragedy *Torrismondo* was published in 1586.

---

[8] Flowering shrub.
[9] Servants.

perfumeries. How many are there who go to the barbers every four days in order to appear close-shaven, rosy-cheeked, and like young men even when they are old? How many dye their beards when the dread arrival of old age causes them to turn white? How many use lead combs to tint their white hairs? How many pluck out their white hairs in order to make it appear that they are in the flower of youth? I pass over the earrings that Frenchmen and other foreigners wear and the necklaces, of Gallic invention, which we read of in Livy.   180

How many spend three or four hours each day combing their hair and washing themselves with those balls of soap sold by mountebanks in the *piazza*[10]? Let us not even mention the time they spend perfuming themselves and putting on their shoes and blaspheming against the saints because their shoes are small and their feet are big, and they want their big feet to get into their small shoes. How ridiculous!

— **Q** **What, according to Marinella, motivates men to slander women?**

— **Q** **How does Marinella defy traditional male attacks on female vanity?**

Machiavelli

The modern notion of progress as an active process of improving the lot of the individual was born during the Renaissance. Repeatedly, Renaissance humanists asserted that society's leaders must exercise *virtù* in order to master Fate (often personified in Western art and literature as a female) and fashion their destinies in their own interests. Balanced against the ideals of human perfectibility championed by Castiglione and Pico were the realities of human greed, ignorance, and cruelty. Such technological innovations as gunpowder made warfare increasingly impersonal and devastating, while the rise of strong national rulers occasioned the worst kinds of aggression and brute force. Even the keepers of the spiritual kingdom on earth—the leaders of the Church of Rome—had become notorious for their self-indulgence and greed, as some Renaissance popes actually took mistresses, led armed attacks upon neighboring states, and lived at shocking levels of luxury.

The most acute critic of these conditions was the Florentine diplomat and statesman Niccolò Machiavelli (1469–1527). A keen political observer and a student of Roman history, Machiavelli lamented Italy's disunity in the face of continuous rivalry among the city-states. He anticipated that outside powers might try to take advantage of Italy's internal weaknesses. The threat of foreign invasion became a reality in 1494, when French armies marched into Italy, thus initiating a series of wars that left Italy divided and impoverished. Exiled from Florence upon the collapse of the republican government he had served from 1498 to 1512 and eager to win favor with the Medici now

that they had returned to power, Machiavelli penned *The Prince*, a political treatise that called for the unification of Italy under a powerful and courageous leader. This notorious little book laid out the guidelines for how an aspiring ruler might gain and maintain political power.

In *The Prince*, Machiavelli argued that the need for a strong state justified strong rule. He pictured the secular prince as one who was schooled in war and in the lessons of history. The ruler must trust no one, least of all mercenary soldiers. He must imitate the lion in his fierceness, but he must also act like a fox to outsmart his enemies. Finally, in the interest of the state, he must be ruthless, and, if necessary, he must sacrifice moral virtue. In the final analysis, the end—that is, the preservation of a strong state—will justify the means of maintaining power, however cunning or violent. As indicated in the following excerpts, Machiavelli formulated the idea of the state as an entity that remains exempt from the bonds of conventional morality.

┌─ **READING 16.7** From Machiavelli's *The Prince* (1513)

XII How Many Different Kinds of Soldiers There Are, 7 and of Mercenaries

. . . a Prince must lay solid foundations since otherwise   1
he will inevitably be destroyed. Now the main
foundations of all States, whether new, old, or mixed, are
good laws and good arms. But since you cannot have the
former without the latter, and where you have the latter,
are likely to have the former, I shall here omit all
discussion on the subject of laws, and speak only of arms.

I say then that the arms wherewith a Prince defends his
State are either his own subjects, or they are
mercenaries, or they are auxiliaries, or they are partly   10
one and partly another. Mercenaries and auxiliaries are
at once useless and dangerous, and he who holds his
State by means of mercenary troops can never be solidly
or securely seated. For such troops are disunited,
ambitious, insubordinate, treacherous, insolent among
friends, cowardly before foes, and without fear of God or
faith with man. Whenever they are attacked defeat
follows; so that in peace you are plundered by them, in
war by your enemies. And this because they have no tie
or motive to keep them in the field beyond their paltry   20
pay, in return for which it would be too much to expect
them to give their lives. They are ready enough,
therefore, to be your soldiers while you are at peace, but
when war is declared they make off and disappear. I
ought to have little difficulty in getting this believed, for
the present ruin of Italy is due to no other cause than her
having for many years trusted to mercenaries, who
though heretofore they may have helped the fortunes of
some one man, and made a show of strength when
matched with one another, have always revealed   30
themselves in their true colors as soon as foreign
enemies appeared. . . .

---

[10] A broad, open public space.

XIV Of the Duty of a Prince in Respect of Military Affairs

A Prince, therefore, should have no care or thought but for war, and for the regulations and training it requires, and should apply himself exclusively to this as his peculiar province; for war is the sole art looked for in one who rules and is of such efficacy that it not merely maintains those who are born Princes, but often enables men to rise to that eminence from a private station; while, on other hand, we often see that when Princes devote themselves rather to pleasure than to arms, they lose their dominions. And as neglect of this art is the prime cause of such calamities, so to be proficient in it is the surest way to acquire power. . . .

XV Of the Qualities in Respect of which Princes are Praised or Blamed

It now remains for us to consider what ought to be the conduct and bearing of a Prince in relation to his subjects and friends. And since I know that many have written on this subject, I fear it may be thought presumptuous in me to write of it also; the more so, because in my treatment of it I depart widely from the views that others have taken.

But since it is my object to write what shall be useful to whosoever understands it, it seems to me better to follow the real truth of things than an imaginary view of them. For many Republics and Princedoms have been imagined that were never seen or known. It is essential, therefore, for a Prince who would maintain his position, to have learned how to be other than good, and to use or not to use his goodness as necessity requires.

Laying aside, therefore, all fanciful notions concerning a Prince, and considering those only that are true, I say that all men when they are spoken of, and Princes more than others from their being set so high, are noted for certain of those qualities which attach either praise or blame. Thus one is accounted liberal, another miserly . . . ; one is generous, another greedy; one cruel, another tender-hearted; one is faithless, another true to his word; one effeminate and cowardly, another high-spirited and courageous; one is courteous, another haughty; one lewd, another chaste; one upright, another crafty; one firm, another facile; one grave, another frivolous; one devout, another unbelieving; and the like. Every one, I know, will admit that it would be most laudable for a Prince to be endowed with all of the above qualities that are reckoned good; but since it is impossible for him to possess or constantly practice them all, the conditions of human nature not allowing it, he must be discreet enough to know how to avoid the reproach of those vices that would deprive him of his government, and, if possible, be on his guard also against those which might not deprive him of it; though if he cannot wholly restrain himself, he may with less scruple indulge in the latter. But he need never hesitate to incur the reproach of those vices without which his authority can hardly be preserved; for if he well

consider the whole matter, he will find that there may be a line of conduct having the appearance of virtue, to follow which would be his ruin, and that there may be another course having the appearance of vice, by following which his safety and well-being are secured.

XVII Whether It is Better to Be Loved Than Feared

[We now consider] the question whether it is better to be loved rather than feared, or feared rather than loved. It might perhaps be answered that we should wish to be both; but since love and fear can hardly exist together, if we must choose between them, it is far safer to be feared than loved. For of men it may generally be affirmed that they are thankless, fickle, false, studious to avoid danger, greedy of gain, devoted to you while you are able to confer benefits upon them, and ready, as I said before, while danger is distant, to shed their blood, and sacrifice their property, their lives, and their children for you; but in the hour of need they turn against you. The Prince, therefore, who without otherwise securing himself builds wholly on their professions is undone. For the friendships which we buy with a price, and do not gain by greatness and nobility of character, though they be fairly earned are not made good, but fail us when we have occasion to use them.

Moreover, men are less careful how they offend him who makes himself loved than him who makes himself feared. For love is held by the tie of obligation, which, because men are a sorry breed, is broken on every whisper of private interest; but fear is bound by the apprehension of punishment which never relaxes its grasp.

Nevertheless a Prince should inspire fear in such a fashion that if he do not win love he may escape hate. For a man may very well be feared and yet not hated, and this will be the case so long as he does not meddle with the property or with the women of his citizens and subjects. And if constrained to put any to death, he should do so only when there is manifest cause or reasonable justification. But, above all, he must abstain from the property of others. For men will sooner forget the death of their father than the loss of their property. . . .

XVIII How Princes Should Keep Faith

Every one understands how praiseworthy it is in a Prince to keep faith, and to live uprightly and not craftily. Nevertheless, we see from what has taken place in our own days that Princes who have set little store by their world, but have known how to overreach men by their cunning, have accomplished great things, and in the end got the better of those who trusted to honest dealing.

Be it known, then, that there are two ways of contending, one in accordance with the laws, the other by force; the first of which is proper to men, the second to beasts. But since the first method is often ineffectual, it becomes necessary to resort to the second. A Prince should, therefore, understand how to use well both the man and the beast . . . of beasts [the Prince should choose as his models] both the lion and the fox; for the lion cannot guard himself from traps, nor the fox from wolves. He must therefore be a fox to discern traps, and a lion to drive off wolves. 140

To rely wholly on the lion is unwise; and for this reason a prudent Prince neither can nor ought to keep his word when to keep it is hurtful to him and the causes which led him to pledge it are removed. If all men were good, this would not be good advice, but since they are dishonest and do not keep faith with you, you, in return, need not keep faith with them; and no Prince was ever at a loss for plausible reasons to cloak a breach of faith. Of 150 this numberless recent instances could be given, and it might be shown how many solemn treaties and engagements have been rendered inoperative and idle through want of faith in Princes, and that he who has best known to play the fox has had the best success.

It is necessary, indeed, to put a good disguise on this nature, and to be skillful in simulating and dissembling. But men are so simple, and governed so absolutely by their present needs, that he who wishes to deceive will never fail in finding willing dupes. . . . 160

And you are to understand that a Prince, and most of all a new Prince, cannot observe all those rules of conduct in respect whereof men are accounted good, being often forced, in order to preserve his Princedom, to act in opposition to good faith, charity, humanity, and religion. He must therefore keep his mind to shift as the winds and tides of Fortune turn, and, as I have already said, he ought not to quit good courses if he can help it, but should know how to follow evil courses if he must. . . . Moreover, in the actions of all men, and most of all 170 Princes, where there is no tribunal to which we can appeal, we look to results. Therefore if a Prince succeeds in establishing and maintaining his authority, the means will always be judged honorable and be approved by every one. For the vulgar are always taken by appearances and by results, and the world is made up of the vulgar, the few only finding room when the many have no longer ground to stand on. . . .

Q **What are the primary qualities of the Machiavellian ruler?**

Q **Why is Machiavelli often called "the first political realist"?**

The advice Machiavelli gives in his handbook of power politics is based on an essentially negative view of humankind: if, by nature, human beings are "thankless," "fickle," "false," "greedy," "dishonest," and "simple" (as

Machiavelli describes them), how better to govern them than by ruthless unlimited power that might keep this "sorry breed" in check? Machiavelli's treatise suggests, furthermore, that personal morality, guided by the principles of justice and benevolence, differs from the morality of the collective entity, the state. It implies, further, that the state, itself an impersonal phenomenon, may be declared amoral, that is, exempt from any moral judgment. In either case, Machiavelli's separation of the value-principles of governance from the principles of Christian morality stunned the European community. The rules of power advertised in *The Prince* appeared to Renaissance thinkers not as idealized notions, but, rather, as expedient solutions based on a realistic analysis of contemporary political conditions. Indeed, Machiavelli's political theories rested on an analysis of human nature not as it should be, but as it was. Throughout *The Prince*, Machiavelli cites examples of power drawn from Roman history and contemporary politics. In defending the successful use of power, for instance, his favorite role model was Cesare Borgia (the illegitimate son of the Renaissance pope Alexander VI), who, along with other thoroughly corrupt and decadent members of his family, exercised a ruthless military campaign to establish a papal empire in central Italy. In such figures, Machiavelli located the heroic aspects of *virtù*: imagination, resilience, ingenuity, and canny intelligence. He provided ample evidence to justify his denunciation of the secular ruler as the divinely appointed model of moral rectitude—a medieval conception staunchly defended by Castiglione.

Machiavelli's profound grasp of past and present history, which he summed up as "knowledge of the actions of man," made him both a critic of human behavior and modern Europe's first political scientist. While his longer and more detailed works—the *History of Florence*, the *Art of War*, and the *Discourses on the First Ten Books of Livy*—summed up his practical experience in government and diplomacy, *The Prince* brought him notoriety. Widely circulated in manuscript form (it was not published until 1532), it was hailed as both a cynical examination of political expediency and as an exposé of real-life politics—so much so that the word "Machiavellian" became synonymous with the evils of political duplicity.

Chronology

434–1454	Cosimo de' Medici rules Florence
1453	fall of Constantinople
1462	Platonic Academy founded in Florence
1469–1492	Lorenzo de' Medici rules Florence
1513	Machiavelli writes *The Prince*

LOOKING BACK

Italy: Birthplace of the Renaissance

- The Renaissance designates that period in European history between roughly 1300 and 1600, during which time the revival of Classical humanism spread from its birthplace in Florence, Italy, throughout Western Europe.
- Florence, a thriving commercial and financial center dominated by a prosperous middle class, found political and cultural leadership in the wealthy and sophisticated Medici family.
- In the climate of intellectual skepticism created by the Great Schism, middle-class men and women challenged canonical sources of authority that frowned upon the accumulation of wealth.
- While Renaissance Italy flourished in the soil of ancient Rome, its political circumstances had much in common with ancient Greece. Independent and disunited, the city-states of Italy, like those of ancient Greece, were fiercely competitive.

Classical Humanism

- Classical humanism, the movement to recover, edit, and study ancient Greek and Latin manuscripts, took shape in fourteenth-century Italy, where it marked the beginnings of the Renaissance.
- Petrarch, the father of humanism, provided the model for Renaissance scholarship and education. He glorified Ciceronian Latin, encouraged the preservation and dissemination of Classical manuscripts, and wrote introspective sonnets that were revered and imitated for centuries to come.
- Classical humanism helped to cultivate a sense of civic pride, a new respect for oral and written eloquence, and a set of personal values that sustained the ambitions of the rising merchant class. Alberti stressed the importance of Classical education and hard work in the cultivation of *virtù*. Ficino translated the entire body of Plato's writings, while Pico della Mirandola applied his vast study of ancient literature to defend free will and the unlimited potential of the individual.
- Renaissance humanists cultivated the idea of the good life. They applied the moral precepts of the Classical past to diplomacy, politics, and the arts. Castiglione's *Book of the Courtier* established a modern educational ideal in the person of *l'uomo universale*—the well-rounded individual.

Renaissance Women

- The Renaissance provided greater opportunities for education and power among upper-class women than were available to their medieval counterparts. While Renaissance women's roles and rights were carefully limited by men, most of whom considered women their social and intellectual inferiors, many reaped the advantages of an increasingly commercialized economy. Some rose to fame as political figures, writers, and portraitists.
- Women humanists usually had access to a family library and a private education. The notable northern Italian humanists, Laura Cereta and Lucretia Marinella, defended women in the face of contemporary misogyny. They brought attention to the achievements of educated women and compared the frivolous pursuits of both sexes.

Machiavelli

- The West's first political scientist, Machiavelli lamented Italy's disunity amidst continuous rivalry among the city-states. He anticipated the invasion of foreign powers that might try to take advantage of Italy's internal weaknesses. His canonical text, *The Prince*, argued the need for a strong state ruled by a strong leader.
- Machiavelli envisioned the secular ruler as ruthless. If necessary, he must sacrifice moral virtue for the good of the state. In his view, the state, an impersonal entity, could not be judged by the standards of human morality.
- The views of Machiavelli and other of the Renaissance humanists would come to shape the modern character of the European West.

Glossary

condottiere (plural *condottieri*) a professional soldier; a mercenary who typically served the Renaissance city-state

intarsia the decoration of wood surfaces with inlay

sonnet a fourteen-line lyric poem with a fixed scheme of rhyming

Chapter 17

Renaissance Artists: Disciples of Nature, Masters of Invention

ca. 1400–1600

"The eye, which is called the window of the soul, is the chief means whereby the understanding may most fully and abundantly appreciate the infinite works of nature."
Leonardo

Figure 17.1 LUCCA DELLA ROBBIA, *Drummers* (detail of the *Cantoria*).
Marble, 3 ft. 6⅛ in. × 3 ft. 4¹⁹⁄₂₀ in. This marble relief panel is one of eight commissioned by Lorenzo de' Medici to adorn the 17-foot-long music gallery of the cathedral of Florence.

LOOKING AHEAD

The Renaissance produced a flowering in the visual arts rarely matched in the annals of world culture. Artists embraced the natural world with an enthusiasm that was equalled only by their ambition to master the lessons of Classical antiquity. The result was a unique and sophisticated body of art that set the standards for most of the painting, sculpture, and architecture produced in the West until the late nineteenth century.

During the Early Renaissance, the period from roughly 1400 to 1490, Florentine artists worked side by side with literary humanists to revive the Classical heritage. These artist–scientists combined their interest in Greco Roman art with an impassioned desire to understand the natural world and imitate its visual appearance. As disciples of nature, they studied its operations and functions; as masters of invention, they devised new techniques by which to represent the visible world more realistically. In the years of the High Renaissance—approximately 1490 to 1530—the spirit of individualism reached heroic proportions, as artists such as Leonardo da Vinci, Raphael, and Michelangelo integrated the new techniques of naturalistic representation with the much respected principles of Classical art.

While the subject matter of Renaissance art was still largely religious, the style was more lifelike than ever. Indeed, in contrast with the generally abstract and symbolic art of the Middle Ages, Renaissance art was concrete and realistic. Most medieval art served liturgical or devotional ends; increasingly, however, wealthy patrons commissioned paintings and sculptures to embellish their homes and palaces or to commemorate secular and civic achievements. Portrait painting, a genre that glorified the individual, became popular during the Renaissance, along with other genres that described the physical and social aspects of urban life. These artistic developments reflect the needs of a culture driven by material prosperity, civic pride, and personal pleasure.

Renaissance Art and Patronage

In the commercial cities of Italy and the Netherlands, painting, sculpture, and architecture were the tangible expressions of increased affluence. In addition to the traditional medieval source of patronage—the Catholic Church—merchant princes and petty despots vied with growing numbers of middle-class patrons and urban-centered guilds whose lavish commissions brought prestige to their businesses and families. Those who supported the arts did so at least in part with an eye on leaving their mark

upon society or immortalizing themselves for posterity. Thus art became evidence of material well-being as well as a visible extension of the ego in an age of individualism.

Active patronage enhanced the social and financial status of Renaissance artists. Such artists were first and foremost craftspeople, apprenticed to studios in which they might achieve mastery over a wide variety of techniques, including the grinding of paints, the making of brushes, and the skillful copying of images. While trained to observe firmly established artistic convention, the more innovative amongst them moved to create a new visual language. Indeed, for the first time in Western history, artists came to wield influence as humanists, scientists, and poets: a new phenomenon of the artist as hero and genius was born. The image of the artist as hero was promoted by the self-publicizing efforts of these artists, as well as by the adulation of their peers. The Italian painter, architect, and critic Giorgio Vasari (1511–1574) immortalized hundreds of Renaissance artists in his monumental biography *The Lives of the Most Excellent Painters, Architects, and Sculptors*, published in 1550. Vasari drew to legendary proportions the achievements of notable Renaissance figures, many of whom he knew personally. Consider, for instance, this terse characterization of Leonardo da Vinci:

> . . . He might have been a scientist if he had not been so versatile. But the instability of his character caused him to take up and abandon many things. In arithmetic, for example, he made such rapid progress during the short time he studied it that he often confounded his teacher by his questions. He also began the study of music and resolved to learn to play the lute, and as he was by nature of exalted imagination, and full of the most graceful vivacity, he sang and accompanied himself most divinely, improvising at once both verses and music. He studied not one branch of art only, but all. Admirably intelligent, and an excellent geometrician besides, Leonardo not only worked in sculpture . . . but, as an architect, designed ground plans and entire buildings; and, as an engineer, was the one who first suggested making a canal from Florence to Pisa by altering the river Arno. Leonardo also designed mills and water-driven machines. But, as he had resolved to make painting his profession, he spent most of his time drawing from life. . . .

The Early Renaissance

The Revival of the Classical Nude

Like the Classical humanists, artists of the Renaissance were the self-conscious beneficiaries of ancient Greek and Roman culture. One of the most creative forces in Florentine sculpture, Donato Bardi, known as Donatello (1386–1466), traveled to Rome to study antique statuary. The works he observed there inspired his extraordinary likeness of the biblical hero David (Figure 17.2). Completed in 1432, Donatello's bronze was the first freestanding, life-sized nude sculpture since antiquity. While not an imitation of any single Greek or Roman statue, the piece reveals an indebtedness to Classical models in its correct anatomical proportions and gentle *contrapposto* stance (compare the *Kritios Boy* and *Doryphorus* in chapter 5). However, the sensuousness of the youthful figure—especially apparent in the surface modeling—surpasses that of any antique statue. Indeed, in this tribute to male beauty, Donatello rejected the medieval view of the human body as the wellspring of sin and anticipated the modern Western exaltation of the body as the seat of pleasure.

Figure 17.2 DONATELLO, *David*, completed 1432. Bronze, height 5 ft. 2 in.

Figure 17.3 ANTONIO POLLAIUOLO, *Hercules and Antaeus*, ca. 1475. Bronze, height 18 in. with base.

Donatello's colleague Lucca della Robbia (1400–1482) would become famous for his enameled terracotta religious figures; but in his first documented commission—the *Cantoria* (Singing Gallery) for the cathedral of Florence—he exhibited his talents as a sculptor of marble and as a student of antiquity (see Figure 17.1). Greco-Roman techniques of high and low relief are revived in the ten panels representing choristers, musicians, and dancers—the latter resembling the *putti* (plump, nude boys), often used to depict Cupid in ancient art. In a spirited display of physical movement, Lucca brought to life Psalm 150, which enjoins one to praise God with "trumpet sound," "lute and harp," "strings and pipe," and "loud clashing cymbals." Just as Donatello conceived the biblical David in the language of Classical antiquity, so Lucca invested the music of Scripture with a lifelike, Classicized vigor.

The Renaissance revival of the Classical nude was accompanied by a quest to understand the mechanics of the human body. Antonio Pollaiuolo (ca. 1431–1498) was among the first artists to dissect human cadavers in order to study anatomy. The results of his investigations are documented in a bronze sculpture depicting the combat between Hercules and Antaeus, a story drawn from Greco-Roman legend (Figure **17.3**). This small but powerful sculpture in the round is one of many examples of the Renaissance use of Classical mythology to glorify human action, rather than as an exemplum of Christian morality. The wrestling match between the two legendary strongmen of antiquity, Hercules (the most popular of all Greek heroes) and Antaeus (the son of Mother Earth), provided Pollaiuolo with the chance to display his remarkable understanding of the human phyique, especially as it responds to stress. Pollaiuolo concentrates on the moment when Hercules lifts Antaeus off the ground, thus divesting him of his maternal source of strength and crushing him in a "body lock." The human capacity for tension and energy is nowhere better captured than in the straining muscles and tendons of the two athletes in combat.

The Classically inspired nude fascinated Renaissance painters as well as sculptors. In the *Birth of Venus* (see Figure 17.4) by Sandro Botticelli (1445–1510), the central image is an idealized portrayal of womankind based on an antique model (see Figure 17.5). Born of sea foam (according to the Greek poet Hesiod), Venus floats on a pearlescent scallop shell to the shore of the island of

MAKING CONNECTIONS

Figure 17.4 SANDRO BOTTICELLI, *Birth of Venus*, after 1482. Tempera on canvas, 5 ft. 9 in. × 9 ft. ¼ in.

Florentine artists, humanists, and their patrons collected Classical statuary, examples of which were recovered and revered during the age of the Renaissance. The life-sized Hellenistic marble sculpture, *Medici Venus* (Figure **17.5**), depicting Aphrodite, the Greek goddess of love, probably a copy of a bronze original, is said to have been found (in fragments) in Rome during the fifteenth century (its exact origin and date of recovery, however, are disputed

Figure 17.5 *Medici Venus*, first century C.E. Marble, height 5 ft. ¼ in.

by scholars). The dolphin at the foot of the sculpture is a reference to the legendary origins of the goddess, who, according to Hesiod (see chapter 4), was generated by the sea foam (or semen) of her mythical father, Uranus. Botticelli's goddess of love (Figure **17.4**) retains the graceful *contrapposto* stance and the modest gesture of the *Medici Venus*, suggesting that he had probably seen the restored sculpture or a similar copy.

Cythera. To her right are two wind gods locked in sensuous embrace, while to her left is the welcoming figure of Pomona, the ancient Roman goddess of fruit trees and fecundity. Many elements in the painting—water, wind, flowers, trees—suggest procreation and fertility, powers associated with Venus as goddess of earthly love. But Botticelli, inspired by a contemporary Neoplatonic poem honoring Aphrodite/Venus as goddess of divine love, renders Venus also as an object of ethereal beauty and spiritual love. He pictorializes ideas set forth at the Platonic Academy of Florence (see chapter 16), particularly the Neoplatonic notion that objects of physical beauty move the soul to desire union with God, divine fount of beauty and truth. Botticelli's wistful goddess assumes the double role accorded her by the Neoplatonists: goddess of earthly love and goddess of divine (or Platonic) love.

Botticelli executed the *Birth of Venus* in tempera on a large canvas. He rendered the figures with a minimum of shading, so that they seem weightless, suspended in space. An undulating line animates the windblown hair, the embroidered robes, and the delicate flowers that lie on the tapestrylike surface of the canvas. Gold accents and pastel colors (including the delicious lime of the water) further remove this idyllic vision from association with the mundane world.

Early Renaissance Architecture

The art of the Early Renaissance was never a mere imitation of antique models (as was often the case with Roman copies of Greek sculpture), but rather an original effort to reinterpret Greco-Roman themes and principles. The same is true of Renaissance architecture. The revival of Classical architecture was inaugurated by the architect, sculptor, and theorist Filippo Brunelleschi (1377–1446). In 1420, Brunelleschi won a civic competition for the design of the dome of Florence Cathedral (Figure **17.6**). His ingeniously conceived dome—the largest since that of the Pantheon in Rome—consisted of two octagonal shells. Each incorporated eight curved panels joined by massive ribs that soar upward from the octagonal **drum**—the section immediately beneath the dome—to converge at an elegant **lantern** through which light enters the interior. In the space between the two shells, Brunelleschi designed an interlocking system of ribs that operate like hidden flying buttresses (Figure **17.7**). To raise the dome, he devised new methods of hoisting stone and new masonry techniques, all of which won him acclaim in Florence. Indeed, Brunelleschi's colleague Alberti hailed the completed dome as "a feat of engineering . . . unknown and unimaginable among the ancients."

Figure 17.6 Florence Cathedral.

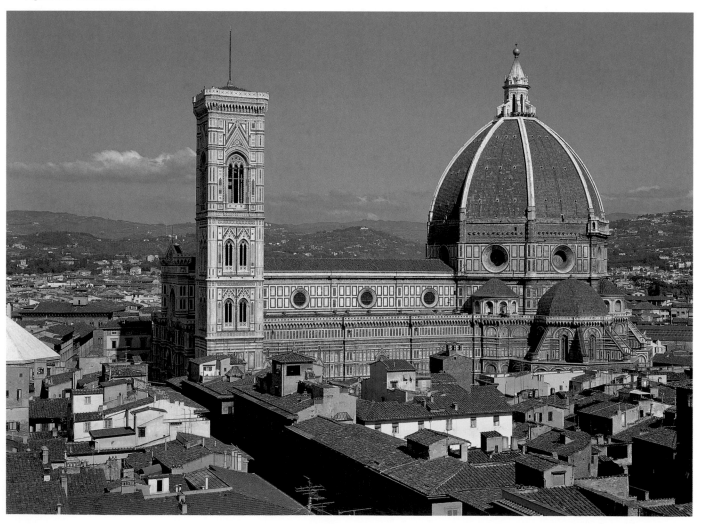

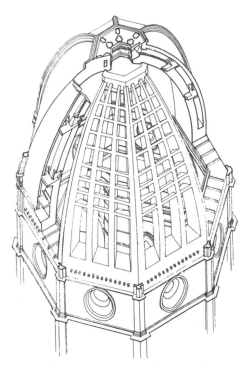

Figure 17.7 Axonometric section of the dome of Florence Cathedral. Cross section at base 11 ft. × 7 ft.

Figure 17.8 FILIPPO BRUNELLESCHI, Pazzi Chapel, cloister of Santa Croce, Florence, ca. 1441–1460.

Figure 17.9 FILIPPO BRUNELLESCHI, Pazzi Chapel, Santa Croce, Florence, ca. 1441–1460.

Brunelleschi was among the first architects of the Renaissance to defend Classical principles of symmetry and proportion in architectural design. In the graceful little chapel he produced for the Pazzi family of Florence (Figure 17.8), he placed a dome over the central square of the inner hall and buttressed the square with two short barrel vaults. Since the exterior of this self-contained structure was later modified by the addition of a portico, it is in the interior that Brunelleschi's break with the medieval past is fully realized (Figure 17.9). Here, the repetition of geometric shapes enforces a new kind of visual clarity wherein all parts of the structure are readily accessible to the eye and to the mind. Gray stone moldings and gray Corinthian **pilasters**—shallow, flattened, rectangular columns that adhere to the wall surface—emphasize the "seams" between the individual segments of the stark white interior, producing a sense of order and harmony that is unsurpassed in Early Renaissance architecture. Whereas the medieval cathedral coaxes one's gaze heavenward, the Pazzi Chapel fixes the beholder decisively on earth.

Brunelleschi's enthusiasm for an architecture of harmonious proportions was shared by his younger colleague, the multitalented Florentine humanist Leon Battista Alberti (see chapter 16). Alberti's scientific treatises on painting, sculpture, and architecture reveal his admiration for Roman architecture and his familiarity with the writings of the Roman engineer Vitruvius (see Reading 5.1). In his *Ten Books on Architecture* (modeled after Vitruvius' *De architectura*), Alberti argued that architectural design should proceed from the square and the circle, the two most perfect geometric shapes. This proposition was the guiding precept for all of Alberti's buildings (a total of only six); it would become the definitive principle of High Renaissance composition (see Figures 17.24, 17.30, 17.31).

In the townhouse Alberti designed for the wealthy Rucellai family of Florence (Figure **17.10**), all the details of the building conform to an elegant uniformity of style that stands in contrast with Michelozzo's more rugged Medici Palace (see Figure 16.4). Lacking direct antique precedents for palace architecture, Alberti reconceived the Classical principles of regularity, symmetry, and proportion. Each story of the palace is identical in height, and each story is

Figure 17.10 LEON BATTISTA ALBERTI (designer) and **BERNARDO ROSSELLINO** (architect), Palazzo Rucellai, Florence, 1446–1451.

ornamented with a different Classical order (see chapter 5). Rows of crisply defined arcaded windows appear on the upper stories, while square windows placed well above the street (for safety and privacy) accent the lowest level. From the Roman Colosseum (see chapter 6), Alberti borrowed the device of alternating arches and engaged columns, flattening the latter into pilasters. Here the principles of clarity and proportion prevail. The building quickly became the model for Renaissance palace architecture.

For the west front of Santa Maria Novella, his second major architectural project in Florence (Figure **17.11**), Alberti produced a striking pattern of geometric shapes ordered by a perfect square: the height of the green and white marble façade (from the ground to the tip of the pediment) exactly equals its width. All parts are related by

Figure 17.11 LEON BATTISTA ALBERTI, Santa Maria Novella, Florence, completed 1470. Green and gray marble. Alberti ingeniously added the volutes in order to conceal the disjunction between the high nave and the lower side aisles of the Gothic structure.

harmonic proportions based on numerical ratios; for instance, the upper portion of the façade is one-fourth the size of the square into which the entire face of the church would fit. Huge **volutes** (scrolls)—imitated by generations of Western architects to come—unite the upper and lower divisions of the façade, while the motif of a triumphal arch dominates the central entrance. At Santa Maria Novella, as in the churches he designed at Rimini and Mantua, Alberti imposed the motifs and the principles of Classical architecture upon the brick Latin cross basilica, thus uniting Greco-Roman and Christian traditions.

Both Alberti and Brunelleschi espoused the Hellenic theory that the human form mirrored the order inherent in the universe. The human microcosm (or "lesser world") was the natural expression of the divine macrocosm (or "greater world"). Accordingly, the study of nature and the understanding and exercise of its underlying harmonies put one in touch with the macrocosm. Rational architecture, reflecting natural laws, would help to cultivate rational individuals. Just as the gentler modes in music elicited refined behavior (the Doctrine of Ethos; see chapter 5), so harmoniously proportioned buildings might produce ideal citizens.

The Renaissance Portrait

The revival of portraiture during the Renaissance was an expression of two impulses: the desire to immortalize oneself by way of one's physical appearance and the wish to publicize one's greatness in the traditional manner of Greek and Roman antiquity. Like biography and autobiography—two literary genres that were revived during the Renaissance—portraiture and self-portraiture were hallmarks of a new self-consciousness. The bronze self-portrait of Alberti, a medal bearing the artist's personal emblem of a winged eye (see Figure 16.8), looks back to the small fourteenth-century portrait profile of King John of France (see Figure

15.15). But the former is more deliberate in its effort to recreate an accurate likeness and, at the same time, more clearly imitative of Roman coins and medals.

While the profile view tended to draft a distinctive likeness (see Figures 16.5 and 16.6), the three-quarter and full-face views gave artists the opportunity to capture the physical presence of the sitter (see Figures 16.9 and 16.10). One of the earliest efforts at realistic representation along these lines came from the Netherlandish artist Jan van Eyck (ca. 1370–1441), discussed more fully in chapter 19. Jan's pioneering use of the technique of thin transparent glazes of pigments bound with linseed oil recreated the naturalistic effects of light, and consequently, achieved a high degree of realism. In his penetrating self-portrait (Figure **17.12**), whose level gaze and compressed lips suggest the personality of a shrewd realist, facial features are finely, almost photographically, detailed. To the Renaissance passion for realistic representation, Jan introduced the phenomenon of the psychological portrait—the portrait that probed the temperament, character, or unique personality of the subject.

Figure 17.12 JAN VAN EYCK, *Man in a Turban* (*Self-Portrait?*), 1433. Tempera and oil on panel, 13⅜ × 10¼ in. The three-quarter view gives the figure an aggressive spatial presence that is further enhanced by the complex folds of crimson fabric in the turban.

While Early Renaissance artists usually represented their sitters in domestic interiors, High Renaissance masters preferred to situate them in *plein-air* (outdoor) settings, as if to suggest human consonance with nature. Leonardo da Vinci's *Mona Lisa* (Figure **17.13**), the world's best-known portrait, brings figure and landscape into exquisite harmony: the pyramidal shape of the sitter (possibly the wife of the Florentine banker Francesco del Giocondo) is echoed in the rugged mountains; the folds of her tunic are repeated in the curves of distant roads and rivers. Soft golden tones, achieved by the application of thin layers of transparent oil paint, bathe the figure, which, like the landscape, is realized in soft, smoky (in Italian, *sfumato*) gradations of light and shade. The setting, a rocky and ethereal wilderness, is as elusive as the sitter, whose eyes and mouth are delicately blurred to produce a facial expression that is almost impossible to decipher—a smile both melancholic and mocking. While the shaved

FIGURE 17.13 LEONARDO DA VINCI, *Mona Lisa*, ca. 1503–1505. Oil on panel, 30¼ × 21 in. Scientific analysis of the painting in 2004 revealed that the figure originally wore a large transparent robe favored by expecting or nursing mothers in Renaissance Italy, a detail that some scholars take to support the thesis that the painting commemorated the birth of the third child of Lisa Gherandini, wife of a Florentine silk merchant.

Figure 17.14 (left and above) **ANDREA DEL VERROCCHIO** (completed by Alessandro Leopardi), equestrian statue of Bartolommeo Colleoni, ca. 1481–1496. Bronze, height approx. 13 ft.

eyebrows and plucked hairline are hallmarks of fifteenth-century female fashion, the figure resists classification by age and (in the opinion of some) by gender. Praised by Renaissance copyists for its "lifelikeness," the *Mona Lisa* has remained an object of fascination and mystery for generations of beholders.

Renaissance portraits often took the form of life-sized sculptures in the round, some of which were brightly painted to achieve naturalistic effects. Such is also the case with the polychrome terracotta likeness of Lorenzo de' Medici (see Figure 16.3), executed by the Florentine sculptor Andrea del Verrocchio (1435–1488), which reveals a spirited naturalism reminiscent of Roman portraiture (see chapter 6). Verrocchio (a nickname meaning "true eye") was the Medici court sculptor and the close companion of Lorenzo, whose luxurious lifestyle and opulent tastes won him the title "Il Magnifico" ("the Magnificent"). Verrocchio immortalized the physical appearance of the Florentine ruler, who was also a humanist, poet, and musician. At the same time, he captured the willful vitality of the man whose *virtù* made him a legend in his time.

Renaissance sculptors revived still another antique genre: the equestrian statue. Verrocchio's monumental bronze statue of the *condottiere* Bartolommeo Colleoni (Figure **17.14**), commissioned to commemorate the mercenary soldier's military victories on behalf of the city of Venice, recalls the Roman statue of Marcus Aurelius on horseback (see Figure 6.23) as well as the considerably smaller equestrian statue of Charlemagne (see Figure 11.8). However, compared with these works, Verrocchio's masterpiece displays an unprecedented degree of scientific naturalism and a close attention to anatomical detail—note the bulging muscles of Colleoni's mount. Verrocchio moreover makes his towering mercenary twist dramatically in his saddle and scowl fiercely. Such expressions of *terribilità*, or awe-inspiring power, typify the aggressive spirit that fueled the Renaissance.

EXPLORING ISSUES

Renaissance Art and Optics

One of the most intriguing debates of the early twenty-first century concerns the question of whether Renaissance artists made use of optical devices in the preparation of their paintings. The British artist David Hockney and the physicist Charles M. Falco (among others) have argued that, as early as the 1430s, artists were able to achieve astounding accuracy of visual representation by using either concave mirrors or refractive lenses to project images of objects onto paper, wooden panels, or canvas. Such optical devices, they argue, enabled artists to trace these projected images preliminary to painting them. An early version of the *camera lucida*, a portable lens and prism device (traditionally associated with later centuries, see chapter 23), would have allowed them to easily transcribe the contours and details of their models onto a two-dimensional surface.

The opponents of the Hockney–Falco thesis contend that there is no corroboratory evidence in literature or legend for the use of such devices during the Renaissance. They maintain that numerous nonoptical factors, such as the new science of geometric perspective, experimentation with the oil medium, and a growing passion for the realistic representation of the physical world, are more likely explanations for the heightened accuracy of Renaissance painting.

Early Renaissance Artist–Scientists

If Renaissance artists took formal and literary inspiration from Classical antiquity, they were equally motivated by a desire to recreate the appearance of the natural world. The empirical study of the physical world—the reliance on direct observation—was the first step in their effort to capture in art the "look" of nature. Medieval artists had little motivation to simulate the world of the senses, a world they regarded as the imperfect reflection of the divine order. For Renaissance artist–scientists, however, the visible, physical world could be mastered only if it were understood. To this end, they engaged in a program of examination, analysis, and record keeping. They drew from live studio models, studied human and animal anatomy, and analyzed the effects of natural light on objects in space. Art became a form of rational inquiry or, as in the case of Leonardo, of scientific analysis.

For Renaissance artists, the painting constituted a window on nature: the **picture plane**, that is, the two-dimensional surface of the panel or canvas, was conceived as a transparent glass or window through which one might perceive the three-dimensional world. Various techniques aided artists in the task of recreating the illusion of reality. The technique of oil painting, refined by Jan van Eyck, was among the first of these. The application of thin oil glazes, which also became popular in Italy, produced a sense of atmospheric space rarely achieved in fresco (see Figure 15.9) or tempera (see Figure 17.4). But the more revolutionary "breakthrough" in Renaissance painting was the invention of **linear perspective**, an ingenious tool for the translation of three-dimensional space onto a two-dimensional surface. Around 1420, inspired, in all likelihood, by Latin translations of Arab-Muslim treatises on optics and optical devices, Brunelleschi formulated the first laws of linear perspective. These laws describe the manner by which all parallel lines in a given visual field appear to converge at a single vanishing point on the horizon (an illusion familiar to anyone who, from the rear of a train, has watched railroad tracks "merge" in the distance). Brunelleschi projected the picture plane as a cross section through which diagonal lines (orthogonals) connected the eye of the beholder with objects along those lines and hence with the vanishing point (Figure **17.15**; see also Figures 17.21, 17.39). The new perspective system, stated mathematically and geometrically by Alberti in 1435 and advanced thereafter by Leonardo and Dürer (see chapter 19), enabled artists to represent objects "in depth" at various distances from the viewer and in correct proportion to one another. Linear perspective satisfied the Renaissance craving for an exact and accurate description of the physical world. It also imposed a fixed relationship—both in time and space—between the image and the eye of the beholder, making the latter the exclusive point of reference within the spatial field and thus, metaphorically, placing the individual at the center of the world.

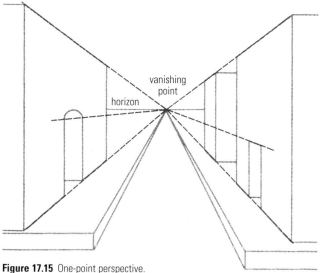

Figure 17.15 One-point perspective.

Figure 17.16 MASACCIO, *Trinity with the Virgin, Saint John the Evangelist, and Donors*, ca. 1426–1427. Fresco (now detached from wall), 21 ft. 10⅝ in. × 10 ft. 4¾ in.

Figure 17.17 MASACCIO, *Trinity with the Virgin, Saint John the Evangelist, and Donors*, showing perspective lines.

Masaccio

The first artist to master Brunelleschi's new spatial device was the Florentine painter Tommaso Guidi, called Masaccio, or "Slovenly Tom" (1401–1428). Before his untimely death (possibly by poison) at age twenty-seven, Masaccio demonstrated his remarkable artistic talents in frescoes he painted for the churches of Florence. Masaccio's *Trinity with the Virgin, Saint John the Evangelist, and Donors* (Figure **17.16**), in Santa Maria Novella, reflects the artist's mastery over the new perspective system: the lines of the painted barrel vault above the *Trinity* recede and converge at a vanishing point located at the foot of the Cross, thus corresponding precisely with the eye-level of viewers standing below the scene in the church itself (Figure **17.17**). Masaccio further enhanced the illusion of real space by placing the figures of the kneeling patrons "outside of" the Classical architectural forms that frame the sacred space.

The cycle of frescoes Masaccio executed for the Brancacci Chapel in Santa Maria del Carmine in Florence represents an even more elaborate synthesis of illusionistic techniques. In *The Tribute Money*, a scene based on the Gospel

Figure 17.18 MASACCIO, *The Tribute Money*, ca. 1425. Fresco (after restoration), 8 ft. 4 in. × 19 ft. 8 in. Seeking to entrap Jesus, a group of Pharisees asked him whether taxes should be paid to Rome. To avoid offending the divergent authorities, Jewish and Roman, Jesus replied, "Render unto Caesar the things that are Caesar's, and unto God the things that are God's" (Matthew 22:21).

story in which Jesus honors the demands of the Roman state by paying a tax or "tribute," the artist combined three related scenes: on the left, the apostle Peter gathers money from the mouth of a fish, as instructed by Jesus, in the center; on the right, Peter is shown delivering the coins to the Roman tax collector (Figure 17.18). Masaccio's application of linear perspective—the orthogonals of the building on the right meet at a vanishing point just behind the head of Jesus—provides spatial unity to the three separate episodes. Tonal unity is provided by means of **aerial perspective**—the subtle blurring of details and diminution of color intensity in objects perceived at a distance. Refining the innovative spatial techniques explored by Giotto at the Arena Chapel in Padua (see Figures 15.1 and 15.9), Masaccio also made use of light and shade (*chiaroscuro*) to model his figures as though they actually stood in the light of the chapel window located to the right of the fresco (Figure 17.19).

Eager to represent nature as precisely as possible, Masaccio worked from live models as well as from the available antique sources. From Classical statuary he borrowed the graceful stance of the Roman tax collector, who is shown twice in the fresco—viewed from front and back. Antique sculpture also probably inspired the Roman togas and the head of John the Evangelist (on Jesus' right). In the Brancacci Chapel frescoes, Masaccio anticipated the three principal features of Early Renaissance painting: the adaptation of Classical prototypes, the empirical study of nature, and the application of the new techniques of spatial illusionism.

Figure 17.19 Brancacci Chapel (after restoration). Masaccio was in his early twenties when he began work in the chapel. *The Tribute Money,* a subject that may have been chosen as a reference to the recent establishment of income tax in Florence, is pictured on the upper left wall.

Figure 17.20 LORENZO GHIBERTI, "Gates of Paradise," 1425–1442. The east portal of the Florentine Baptistry contains Lorenzo Ghiberti's immense (18 ft. 6 in. tall) gilt-bronze doors, brilliantly depicting in low relief ten episodes from the Old Testament. Ghiberti pictured himself in the roundel at the middle of the left door. Other figures depict his son, Vittorio, biblical prophets, and heroines. In 1990, the doors were removed for restoration. They now reside in the Museo del Duomo in Florence; copies have replaced the originals on the baptistry.

Ghiberti

Masaccio was not alone in the rush to explore the new illusionism. Artists throughout Italy found numerous opportunities to devise *trompe l'oeil* ("fool-the-eye") illusions such as those that delighted visitors to the *studiolo* of Federico da Montefeltro (see Figure 16.7). In the domain of sculpture, the Early Renaissance master of pictorial illusionism was the Florentine goldsmith Lorenzo Ghiberti (1378–1455). After winning the civic competition (his competitor was the eminent Brunelleschi) for a set of bronze relief panels to adorn the north door of the Florentine baptistry of San Giovanni, Ghiberti was commissioned to prepare a second set for the east doorway of the building, which faced the Duomo. He spent twenty-seven years creating the ten panels for the monumental 3-ton, 20-foot-tall door (Figure **17.20**).

The panels were executed by means of the lost-wax process (see Figure 0.18): each detailed beeswax model was embedded in a clay mold; when the mold was fired and the wax melted away, liquid bronze was poured into the mold. The panels bring to life ten milestones of the Hebrew Bible, from the creation of Adam and Eve to the reign of Solomon. They make brilliant use of linear perspective to stage dramatic narratives filled with graceful figures and fine atmospheric details. The bottom panel on the right, which depicts the meeting of Solomon and Sheba (**Figure 17.21**), engages one-point perspective to give dramatic focus to the event. Overwhelmed by the majesty of these doors, the great sculptor of the next generation, Michelangelo, pronounced them worthy of being the Gates of Paradise. In their splendid union of naturalism

Figure 17.21 LORENZO GHIBERTI, *Meeting of Solomon and Sheba* (single panel of the "Gates of Paradise," Figure 17.20). Gilt-bronze relief, 31¼ × 31¼ in.

and idealization, and in their masterful casting, Ghiberti's doors established a benchmark in the art of Renaissance sculpture.

Leonardo da Vinci as Artist–Scientist

Among the artist–scientists of the Renaissance, Leonardo da Vinci (1452–1519) best deserves that title. A diligent investigator of natural phenomena, Leonardo examined the anatomical and organic functions of plants, animals, and human beings. He also studied the properties of wind and water and invented several hundred ingenious mechanical devices, including an armored tank, a diving bell, and a flying machine, most of which never left the notebook stage. Between 1489 and 1518, Leonardo produced thousands of drawings accompanied by notes (Figure **17.22**) written in mirror-image script (devised perhaps to discourage imitators and plagiarists). This annotated record of the artist–scientist's passion to master nature includes anatomical drawings whose accuracy remained unsurpassed until 1543, when the Flemish physician Andreas Vesalius published the first medical illustrations of the human anatomy. Some of Leonardo's studies explore ideas—for example, the mechanics of flight (Figure **17.23**)—and the standardization of machine parts that were far in advance of their time. Although Leonardo's notebooks (unpublished until 1898) had little influence upon European science, they remain a symbol of the Renaissance imagination and a timeless source of inspiration.

Figure 17.22 LEONARDO DA VINCI, *Embryo in the Womb*, ca. 1510. Pen and brown ink, 11¾ × 8½ in.

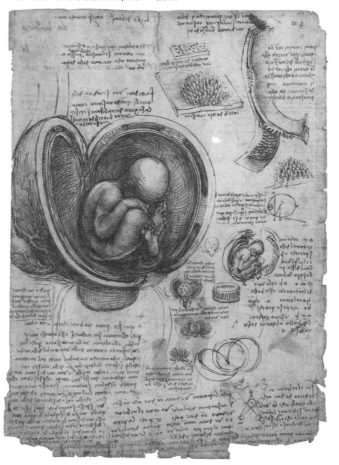

Following Alberti, Leonardo maintained that a universal system of proportion governed both nature and art. Indeed, Leonardo's quest for a governing order led him to examine the correspondence between human proportions and ideal geometric shapes, as Vitruvius and his followers had advised. Leonardo's so-called "Vitruvian Man" (Figure **17.24**), whose strict geometry haunts the compositions of High Renaissance painters and architects, is the metaphor for the Renaissance view of the microcosm as a mirror of the macrocosm. Yet, more than any other artist of his time, Leonardo exalted the importance of dependence on the senses for discovering the general rules of nature. Critical of abstract speculation bereft of sensory confirmation, he held that the human eye was the most dependable instrument for obtaining true knowledge of nature. When Leonardo wrote, "That painting is the most to be praised which agrees most exactly with the thing imitated," he was articulating the Renaissance view of art as the imitation of nature. Although Leonardo never established a strict methodology for the formulation of scientific laws, his insistence on direct experience and experimentation made him the harbinger of the Scientific Revolution that would sweep through Western Europe during the next two centuries. In the following excerpts from his notebooks, Leonardo defends the superiority of sensory experience over "book learning" and argues that painting surpasses poetry as a form of human expression.

READING 17.1 From Leonardo da Vinci's *Notes* (ca. 1510)

I am fully aware that the fact of my not being a man of   1
letters may cause certain arrogant persons to think that
they may with reason censure me, alleging that I am a man
ignorant of book-learning. Foolish folk! Do they not know
that I might retort by saying, as did Marius to the Roman
Patricians, "They who themselves go about adorned in the
labor of others will not permit me my own." They will say
that because of my lack of book-learning, I cannot properly
express what I desire to treat of. Do they not know that
my subjects require for their exposition experience rather   10
than the words of others? And since experience has been
the mistress of whoever has written well, I take her as my
mistress, and to her in all points make my appeal.

I wish to work miracles. . . . And you who say that it is
better to look at an anatomical demonstration than to see
these drawings, you would be right, if it were possible to
observe all the details shown in these drawings in a single
figure, in which, with all your ability, you will not see nor
acquire a knowledge of more than some few veins, while,
in order to obtain an exact and complete knowledge of   20
these, I have dissected more than ten human bodies,
destroying all the various members, and removing even
the very smallest particles of the flesh which surrounded
these veins without causing any effusion of blood other
than the imperceptible bleeding of the capillary veins. And,
as one single body did not suffice for so long a time, it
was necessary to proceed by stages with so many bodies

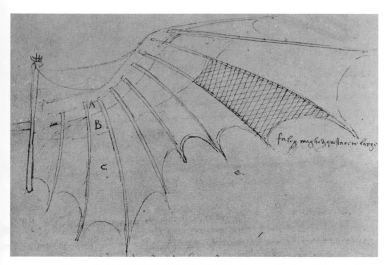

Figure 17.23 LEONARDO DA VINCI, *Wing Construction for a Flying Machine*, ca. 1500. Pen and brown ink. The comic book hero Batman, according to its twentieth-century creator, Bob Kane, was born when Kane first viewed Leonardo's notebook drawings that described the mechanics of flight.

as would render my knowledge complete; and this I repeated twice over in order to discover the differences. . . .

The eye, which is called the window of the soul, is the chief means whereby the understanding may most fully and abundantly appreciate the infinite works of nature; and the ear is the second inasmuch as it acquires its importance from the fact that it hears the things which the eye has seen. If you historians, or poets, or mathematicians had never seen things with your eyes you would be ill able to describe them in your writings. And if you, O poet, represent a story by depicting it with your pen, the painter with his brush will so render it as to be more easily satisfying and less tedious to understand. If you call painting "dumb poetry," then the painter may say of the poet that his art is "blind painting." Consider then which is the more grievous affliction, to be blind or be dumb! Although the poet has as wide a choice of subjects as the painter, his creations fail to afford as much satisfaction to mankind as do paintings, for while poetry attempts with words to represent forms, actions, and scenes, the painter employs the exact images of the forms in order to reproduce these forms. Consider, then, which is more fundamental to man, the name of man or his image? The name changes with change of country; the form is unchanged except by death.

And if the poet serves the understanding by way of the ear, the painter does so by the eye which is the nobler sense. I will only cite as an instance of this how if a good painter represents the fury of a battle and a poet also describes one, and the two descriptions are shown together to the public, you will soon see which will draw most of the spectators, and where there will be most discussion, to which most praise will be given and which will satisfy the more. There is no doubt that the painting which is by far the more useful and beautiful will give the greater pleasure. Inscribe in any place the name of God and set opposite to it his image, you will see which will be held in greater reverence!. . .

30

40

50

60

If you despise painting, which is the sole imitator of all the visible works of nature, it is certain that you will be despising a subtle invention which with philosophical and ingenious speculation takes as its theme all the various kinds of forms, airs, and scenes, plants, animals, grasses and flowers, which are surrounded by light and shade. And this truly is a science and the true-born daughter of nature, since painting is the offspring of nature. But in order to speak more correctly we may call it the grandchild of nature; for all visible things derive their existence from nature, and from these same things is born painting. So therefore we may justly speak of it as the grandchild of nature and as related to God himself.

70

Q How does this reading illustrate Leonardo's role as an artist–scientist?

Q In what ways is painting, according to Leonardo, superior to poetry?

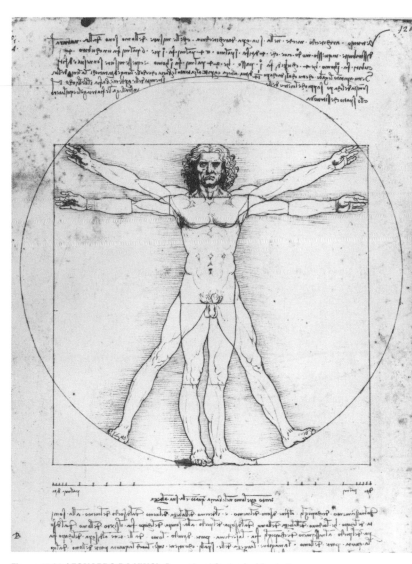

Figure 17.24 LEONARDO DA VINCI, *Proportional Study of a Man in the Manner of Vitruvius*, ca. 1487. Pen and ink, 13½ × 9⅝ in. Leonardo's famous figure indicates that man's proportions are regular, reflecting Vitruvian "divine" geometry: the outstretched arms make the figure a square; at a diagonal they center a circle.

The High Renaissance

Leonardo

By the end of the fifteenth century, Renaissance artists had mastered all of the fundamental techniques of visual illusionism, including linear and aerial perspective and the use of light and shade. They now began to employ these techniques in ever more heroic and monumental ways. To the techniques of scientific illusionism they wedded the Classical principles of clarity, symmetry, and order, arriving at a unity of design that would typify High Renaissance art. The two artists whose paintings best represent the achievements of the High Renaissance are Leonardo da Vinci and Raphael.

In his few (and largely unfinished) religious narratives, Leonardo da Vinci fused narrative and symbolic content to achieve an ordered, grand design. The classic example is his *Last Supper*, executed in the late 1490s to adorn the wall of the refectory (the monastery dining room) of Santa Maria delle Grazie in Milan (see Figure 17.25). The *Last Supper* is one of the great religious paintings of all time. Leonardo intended that the sacred event (appropriate for meditation by the monks at table) *appear* to take place within the monastic dining room. The receding lines of the ceiling beams and side-wall tapestries create a sense of spatial depth and link the scene illusionistically with the interior walls of the refectory. Leonardo

EXPLORING ISSUES

The *Last Supper:* Restoration or Ruin?

Figure 17.25 LEONARDO DA VINCI, *Last Supper*, ca. 1485–1498. Fresco: oil, tempera, and varnish on plaster, 15 ft. 1⅛ in × 28 ft. 10½ in. This shows the fresco before restoration.

Slow in his working methods, Leonardo rejected the traditional (fast-drying) *buon fresco* technique of applying paint to a wet-plastered wall. Instead, he experimented with a mixture of oil, tempera, and varnish that proved to be nondurable. The use and abuse of the Santa Maria delle Grazie refectory over the centuries—especially after it was

hit by an Allied bomb in 1943—further precipitated the deterioration of the *Last Supper*. Between the eighteenth and twentieth centuries, the fresco underwent many retouchings, repaintings, and cleanings, the most recent of which was a twenty-two-year Italian-led rehabilitation enterprise (completed in 1999) that made use of various technologies, fixed the vanishing point at the center of the composition directly behind the head of Jesus (see Figure 17.15). Topped by a pediment, the open doorway (one of three, symbolic of the Trinity) acts as a halo, reinforcing the centrality of Christ and his mission as "light of the world." The formal elements of the composition thereby underscore the symbolic aspects of the religious narrative. To this masterful rationalization of space, Leonardo added high drama: he divided the apostles into four groups of three who interact in response to the Master's declaration that one of his followers would betray him (Matthew 26:21). The somber mood, enhanced by Christ's meditative look and submissive gesture indicating the bread and

wine as symbols of the Eucharist, is heightened by the reactions of the apostles—astonishment, anger, disbelief—appropriate to their biblical personalities. (The quick-tempered Peter, for instance—fifth from the left— wields the knife he later uses to cut off the ear of Christ's assailant, Malchus.)

Leonardo seems to have completed the figures of all the apostles before portraying Jesus and Judas. His habit of coming into the refectory and gazing thoughtfully at the work for hours, sometimes without picking up a brush, infuriated the monastery's prior. Vasari, the enthusiastic admirer of Leonardo's fresco, recounts the details.

Figure 17.26 LEONARDO DA VINCI, *Last Supper*, ca. 1485–1498. This shows the fresco in Figure 17.25 after the restoration was completed in 1999.

but left many of the figures with no facial features (Figure **17.26**). Bitter controversy surrounded the issue of restoring this and other landmark works, such as the Sistine Chapel ceiling (see Figure 17.34). While some scholars praise the restoration of the *Last Supper*, others claim that the cleaning has done additional damage and has distorted Leonardo's

colors beyond repair. Some art historians vehemently refuse to show the restored version in their books and classrooms, claiming that the precleaned fresco (see Figure **17.25**) is closer to Leonardo's original intentions. Most agree, however, that what is left of the masterpiece is not much more than a ghost of the original.

Science and Technology

1494	Leonardo devises plans to harness the waters of the Arno River
1508	Leonardo records the results of cadaver dissections and analyzes the movements of birds in flight, in unpublished manuscripts
1513	Leonardo undertakes scientific studies of botany, geology, and hydraulic power

READING 17.2 From Vasari's *Lives of the Most Excellent Painters, Architects, and Sculptors* (1550)

Biography of Leonardo da Vinci

The master gave so much beauty and majesty to the   1
heads of the Apostles that he was constrained to leave
the Christ unfinished, convinced as he was that he could
not render the divinity of the Redeemer. Even so, this
work has always been held in the highest estimation by
the Milanese and by foreigners as well. Leonardo
rendered to perfection the doubts and anxieties of the
Apostles, their desire to know by whom their Master is to
be betrayed. All their faces show their love, terror, anger,
grief, or bewilderment, unable as they are to fathom the   10
meaning of the Lord. The spectator is also struck by the
determination, hatred, and treachery of Judas [fourth
figure from the left]. The whole is executed with the
most minute exactitude. The texture of the tablecloth
seems actually made of linen.

The story goes that the prior was in a great hurry to see
the picture done. He could not understand why Leonardo
should sometimes remain before his work half a day
together, absorbed in thought. He would have him work
away, as he compelled the laborers to do who were   20
digging in his garden, and never put the pencil down.
Not content with seeking to hurry Leonardo, the prior
even complained to the duke, and tormented him so
much that, at length, he sent for Leonardo and
courteously entreated him to finish the work. Leonardo,
knowing the duke to be an intelligent man, explained
himself as he had never bothered to do to the prior. He
made it clear that men of genius are sometimes
producing most when they seem least to labor, for their
minds are then occupied in the shaping of those   30
conceptions to which they afterward give form. He told
the duke that two heads were yet to be done: that of the
Savior, the likeness of which he could not hope to find
on earth and had not yet been able to create in his
imagination in perfection of celestial grace: and the
other, of Judas. He said he wanted to find features fit to
render the appearance of a man so depraved as to betray

his benefactor, his Lord, and the Creator of the world. He
said he would still search but as a last resort he could
always use the head of the troublesome and impertinent   40
prior. This made the duke laugh with all his heart. The
prior was utterly confounded and went away to speed the
digging in his garden. Leonardo was left in peace.

Q **What aspects of Leonardo's Last Supper does Vasari admire? What does this suggest about Renaissance standards in the visual arts?**

Raphael

The second of the great High Renaissance artists was Urbino-born Raphael (Raffaello Sanzio; 1483–1520). Less devoted to scientific speculation than Leonardo, Raphael was first and foremost a master painter. His fashionable portraits were famous for their verisimilitude and incisiveness. A case in point is the portrait of Raphael's lifelong friend Baldassare Castiglione (see Figure 16.9), which captures the self-confidence and thoughtful intelligence of this celebrated Renaissance personality.

Raphael's compositions are notable for their clarity, harmony, and unity of design. In *The Alba Madonna* (Figure **17.27**), one of Raphael's popular renderings of the Madonna and Child, the artist sets the figures in a landscape framed by the picturesque hills of central Italy. Using clear, bright colors and precise draftsmanship, he organized the **tondo** (round picture) by way of simple geometric shapes: the triangle (formed by the Virgin, Christ Child, and the infant John the Baptist), the circle (the head of the Virgin), and the trapezoid (one length of which is formed by the Virgin's outstretched leg). Despite the formality of the composition and the nobility of the figures, the scene might be construed as a record of an ordinary woman with two children in a landscape, for Raphael has avoided obvious religious symbolism, such as the traditional halo. Raphael's religious figures, notable for their serenity and grace, occupy a world of sweetness and light. His female saints, often posed theatrically, are idealized creatures with gentle expressions. Such features were often taken to sentimental extremes by the artist's many imitators.

In 1510 Pope Julius II, the greatest of Renaissance church patrons, commissioned Raphael to execute a series of frescoes for the Vatican Stanza della Segnatura—the pope's personal library and the room in which official church papers were signed. The paintings were to represent the four domains of human learning: theology, philosophy, law, and the arts. To illustrate philosophy, Raphael painted *The School of Athens*. In this landmark fresco, the artist immortalized the company of the great philosophers and scientists of ancient history. At the center of the composition appear, as if in scholarly debate, the two giants of Classical philosophy: Plato, who points heavenward to indicate his view of reality as fixed in universal Forms, and Aristotle, who points to the earth to indicate that universal truth depends on the study of nature. Framed by a series

Figure 17.27 RAPHAEL, *The Alba Madonna*, ca. 1510.
Oil on wood transferred to canvas, diameter 37¼ in.

of receding arches, the two philosophers stand against the bright sky, beneath the lofty vaults of a Roman basilica that resembles the newly remodeled Saint Peter's Cathedral (Figure 17.28). Between their heads lies the invisible vanishing point at which all the principal lines of sight converge. On either side of the great hall appear historical figures belonging to each of the two philosophic "camps": the Platonists (left) and the Aristotelians (right).

The School of Athens is a portrait gallery of Renaissance artists whose likenesses Raphael borrowed to depict his Classical heroes. The stately, bearded Plato is an idealized portrait of Leonardo, who was visiting Rome while Raphael was at work in the Vatican. The balding Euclid, seen bending over his slate in the lower right corner of the composition, resembles Raphael's good friend, the architect Bramante. In the far right corner, Raphael himself (wearing a dark hat) appears discreetly among the Aristotelians. And in final revisions of the fresco, Raphael added to the left foreground the likeness of Michelangelo

in the guise of the brooding and solitary Greek philosopher Heraclitus. *The School of Athens* is the ultimate tribute to the rebirth of Classical humanism in the age of the Renaissance, for here, in a unified, imaginary space, the artists of Raphael's day are presented as the incarnations of the intellectual titans of antiquity.

In the restrained nobility of the near life-sized figures and the measured symmetry of the composition, Raphael's *School of Athens* marked the culmination of a style that had begun with Giotto and Masaccio; here, Raphael gave concrete vision to a world purged of accident and emotion. Monumental in conception and size and flawless in execution, *The School of Athens* advanced a set of formal principles that came to epitomize the *Grand Manner*: spatial clarity, decorum (that is, propriety and good taste), balance, unity of design, and grace (the last especially evident in the subtle symmetries of line and color). These principles remained touchstones for Western academic art until the late nineteenth century.

Figure 17.28 RAPHAEL, *The School of Athens*, 1509–1511. Fresco, 26 ft. × 18 ft.

1 Apollo
2 Alcibiades or Alexander
3 Socrates
4 Plato (Leonardo)
5 Aristotle
6 Minerva
7 Sodoma
8 Raphael
9 Ptolemy
10 Zoroaster (Pietro Bembo?)
11 Euclid (Bramante)
12 Diogenes
13 Heraclitus (Michelangelo)
14 Parmenides, Xenocrates
   or Aristossenus
15 Francesco Maria della
   Rovere
16 Telauges
17 Pythagoras
18 Averhöes
19 Epicurus
20 Federigo Gonzaga
21 Zeno

Architecture of the High Renaissance: Bramante and Palladio

During the High Renaissance, the center of artistic activity shifted from Florence to Rome as the popes undertook a campaign to restore the ancient city of Rome to its original grandeur as the capital of Christendom. When Pope Julius II commissioned Donato Bramante (1444–1514) to rebuild Saint Peter's Cathedral, the architect designed a monumentally proportioned, centrally planned church to be capped by an immense dome. Bramante's plan was much modified in the 120 years it took to complete the new Saint Peter's. But his ideal building—organized so that all structural elements were evenly disposed around a central point—took shape on a smaller scale in his Tempietto, the "little temple" that marked the site of Saint Peter's martyrdom in Rome (Figure **17.29**). Modeled on the Classical tholos (see chapter 5), Bramante's fine-standing circular stone chapel is ringed by a simple Doric colonnade and topped by a dome elevated upon a niched drum. Although the interior affords little light and space, the exterior gives the appearance of an elegant marble reliquary. It embodies the High Renaissance ideals of clarity, mathematical order, and unity of design.

The Renaissance passion for harmonious design had an equally powerful influence on the history of domestic architecture, a circumstance for which the Italian architect Andrea Palladio (1518–1580) was especially responsible. In his *Four Books on Architecture*, published in Venice in 1570, Palladio defended symmetry and centrality as the controlling elements of architectural design. He put his ideals into practice in a number of magnificent country houses he built for patrons in northern Italy. The Villa Rotonda near Vicenza—a centrally planned, thirty-two-room country house—is a perfectly symmetrical structure featuring a central room (or rotunda) covered by a dome (Figure **17.30**). All four façades of the villa are identical, featuring a projecting Ionic portico approached by a flight of steps (Figure **17.31**). In its geometric clarity, its cool elegance, and its dominance over its landscape setting, the Villa Rotonda represents the Renaissance distillation of Classical principles as applied to secular architecture. With this building, Palladio established the definitive ideal in domestic housing for the wealthy and provided a model of solemn dignity that would inspire generations of Neoclassical architects in England and America (see chapter 26).

Figure 17.29 DONATO BRAMANTE, Tempietto, San Pietro in Montorio, Rome, 1502. Height 46 ft., external diameter 29 ft.

Figure 17.30 ANDREA PALLADIO (Andrea di Pietro Gondola), Villa Rotonda, Vicenza, Italy, completed 1569.

Figure 17.31 Plan of the Villa Rotonda, Vicenza, Italy.

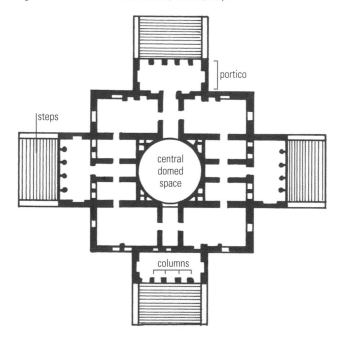

Michelangelo and Heroic Idealism

The works of the High Renaissance master Michelangelo Buonarroti (1475–1564) are some of the most heroic in Renaissance art. An architect, poet, painter, and engineer, Michelangelo regarded himself first and foremost as a sculptor. At the age of twenty-one, he launched his career with a commission for a marble *Pietà* that would serve as a tomb monument in Old Saint Peter's Cathedral in Rome

(Figure **17.32**). Boasting that he would produce the most beautiful marble sculpture in Rome, Michelangelo carved the image of the young Virgin holding the lifeless body of Jesus (as was traditional to this subject), but, at the same time, caught in a moment of sorrowful meditation. The figure of Mary, disproportionately large in comparison with that of Jesus, creates a protective pyramidal shape that not only supports, but enfolds the Son. All elements of the composition—the position of the left arm of Jesus, the angles formed by his knees, and the folds of Mary's drapery—work toward a gentle unity of design that contrasts sharply with earlier versions of the subject (see Figure 15.10). Indeed, Michelangelo's *Pietà* transformed the late medieval devotional image into a monumental statement on the meaning of Christian sacrifice.

Michelangelo went on to establish his reputation in Florence at the age of twenty-seven, when he undertook to carve a freestanding larger-than-life statue of the biblical David from a gigantic block of Carrara marble that no other sculptor had dared to tackle (Figure **17.33**). When Michelangelo completed the statue in 1504, the rulers of Florence placed it at the entrance to the city hall as a symbol of Florentine vigilance. Compared to Donatello's lean and introspective youth (see Figure 17.2), Michelangelo's *David* is a defiant presence—the offspring of a race of giants. While indebted to Classical tradition, Michelangelo deliberately violated Classical proportions by making the head and hands of his figure too large for his trunk. The body of the fearless adolescent, with its swelling veins and taut muscles, is tense and brooding, powerful rather than graceful. Indeed, in this image, Michelangelo drew to heroic proportions the Renaissance ideals of *terribil-ità* and *virtù*.

Although Michelangelo considered himself primarily a sculptor, he spent four years fulfilling a papal commission to paint the 5760-square-foot ceiling of the Vatican's Sistine Chapel (Figure **17.34**). The scope and monumentality of this enterprise reflect both the ambitions of Pope Julius II and the heroic aspirations of Michelangelo himself. Working from scaffolds poised some 70 feet above the floor, Michelangelo painted a vast scenario illustrating the Creation and Fall of Humankind as recorded in Genesis (1:1 through 9:27; Figure **17.35**). In the nine principal scenes, as well as in the hundreds of accompanying prophets and sibyls, he used high-keyed, clear, bright colors (restored by recent cleaning). He overthrew many traditional constraints, minimizing setting and symbolic details and maximizing the grandeur of figures that—like those he carved in stone—seem superhuman in size and spirit.

A significant archeological event influenced Michelangelo's treatment of the figure after 1506: in that year, diggers working in Rome uncovered the *Laocoön* (see Figure 5.33), the celebrated Hellenistic sculpture that had been known to Western scholars only by way of the Roman

Figure 17.32 MICHELANGELO, *Pietà*, 1497–1500. Marble, 15 ft 8½ in.

Figure 17.33 MICHELANGELO, *David*, 1501–1504. Marble, height 13 ft. 5 in.

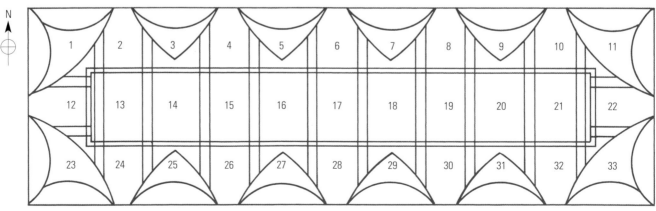

Figure 17.34 MICHELANGELO, Sistine Chapel ceiling (after cleaning), Vatican, Rome, 1508–1512. Fresco, 45 ft. × 128 ft.

Figure 17.35, *facing page,* Sistine Chapel ceiling, plan of scenes (after Hibbard).

1 death of Haman	14 creation of Sun, Moon, planets	27 Asa
2 Jeremiah	15 separation of land from water	28 Cumaean Sibyl
3 Salmon	16 creation of Adam	29 Ezekias
4 Persian Sibyl	17 creation of Eve	30 Isaiah
5 Roboam	18 temptation and expulsion	31 Josiah
6 Ezekiel	19 sacrifice of Noah	32 Delphic Sibyl
7 Ozias	20 the flood	33 Judith and Holofernes
8 Eritrean Sibyl	21 drunkenness of Noah	
9 Zorobabel	22 Zacharias	
10 Joel	23 Moses and the serpent of brass	
11 David and Goliath	24 Libyan Sibyl	
12 Jonah	25 Jesse	
13 separation of light from darkness	26 Daniel	

writer, Pliny. The sculpture—with its bold contortions and its powerfully rendered anatomy—had as great an impact on Michelangelo and the course of High Renaissance art as Cicero's prose had exercised on Petrarch and Early Renaissance literature. Indeed, the twisted torsos, taut muscles, and stretched physiques of the Sistine Chapel figures reflect the influence of the *Laocoön* and other recovered Classical antiquities. In the *Creation of Adam* (Figure **17.36**), God and Man—equal in size and muscular grace—

confront each other like partners in the divine plan. Adam reaches longingly toward God, seeking the moment of fulfillment, when God will charge his languid body with celestial energy. If the image depicts Creation, it is also a metaphor for the Renaissance belief in the potential divinity of humankind—the visual analogue of Pico's *Oration on the Dignity of Man* (see chapter 16).

Creation and creativity are themes that dominate Michelangelo's sonnets. In some of the sonnets, he likens

Figure 17.36 MICHELANGELO, *Creation of Adam*, detail of Figure 17.34.

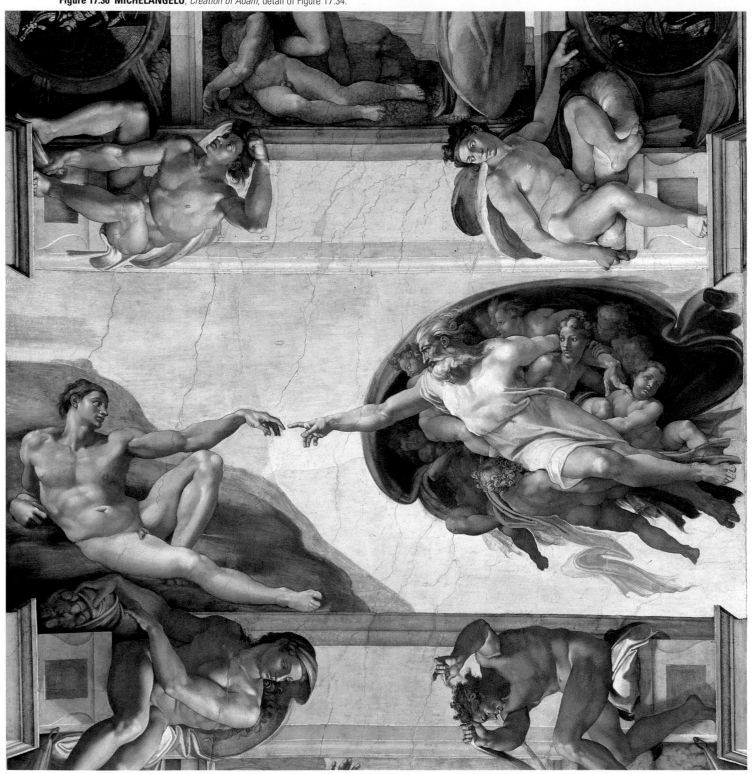

the creative act to the workings of Neoplatonic love, which move to purge the base (or lower) elements of the human being. In others, he suggests that the task of the sculptor is to "liberate" the "idea" that is embedded within the marble block. Hailed as a major poet even in his own time, Michelangelo reflected upon all aspects of the creative life; reflecting on the Sistine Chapel ceiling, he describes his hardships with comic eloquence:

> In this hard toil I've such a goiter grown,
> Like cats that water drink in Lombardy,
> (Or wheresoever else the place may be)
> That chin and belly meet perforce in one.
> My beard doth point to heaven, my scalp its place
> Upon my shoulder finds; my chest, you'll say,
> A harpy's is, my paint-brush all the day
> Doth drop a rich mosaic on my face.
> My loins have entered my paunch within,
> My nether end my balance doth supply,
> My feet unseen move to and fro in vain.
> In front to utmost length is stretched my skin
> And wrinkled up in folds behind, while I
> Am bent as bowmen bend a bow in [Spain].

In 1546, Michelangelo accepted the papal commission to complete the dome and east end of the new Saint Peter's Cathedral in Rome—a project that followed numerous earlier efforts to make the basilica a centrally planned, domed church (Figure **17.37**). For Saint Peter's, Michelangelo designed an elliptically shaped dome on a huge drum ornamented with double columns of the "colossal order" (Figure **17.38**). He lived to build the drum, but it was not until

1590 that the dome was completed. Rising some 450 feet from the floor of the nave to the top of its tall lantern, Michelangelo's dome was heroic in size and dramatic in contour. But its enormous double shell of brick and stone proved impractical: cracks in the substructure appeared less than ten years after completion, and the superstructure had to be bolstered repeatedly over the centuries, most recently by means of chains. Nevertheless, the great dome

Figure 17.37 MICHELANGELO, plan for the new Saint Peter's, Vatican, Rome, ca. 1537–1550. Michelangelo revived the Greek cross plan originally projected by Bramante. He brought drama to the façade by adding a portico with two sets of columns and a massive flight of steps.

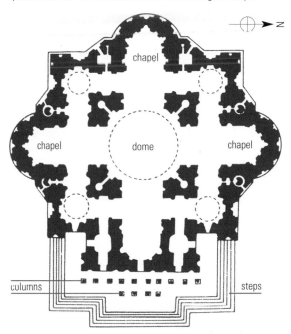

Figure 17.38 MICHELANGELO, dome of Saint Peter's, Vatican, Rome, ca. 1546–1564 (view from the south). Dome completed by Giacomo della Porta, 1590.

inspired numerous copies, such as that of Saint Paul's Cathedral in London (see Figure 22.3) and the United States Capitol in Washington, D.C.

Michelangelo shared the Neoplatonic belief that the soul, imprisoned in the body, yearned to return to its sacred origins. In his last works of art, as in his impassioned sonnets, he explored the conflict between flesh and spirit that had burdened many humanists, including Petrarch. The restless, brooding figures of Michelangelo's late works, especially those conceived for the Last Judgment fresco of the Sistine Chapel (see Figure 20.4)—unveiled twenty-nine years after the completion of the ceiling—mark a new direction in his art. As if burdened by a deeply troubled spirituality, these figures writhe and twist, like spirits trying to free themselves of physical matter. Ever the master of invention, the aging Michelangelo moved the gravity and solemnity of High Renaissance art in the direction of mannered theatricality.

The High Renaissance in Venice

The most notable artworks of the High Renaissance did not come from Florence, which suffered severe political upheavals at the end of the fifteenth century, but from the cities of Rome, Milan, and Venice. Venice, the Jewel of the Adriatic and a thriving center of trade, was a cluster of islands whose main streets consisted of canals lined with richly ornamented palaces. The pleasure-loving Venetians, governed by a merchant aristocracy, regularly imported costly tapestries, jewels, and other luxury goods from all

parts of Asia. During the sixteenth century, Venice outshone all of the other city-states of Italy in its ornate architecture and its taste for pageantry. Both of these features are recreated in the *Procession of the Reliquary of the Cross in Piazza San Marco* (Figure **17.39**) painted by one of Venice's leading artists, Gentile Bellini (1429?–1507). In this panoramic canvas, Bellini employed the new system of one-point perspective to dramatize the union of civic and religious ritual: the annual celebration of the feast day of Saint Mark, patron saint of Venice, and the elevation of the True Cross, the prized relic said to have miraculously cured a dying Venetian child. At the far end of the *piazza* stands the cathedral of Saint Mark, a monumental counterpart of the ornate reliquary shrine carried in the foreground.

A symbol of Venetian opulence and one of the city's most prized architectural treasures, San Marco epitomizes the cross-cultural heritage of Byzantine, Islamic, and Western Christian decorative styles. The multidomed cathedral was begun during the eleventh century and ornamented over many centuries with dazzling mosaics that adorn both the interior and the exterior. As befitting this city of jeweled altarpieces, radiant mosaics, and sparkling lagoons, Renaissance Venice produced an art of color and light. While Florentine artists depended primarily on *line* as fundamental to design and the articulation of form, the Venetians delighted in the affective power of *color*. In preference to fresco-painting and tempera applied on wood panels, they favored the oil medium, to build up thin color glazes on rough canvas surfaces.

Figure 17.39 GENTILE BELLINI, *Procession of the Reliquary of the Cross in Piazza San Marco*, 1496. Oil on canvas, 12 ft. ½ in. × 24 ft. 5¼ in. The white-robed members of the religious confraternity dedicated to Saint John the Evangelist are shown in the foreground. In the middle and background are seen groups of ambassadors from Germany, Bohemia, and elsewhere. The red-robed father of the boy cured by the miraculous True Cross kneels in thanks just behind the canopied relic.

Figure 17.40 TITIAN (begun by Giorgione), *Pastoral Concert*, ca. 1505. Oil on canvas, 3 ft. 7¼ in. × 4 ft. 6¼ in. Some scholars interpret this painting as an allegory on the creation of poetry. The nude women, who seem to be invisible to the poets, may be viewed as their muses.

Giorgione and Titian

The two greatest Venetian colorists were Giorgio Barbarelli, known as Giorgione (ca. 1477–1511), and Tiziano Vecelli, called Titian (ca. 1488–1576). Little is known of Giorgione's life, but his influence on his younger colleague was significant. The *Pastoral Concert* (Figure **17.40**), a work that some scholars hold to be an early Titian, was probably begun by Giorgione and completed by Titian. This intriguing canvas shows two magnificently dressed Venetian courtiers—one playing a lute—in the presence of two female nudes. One woman holds a recorder, while the other pours water into a well. The precise subject of the painting is unclear, but its sensuousness—more a product of mood than of narrative content—is enhanced by textural and color contrasts: the red satin costume of the lute player versus the soft golden flesh of the women, the dense green foliage of the middle ground versus the thin gray atmosphere on the distant horizon, and so forth. In its evocation of untroubled country life, *Pastoral Concert* may be considered the visual equivalent of pastoral verse, a genre that became popular among Renaissance humanists. But the painting also introduces a new subject that would become quite fashionable in Western art: the nude in a landscape setting.

During the sixteenth century, the female nude—often bearing the name of a Classical goddess—became a favorite subject of patrons seeking sensuous or erotic art for private enjoyment. The most famous of such commissions, the so-called *Venus of Urbino* (Figure **17.41**), was painted for Guidobaldo della Rovera, the Duke of Urbino, during the last stage of Titian's artistic career. Here, a curvaceous nude reclines on a bed in the curtained alcove of a typical upper-class Venetian palace. The tiny roses in her hand, the myrtle plant (a symbol of Venus, goddess of love and fertility) on the window sill, the smooth dog at her feet (symbolic of fertility), and the servants who rummage in the nearby wedding chest all suggest impending marriage, while her seductive pose and arresting gaze are manifestly sexual. Titian enhanced the sensuality of the image by means of exquisitely painted surfaces: the delicate nuances of creamy skin modeled with glowing pinks, the reddish blond locks of hair, the deep burgundies of tapestries and cushions, and the cooler bluish whites of the sheets—all bathed in a pervasive golden light. Titian, who worked almost exclusively in oils, applied paint loosely, building up forms with layers of color so that contours seem to melt into each other, a technique best described as "painterly." He preferred broken and subtle tones of color to the flat, bright hues favored by such artists as Raphael. Titian's

Figure 17.41 TITIAN, *Venus of Urbino*, 1538–1539. Oil on canvas, 3 ft. 11 in. × 5 ft. 5 in. Microscopic analysis of Venetian oil painting reveals that artists often mixed pulverized glass into their paints; these small bits of powdered colored glass reflect and disperse light prismatically, giving the paintings their "glowing" appearance.

painterly style became the definitive expression of the coloristic manner in High Renaissance painting and a model for such artists as Rubens in the seventeenth century and Delacroix in the nineteenth.

The Music of the Renaissance

Like Renaissance art, Renaissance music was increasingly secular in subject matter and function. However, the perception of the Renaissance as a time when secular music overtook ecclesiastical music may be due to the fact that after 1450 more secular music was committed to paper. The printing press, perfected in Germany in the mid-fifteenth century, encouraged the preservation and dissemination of all kinds of musical composition. With the establishment of presses in Venice in the late fifteenth century, printed books of lute music and partbooks for individual instruments appeared in great numbers. (Most music was based on preexisting melodies, and manuscripts normally lacked tempo markings and other indications as to how a piece was to be performed.) Publishers also sold handbooks that offered instructions on how to play musical instruments. It is no surprise, then, that during the Renaissance, music was composed by both professional and amateur musicians. Indeed, Castiglione observed that making music was the

function of all well-rounded individuals. Music was an essential ingredient at intimate gatherings, court celebrations, and public festivals (Figure **17.42**). And virtuosity in performance, a hallmark of Renaissance music, was common among both amateurs and professionals. Along with the poets of his court, the talented Lorenzo de' Medici took pleasure in writing lively vernacular songs for the carnivals that traditionally preceded the Lenten season. On pageant wagons designed for holiday spectacles in Florence and other cities, masked singers, dancers, and mimes enacted mythological, religious, and contemporary tales in musical performance.

While the literary and visual evidence of Classical antiquity was readily available to the humanists of the Renaissance, few musical examples had survived, and none could be accurately deciphered. For that reason, medieval tradition maintained a stronger influence in the development of music than it did in art and literature. (Not until the late sixteenth century did composers draw on Greek drama as the inspiration for a new genre: opera—discussed in chapter 20.) Moreover, perhaps because performing music was believed to be within everyone's reach, musicians were not held in such high esteem as painters, sculptors, or architects of the Renaissance. Most theorists, including Leonardo da Vinci (himself a musician of some renown),

Figure 17.42 LORENZO COSTA, *The Concert,* ca. 1485–95. Oil on poplar, 3 ft. 1½ in. × 29¾ in.

considered poetry—and by extension, music—inferior to painting. Nevertheless, just as Renaissance artists pursued a more "natural-looking" art, Renaissance composers sought a more "natural-sounding" music. By the early fifteenth century, the trend toward consonant sounds encouraged the use of **intervals** of thirds in place of the traditional medieval (and ancient) intervals of fourths and fifths. And in the lighthearted songs written by Lorenzo de' Medici, an emphasis on melody and clear harmonic structure—a dramatic departure from complex polyphony—are apparent.

Early Renaissance Music: Dufay

While in the visual arts Italy took the lead, in music, French and Franco-Flemish composers outshone their Italian counterparts. During the fifteenth and much of the sixteenth centuries, composers from Burgundy and Flanders dominated the courts of Europe, including those of Italy. The leading Franco-Flemish composer of the fifteenth century, Guillaume Dufay (1400–1474), spent more than thirteen years of his career in Italy, during which time he set to music the verses of Petrarch and Lorenzo de' Medici (unfortunately, the latter compositions have been lost). In Dufay's more than two hundred surviving vocal and instrumental compositions, including motets, Masses, and *chansons* (secular songs), he made extensive use of late medieval polyphonic techniques. At the same time, he introduced a close melodic and rhythmic kinship between all parts of a musical composition.

Just as religious subject matter inspired much of the art of Renaissance painters and sculptors, so religious music—

and especially compositions for the Mass—held a prominent place in Dufay's output. However, sacred and secular themes are often indistinguishable in Dufay's works, and both are suffused by warmth of feeling. For his Mass settings, Dufay followed the common practice of borrowing melodies from popular folk tunes. In the *Missa L'homme armé*, for instance, he employed the best known of all fifteenth-century French folksongs, "The Armed Man," as the *cantus firmus* for all sections of the piece.

The Madrigal

During the sixteenth century, the most popular type of vernacular song was the **madrigal**, a composition for three to six unaccompanied voices. Usually polyphonic in texture, the madrigal often incorporated a large degree of vocal freedom, including the playful use of imitation and word painting. An intimate kind of musical composition, the madrigal might develop a romantic theme from a sonnet by Petrarch or give expression to a trifling and whimsical complaint. The Flemish composer Roland de Lassus (Orlando di Lasso; 1532–1594), who graced princely courts throughout Renaissance Europe, produced almost 200 madrigals among his more than 2000 compositions. In 1550, at age eighteen, Lassus wrote one of the most delightful vernacular songs of the Renaissance: "Matona, mia cara" ("My lady, my beloved"). The piece, a **villanella** (a light, dancelike song similar to the madrigal), describes a suitor's effort to seduce his ladyfriend; it ends each stanza with a frivolous group of nonsense syllables.

> My lady, my beloved,
> Such pleasure would I choose
> To sing beneath your window
> Of love you'll never lose.
>
> > *Dong, dong, dong, derry, derry,*
> > *Dong, dong, dong, dong.*
>
> I beg you, only hear me,
> This song of sweetest news,
> My love for you is boundless
> Like lovebirds I enthuse.
>
> > *Dong, dong, dong, derry, derry,*
> > *Dong, dong, dong, dong.*
>
> For I would go a-hunting
> And falcons I would use
> To bring you spoils a-plenty
> Plump woodfowl as your dues.
>
> > *Dong, dong, dong, derry, derry,*
> > *Dong, dong, dong, dong.*
>
> But though my words should fail me,
> Lest fear my cause should lose,
> E'en Petrarch could not help me
> Nor Helicon's fair Muse.
>
> > *Dong, dong, dong, derry, derry,*
> > *Dong, dong, dong, dong.*

> But only say you'll love me
> And if you'll not refuse
> I'll boldly sing of my love
> Night long until the dews.
>
> > *Dong, dong, dong, derry, derry,*
> > *Dong, dong, dong, dong.*

Madrigals flourished primarily in the courts of Italy and England. At the fashionable court of Queen Elizabeth I of England, the madrigal became the rage. Usually based on Italian models, the English madrigal was generally lighter in mood than its Italian counterpart and often technically simple enough to be performed by amateurs. Two of the most popular Elizabethan composers, John Dowland (1563–1626) and Thomas Morley (1557–1602), composed English-language solo songs and madrigals that are still enjoyed today.

High Renaissance Music: Josquin

The outstanding figure in High Renaissance music was Josquin des Prez (ca. 1440–1521). Josquin followed the example of his Franco-Flemish predecessors by serving at the courts of France and Italy, including that of the papacy. A master of Masses, motets, and secular songs, he earned international recognition as "the prince of music." Like Dufay, Josquin unified each polyphonic Mass around a single musical theme, but, more in the grand style of the painter Raphael, Josquin contrived complex designs in which melody and harmony were distributed symmetrically and with "geometric" clarity. He might give focus to a single musical phrase in the way that Raphael might center the Virgin and Child within a composition. And, in an effort to increase compositional balance, he might group voices into pairs, with the higher voices repeating certain phrases of the lower ones.

The expressive grace of Josquin's music followed from the attention he gave to the relationship between words and music. He tailored musical lines so that they followed the natural flow of the words, a device inspired perhaps by his appreciation of the classical kinship of song and text. Josquin was among the first to practice **word painting**, the manipulation of music to convey the literal meaning of the text—as, for example, where the text describes a bird's ascent, the music might rise in pitch. Word painting characterized both the religious and secular music of the Renaissance.

In music, as in the visual arts, composers of the Renaissance valued unity of design. Josquin achieved a homogeneous musical texture by the use of **imitation**, a technique whereby a melodic fragment introduced in the first voice is repeated closely (though usually at a different pitch) in the second, third, and fourth voices, so that one overlaps the next. Simple rhythmic lines and the ingenious use of imitation contributed to the smooth and sonorous style of such motets as "Tulerunt Dominum

---

 See Music Listening Selections at end of chapter.

meum," his eight-voice setting of a New Testament text from the Gospel of John. A master of the integration of multiple voice lines—one of his motets has as many as twenty-four parts—Josquin wrote motets that featured a continuous flow of interwoven melodies and a graceful design comparable to the best of Raphael's High Renaissance compositions.

Women and Renaissance Music

Following the tradition of the female *troubadours* (see chapter 11) and the recommendations of Castiglione, many Renaissance women were accomplished in both playing and composing music. The Venetian aristocrat, Madalena Casulana (ca. 1540–ca. 1590), was the first professional female composer to witness the publication of her works, mainly madrigals. In these vernacular songs, she made active use of word painting to heighten the text in mood and meaning.

Women also played a significant role as professional performers. The *Concerto delle donne* (Consort of Ladies) was a group of professional singers who entertained at the late sixteenth-century court of Ferrara. Famous for their technical and artistic virtuosity, and for such musical innovations as the multiplication of ornamented upper voice parts, they became the model for similar all-female ensembles in Florence and elsewhere. By 1600, talented women, who were often brought to court to train as professional

musicians, held independent careers in musical performance and composition. They sang their own repertory of songs from memory and sight-read others from popular partbooks.

Instrumental Music of the Renaissance

Although most Renaissance music was composed to be sung, the sixteenth century made considerable advances in the development of instrumental music. Music for solo instruments was popular, with the lute still the favorite. In London, its popularity as a solo instrument and to accompany madrigals (see Figure 17.42) warranted the importation of almost 14,000 lute strings in the one-year period between 1567 and 1568. A wide variety of other instruments, such as shawms, cromornes, cornets, trumpets, trombones, stringed instruments, and drums, were used for accompaniment and in small instrumental ensembles (Figure **17.43**).

Renaissance composers wrote music for portable **organs** (popular in private homes and princely courts) and for two other types of keyboard instrument: the **clavichord** and the **harpsichord** (also called the *spinet*, the *clavecin*, and the *virginal*—the last possibly after the "Virgin Queen," Elizabeth I of England, who was an accomplished musician). Harpsichord sounds are made by quills that pluck a set of strings, while clavichord notes are produced by metal tangents that strike the strings. Such instruments create

bright, sharp sounds, somewhat more robust in the harpsichord. Since Renaissance instruments produce a less dynamic and smaller range of sound than do modern instruments, they demand greater attention to nuances of *timbre*—the "color" or quality of musical sound.

During the Late Middle Ages, instruments occasionally took the place of one or more voice parts. It was not until the Renaissance, however, that music for instruments alone regularly appeared. Instrumental compositions developed out of dance tunes with strong rhythms and distinctive melodic lines. Indeed, the earliest model for the instrumental

Figure 17.43 HANS BURGKMAIR, *The Music Room,* from *Der Weiss Kunig,* late sixteenth century. This woodcut illustrates the musical education of the Holy Roman emperor Maximilian I (1459–1519). The instruments shown include the organ (lower left), harp, trumpet, drums, recorders, crumhorn (a curved reed instrument), and violin.

suite was a group of dances arranged according to contrasting rhythms. Instrumental music was characterized by the same kind of complex invention that marked the vocal compositions of Josquin, and the skillful performance of difficult instrumental passages brought acclaim to both performer and composer.

Renaissance Dance

In the Renaissance, dance played an important role in all forms of entertainment: town pageants, courtly rituals, festal displays sponsored by trade and merchant guilds, and in almost all nonecclesiastical celebrations. Folk dancing, of the kind illustrated by the Flemish painter Pieter Brueghel (see Figure 19.15), was a collective public experience that fostered a powerful sense of community. In contrast with folk dances, court dances stressed individual grace and poise. Renaissance dancing masters distinguished folk dance from courtly dance, a move that eventually resulted in the development of dance as a form of theatrical entertainment.

The Renaissance witnessed the first efforts to establish dance as an independent discipline. Guglielmo Ebreo (1439–1482), dancing master at the court of Urbino, wrote one of the first treatises on the art of dancing. He emphasized the importance of grace, the memorization of fixed steps, and the coordination of music and motion. Guglielmo also choreographed a number of lively dances or *balli*—the Italian word from which the French *ballet* derives. Three favorite forms of Italian court dance were the *basse* (a slow, solemn ceremonial dance), the *saltarello* (a vigorous, three-beat dance featuring graceful leaps), and the *piva* (a dance in rapid tempo with double steps). In Guglielmo's day, such dances were still performed by members of the court, rather than by professional dancers.

Chronology

1425–1442	Ghiberti creates the "Gates of Paradise"
1436	Brunelleschi completes the dome of Florence Cathedral
1495–1498	Leonardo paints the *Last Supper*
1512	Michelangelo completes the Sistine Chapel ceiling
1550	Vasari publishes the *Lives of Most Excellent Painters*

LOOKING BACK

Renaissance Art and Patronage

- In the commercial cities of Italy and the Netherlands, the arts became tangible expressions of increased affluence. Merchant princes and petty despots vied with growing numbers of middle class patrons and urban guilds whose lavish commissions brought prestige to their cities, their businesses, and their families.
- No longer regarded as a mere craftsperson, the artist was now regarded as a hero and genius, celebrated for his talents and powers of invention.

The Early Renaissance

- Renaissance artists were disciples of nature: they brought scientific curiosity to the study of the natural world and worked to understand its operations.
- The Early Renaissance artists Donatello, Masaccio, Ghiberti, and Brunelleschi studied the mechanics of the human body,

the effects of light on material substances, and the physical appearance of objects in three-dimensional space.
- Renaissance artists were also masters of invention: they perfected the technique of oil painting, formulated laws of perspective, and applied the principles of Classical art to the representation of Christian and contemporary subjects.

The High Renaissance

- The art of the High Renaissance marks the culmination of a hundred-year effort to wed the techniques of naturalistic representation to Classical ideals of proportion and order.
- Leonardo da Vinci, the quintessential artist–scientist, tried to reconcile empirical experience with abstract principles of design. The art of Raphael, characterized by monumental grace and unity of design, provided the standard for the Grand Manner, the touchstone of academic art for centuries to come.
- Architect, sculptor, and painter, Michelangelo brought a heroic

dimension, both in size and execution, to the treatment of traditional Christian and Classical subjects.

- The centrally planned buildings of Bramante and Palladio exemplified the ideals set forth by their predecessors, Brunelleschi and Alberti, for an architecture of harmony, balance, and clarity.
- In Venice, Giorgione and Titian achieved fame for their painterly renderings of sensuous female nudes occupying landscapes and rich interiors.

The Music of the Renaissance

- During the Renaissance, secular compositions began to outnumber religious ones. Printed sheet music helped to popularize the madrigal and other vernacular song forms.

- The Franco-Flemish composers Guillaume Dufay and Josquin des Prez outshone their Italian counterparts, providing religious and secular compositions for Church and court patrons.
- The techniques of imitation and word painting invested both religious and secular music with homogeneity and increased expressiveness. Madrigals and other vernacular songs regularly employed these techniques.
- The sixteenth century saw the emergence of women as professional composers and professional performers.
- The development of instrumental music as an independent genre went hand in hand with the refinement of musical instruments, such as the clavichord and the harpsichord. During the Renaissance, dance emerged as an independent genre, and the first treatises were written on the art of dancing.

Music Listening Selections

CD One Selection 17 Guillaume Dufay, *Missa L'homme armé (The Armed Man Mass)*, "Kyrie I," ca. 1450.

CD One Selection 18 Roland de Lassus (Orlando di Lasso), Madrigal, "Matona, mia cara" ("My lady, my beloved"), 1550.

CD One Selection 19 Thomas Morley, Madrigal, "My bonnie lass she smileth," 1595.

CD One Selection 20 Josquin des Prez, Motet, "Tulerunt Dominum meum," ca. 1520.

Glossary

aerial perspective the means of representing distance that relies on the imitation of the ways atmosphere affects the eye—outlines are blurred, details lost, contrasts of light and shade diminished, hues bluer, and colors less vivid; also called "atmospheric perspective"

clavichord (French, *clavier*, meaning "keyboard") a stringed keyboard instrument widely used between the sixteenth and eighteenth centuries; when the player presses down on a key, a brass tangent or blade rises and strikes a string

contrapposto (Italian, "counterpoised") a position assumed by the human body

in which one part is turned in opposition to another part

drum the cylindrical section immediately beneath the dome of a building

harpsichord a stringed keyboard instrument widely used between the sixteenth and eighteenth centuries; when the player presses down on a key, a quill, called a plectrum, plucks the string

imitation a technique whereby a melodic fragment introduced in the first voice of a composition is repeated closely (though usually at a different pitch) in the second, third, and fourth voices, so that one voice overlaps the next; the repetition may be exactly the same as the original, or it may differ somewhat

interval the distance between the pitches of two musical tones

lantern a small, windowed tower on top of a roof or dome that allows light to enter the interior of a building

linear perspective (or **optical perspective**) a method of creating the semblance of three-dimensional space on a two-dimensional surface; it derives from two optical illusions: (1) parallel lines appear to converge as they recede toward a vanishing point on a horizon level with the viewer's eye, and (2) objects appear to shrink and move closer together as they recede from view

madrigal a vernacular song, usually composed for three to six unaccompanied voices

organ a keyboard instrument in which keyboards and pedals are used to force air into a series of pipes, causing them to sound

picture plane the two-dimensional surface of a panel or canvas

pilaster a shallow, flattened, rectangular column or pier attached to a wall surface

tondo a circular painting or relief sculpture

villanella a light, dancelike song related to the madrigal

volute a scroll-shaped architectural ornament

word painting the manipulation of music to convey a specific object, thought, or mood—that is, the content of the text

Chapter 18

Cross-Cultural Encounters: Asia, Africa, and the Americas

ca. 1300–1600

". . . the world is old, but the future springs from the past."
Sundiata: An Epic of Old Mali

Figure 18.1 Tapestry weave Inca tunic, from the south coast of Peru, 1440–1540. Camelid fiber and cotton, 35⅞ × 30 in. Members of the camel family, llamas and alpacas provided fibers used for tunics like this one. Its designs belong to a heraldic or totemic code that remains undeciphered.

LOOKING AHEAD

A constellation of circumstances drove Westerners to undertake a program of exploration and expansion in the fifteenth century. The threat to previously established overland trade routes posed by the expanding Ottoman Empire was a major concern to the West. But other, more positive developments were equally significant: the growing enthusiasm for travel (made possible by advances in the science of navigation and the technology of shipbuilding), rising ambition for the accumulation of personal wealth, and the fundamental spirit of intellectual curiosity that marked the Age of the Renaissance.

Europe's overseas ventures would lead ultimately to a more accurate understanding of world geography. The proliferation of commercial exchange would work to establish a new set of trade networks. But perhaps the most compelling aspect of the enterprise of Western exploration was its human dimension: the cross-cultural encounters between Europe, Africa, East Asia, and the Americas. These encounters would set in motion a pattern of colonialism that disrupted older traditions and inaugurated new social, political, and cultural institutions. Sadly, some aspects of that contact would transform and even devastate the populations of Africa and the Americas. Ultimately, cross-cultural exchange brought massive economic transformation to all parts of the modern world. In order to better understand how the populations of Africa and the Americas were affected by European intrusion, it is necessary to examine the cultures of each in the centuries immediately prior to their contact with the Europeans.

Global Travel and Trade

The period between 1400 and 1600 was the greatest age of trans-Eurasian travel since the days of the Roman Empire. However, even earlier, and especially after 1000 C.E., long-range trade, religious pilgrimage, missionary activity, and just plain curiosity had stimulated cross-cultural contact between East and West. Arab merchants dominated North African trade routes. Converts to Islam—especially Turks and Mongols—carried the Muslim faith across Asia into India and Anatolia. Mongol tribes traversed the vast overland Asian Silk Road, which stretched from Constantinople to the Pacific Ocean. Enterprising families, like that of the Venetian merchant Marco Polo (ca. 1254–1324), established cultural and commercial links with the court of the Mongol emperor of China, Kublai Khan. Boasting that "brotherhood among peoples" had reached a new height during his rule (1260–1294), Kublai encouraged long-distance travel and cross-cultural dialogue. The same roads that brought

thirteenth-century Franciscan and Dominican monks into China sped the exchange of goods and religious beliefs between Muslims and Hindus, Confucians and Buddhists.

Although the great plague that swept through Asia and Europe interrupted long-established patterns of East–West exchange, the appearance of fourteenth-century handbooks, such as that written by the Florentine merchant Francesco Pegolotti, suggests that global travel did not completely disappear (Pegolotti journeyed as far as China). Nor did regional travel cease: Chaucer's pilgrims traveled to local Christian shrines, while Buddhists visited their sanctuaries throughout East Asia, and Muslims often made even longer journeys to participate in the ritual of the *hajj*, that is, the pilgrimage to Mecca.

China's Treasure Ships

While the Mongols had encouraged long-distance travel, their policy of outreach took a bold direction under their followers. Eager to reinstate foreign trade and unite "the four seas," the young prince Zhu Di (1368–1424) of the newly established Ming dynasty (1368–1644) ordered the construction of a fleet larger than any in history: 317 wooden treasure ships, each more than 400 feet long (four times the length of Columbus' *Santa Maria*), were constructed between 1405 and 1433. Boasting tall prows, nine masts, and red silk sails, and painted with dragons and phoenixes, the "Dragon Ships"—the largest sail-powered fleet ever constructed—carried cargoes of silk, porcelain, iron, and tea, which were traded for spices, precious gems, incense, exotic animals, ivory, and rare woods. Along with translators and astrologers, 28,000 Chinese sailors crossed the Indian Ocean to trade at the port cities of Africa, India, and Arabia; eastward, they worked the ports of China, Sumatra, and Borneo. The death of Zhu Di and his followers brought an abrupt end to the enterprise, but their ambitious legacy endures in a document that boasts, "We have set eyes on barbarian regions far away . . . traversing the savage waves as if we were treading a public thoroughfare."

European Expansion

In 1453 the highly disciplined armies of the Ottoman Empire, using new gunpowder weaponry, captured Constantinople, renaming it Istanbul. By the end of the century, this Islamic empire had become the greatest power bloc in the world. Stretching from Eastern Europe across the Eurasian steppes, into sub-Saharan Africa, it threatened the safety of European overland caravans to the East. Western rulers explored two main offensive strategies: warfare against the Turks and the search for all-water routes to the East. The first strategy yielded some success when the allied forces of Venice, Spain, and the papacy defeated the Ottoman navy in western Greece at the Battle of Lepanto in 1571. Although this event briefly reduced the Ottoman presence in the Mediterranean—the Turks quickly rebuilt their navy—it did not answer the need for faster and more efficient trade routes to the East. Greed for gold, slaves, and spices—the major commodities of Africa and Asia—

Science and Technology

1405	China launches the first of seven overseas expeditions with over 300 of the largest wooden ships ever built
1418	Prince Henry of Portugal opens a school of navigation
1420	the Portuguese develop the three-masted caravel for ocean travel
1448	Andreas Walsperger (Flemish) uses the coordinates of longitude, latitude, and climatic divisions in his *mappa mundi* (world map)
1522	the circumnavigation of the globe (begun by Magellan) is completed

also encouraged the emerging European nations to compete with Arab and Turkish traders for control of foreign markets.

The technology of navigation was crucial to the success of these ventures. With the early fifteenth-century Latin translation of Ptolemy's *Geography*, map-makers began to order geographic space with the coordinates of latitude and longitude. The Portuguese, encouraged by Prince Henry the Navigator (1394–1460), came to produce maps and charts that exceeded the accuracy of those drafted by Classical and Muslim cartographers. Renaissance Europeans improved such older Arab navigational devices as the compass and the astrolabe (an instrument that measures the angle between the horizon and heavenly bodies and thus fixes latitude; see chapter 10).

Portugal and Spain adopted the Arab lateen sail and built two- and three-masted caravels with multiple sails—ships that were faster, safer, and more practical for rough ocean travel than the oar-driven galleys that sailed the Mediterranean Sea (Figure **18.2**). The new caravels were outfitted with brass cannons and sufficient firepower to fend off severe enemy attack. Christopher Columbus (1451–1506), a Genoese explorer in the employ of Spain, sailed west in search of an all-water route to China and India. His discovery of the Americas—the existence of which no Europeans had ever suspected—was to change the course of world history.

While the Spanish sought to reach China by sailing across the Atlantic Ocean, the Portuguese set off down the coast of Africa (Map **18.1**). In 1488, Bartholomeu Dias (1450–1500) rounded the southernmost tip of Africa and entered the Indian Ocean; the sixteen-month journey confirmed that India could be reached by sailing east. By 1498,

Map 18.1 World Exploration, 1271–1295; 1486–1611. The map shows both the overland expeditions of the thirteenth century and the principal sea voyages of the fifteenth and sixteenth centuries. The date of each expedition follows the name of the navigator.

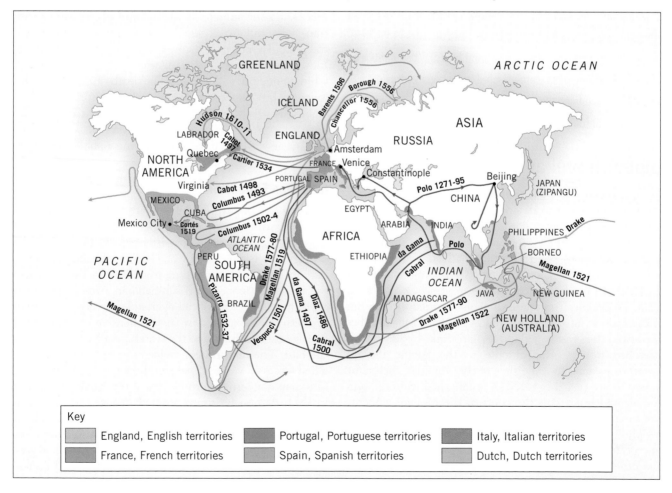

Key

England, English territories Portugal, Portuguese territories Italy, Italian territories

France, French territories Spain, Spanish territories Dutch, Dutch territories

Figure 18.2 ALEJO FERNANDEZ, *Our Lady of the Navigators*, 1535. The painting, which celebrates the Spanish conquest of the Americas, was commissioned for a chapel in Seville. Pictured as the Madonna of Mercy, the Virgin shelters the faithful within her cloak. While none of the figures has been securely identified, the worshiper kneeling at the far left is probably Christopher Columbus.

Vasco da Gama (1460–1524) made a similar journey that allowed him to establish Portuguese trading posts in India. When, in the 1540s, a Portuguese vessel was blown off course by a typhoon, sailors found their way to the southernmost tip of Japan. Soon after, Portuguese vessels, carrying exotic cargo for trade and small groups of Jesuit missionaries (see chapter 20), arrived in Japan. The presence of these "barbarians from the south," (in Japanese, *nanbanjin*), as depicted in at least seventy multipaneled screens, painted for Japan's wealthy merchants between the 1590s and 1630s (Figure **18.3**). European firearms had a major impact on Japanese warfare, as musket-bearing foot soldiers came to replace earlier modes of combat. These enterprises initiated an era of global travel and cross-cultural encounter the consequences of which would transform the destinies of Asia, Africa, and the Americas. Indeed, the age of expansion would mark the beginning of a modern world-system dominated by the West.

Figure 18.3 Six-fold Japanese screen, ca. 1630. In the panels on the left side of this six-fold *nanban* screen, the Japanese are seen greeting a three-masted Portuguese vessel. Richly dressed traders and a group of Jesuit missionaries flank the captain, who is seated on a thronelike chair beneath a canopy. Small ships carry to shore cargo, which is eagerly examined by Japanese merchants.

Map 18.2 Africa, 1000–1500. While the text focuses on the history of West African kingdoms and empires, the map shows the entire continent. Note that the kingdoms of Ife and Benin lay outside of direct Muslim influence.

The African Cultural Heritage

Diversity characterizes all aspects of Africa's history and culture. A vast continent, comprising widely varying geographic regions, the sub-Saharan region alone is host to more than 800 different spoken languages. From Southern Africa came our earliest known ancestors; and in the northeast, the ancient civilizations of Egypt and Nubia flourished thousands of years ago. For centuries, most of Africa consisted of farming villages like that of Nok (discussed in chapter 2), located at the Niger River in present-day Nigeria (Map 18.2). After ca. 1000, however, some of these villages grew into city-states that controlled the surrounding countryside; groups of villages might form a district, while others consolidated to emerge as local kingdoms or regional states, and by the fourteenth century, empires. These societies, much like the complex societies of Eurasian states, involved clearly defined classes: a ruling elite, military and administrative nobility, religious authorities, merchants, commoners, peasants, and slaves.

Despite their geographic and linguistic diversity, African societies share some distinct cultural characteristics that provide a context for our understanding of African culture prior to the European encounter. The most notable of these is a kinship system that emphasizes the importance and well-being of the group as essential to that of the individual. Historically, the African kinship system was based on the extended family, a group of people who were both related to each other and dependent on each other for survival. A village might consist of several extended families or clans ruled by chiefs or elders—either hereditary or elected—who usually held semidivine status. All those who belonged to the same family, clan, or tribe—the living, the dead, and the yet unborn—made up a single cohesive community irrevocably linked in time and space. While this form of social organization was not unique to Africa—indeed, it has characterized most agricultural societies in world history—it played an especially important role in shaping the character of African society and culture. While African social structures might differ from century to century, these kin-based societies did not disappear with the emergence of regional states or empires, nor with the arrival of Muslims (see chapter 10) and Christians.

From earliest times, most African societies maintained the animistic belief that powerful spirits inhabit the natural world. They honored a single creator god, but they addressed his powers indirectly through spirits associated with nature and the souls of departed ancestors. The spirits of the deceased, as well as local divinities were called on in rituals designed to seek protection, resolve conflicts, or fulfill the special needs of the community. Ceremonies marking crucial life transitions—birth, puberty, marriage, death—were orchestrated by shamans or priests who held prominent positions in African society.

Ghana

In the ninth century, a number of African states emerged in the *Sudan* (the word means "Land of the Blacks"): the region that stretches across Africa south of the Sahara Desert (see Map **18.2**). Encouraged by the activities of Muslim merchants and lucrative trans-Saharan trade, some of West Africa's commercial centers grew into regional states. The first of these was Ghana (the name means "war chief"), whose empire came to flourish under the influence of powerful rulers, who extended their authority over the surrounding villages. Located in the forested region between the Senegal and Niger Rivers, Ghana was the center of the gold trade. Its rulers, who were presumed to have divine ancestors, regulated the exportation of gold to the north and the importation of salt from the desert fringes. These two products—gold and salt—along with iron, slaves, and ivory, were the principal African commodities. After Ghana fell to the Muslims in the eleventh century, its native kings, along with much of the local culture, came under Muslim influence. The history of Ghana and other ancient African kingdoms is recorded primarily in Arabic sources describing the courts of kings, but little is known of African life in areas removed from the centers of power.

Figure 18.4 Great Mosque, Djenne, Mali, 1906–1907. Djenne is the oldest known city in sub-Saharan Africa; under the Muslims it became a center of trade and learning. Originally built around 1220, the mosque pictured here dates from 1907 and is the third on this site.

Mali and Songhai

During the thirteenth century, West Africans speaking the Mande language brought much of the Sudan under their dominion to form the Mali Empire. This dramatic development is associated with the powerful warrior-king Sundiata, who ruled Mali from around 1230 to 1255. The wealth and influence of the Mali Empire, which reached its zenith in the early fourteenth century, derived from its control of northern trade routes. On one of these routes lay the prosperous city of Timbuktu (see Map 18.2), the greatest of early African trading centers and the site of a flourishing Islamic university. In Mali, as in many of the African states, the rulers were converts to Islam; they employed Muslim scribes and jurists and used Arabic as the language of administration. The hallmarks of Islamic culture—its great mosques (Figure **18.4**) and libraries and the Arabic language itself—did not penetrate deeply into the vast interior of Africa, however, where native African traditions dominated everyday life.

When the Mali Empire began to weaken in the fifteenth century, the small state of Songhai within its borders broke away, soon to emerge as the ruling power in the central Niger valley. With his capital at Gao, the first king of Songhai took control of the critical trade routes and major cities, including Timbuktu. At its height in the early sixteenth century, Songhai, under the leadership of its Muslim emperors, dominated all of West Africa in wealth and power.

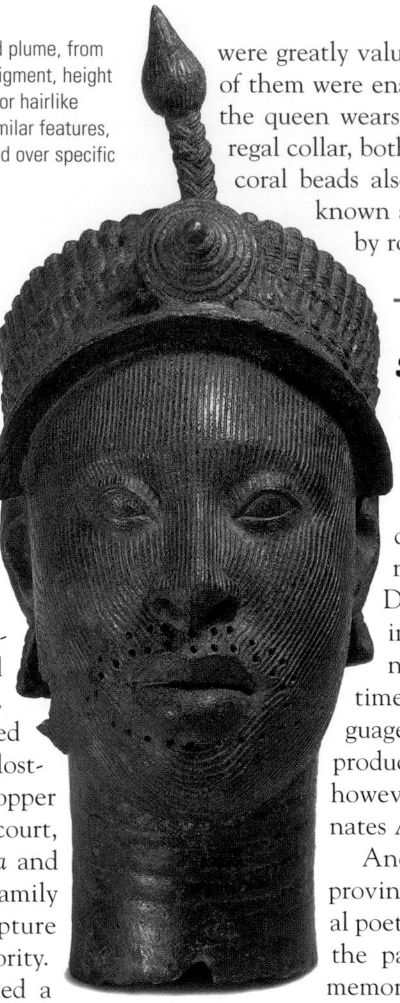

Figure 18.5 The *oba* (ruler) of Ife wearing a bead crown and plume, from Benin, twelfth to fourteenth centuries. Cast brass with red pigment, height 14⅛ in. The holes around the mouth once probably held hair or hairlike additions. Because many of the Benin male portraits bear similar features, it is likely that an idealized notion of a royal face was favored over specific characterization.

Benin

Prior to the fourteenth century, neither Arabs nor Europeans traveled to the thickly vegetated area of tropical rainforest south of the great savanna. Here, at the mouth of the Niger, in the area of present-day Nigeria, emerged the kingdom of Benin. Governed, beginning in the late twelfth century, by the young son of the Yoruba ruler at Ife, Benin came to dominate most of the West African territories north of the Niger delta. The Benin *obas* (rulers) established an impressive royal tradition, building large, walled cities and engaging in trade with other African states.

Guilds of artists, trained in the techniques of lost-wax bronze and copper casting, served the court, immortalizing the *oba* and members of the royal family in portraits that capture their dignity and authority. These works perpetuated a tradition of portraiture that can be traced back to the terracotta figures found in the ancient village of Nok (see Figure 2.24), and more immediately, to the highly refined metal-cast portraits produced in Ife. The *oba* pictured in Figure **18.5**, wearing a beaded crown and a plume, bears the thin, parallel lines of **scarification** (the process of incising the skin) that functioned as a type of body art, but also often designated membership or status within a particular group.

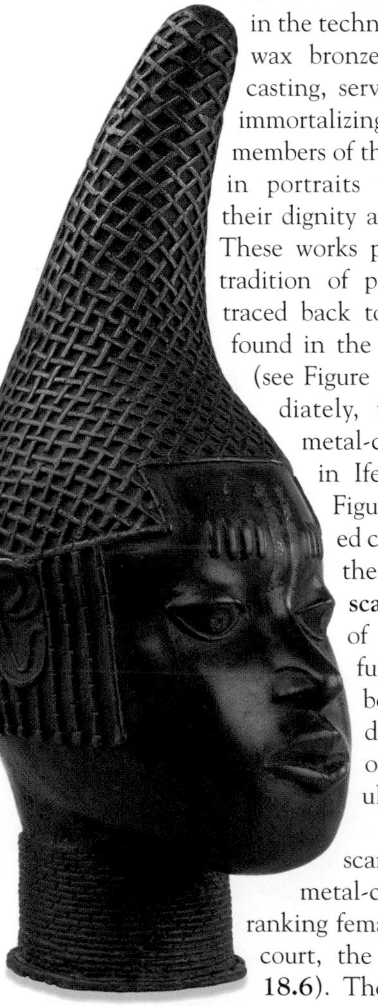

Figure 18.6 Queen mother head, ca. 1500–1550. Brass, height 15½ in. In its subtle blend of realism and idealization, the portrait calls to mind the ancient Egyptian head of Nefertiti (see Figure 2.17). Images like this one stood on the royal altar for some 300 years after Benin culture reached its peak in the sixteenth century.

Yet another kind of scarification is seen in the metal-cast image of the highest ranking female member of the royal court, the queen mother (Figure **18.6**). Those who bore this title were greatly valued as advisors, and numerous likenesses of them were enshrined on royal altars. In this example, the queen wears a tall, conical, netted headdress and a regal collar, both made of coral beads; vertical strands of coral beads also frame the face. The unique coiffure, known as the "chicken's beak," was being worn by royal wives well into the late 1990s.

The Arts of Africa

Sundiata

Africa transmitted native folk traditions orally rather than in writing. As a result, the literary contributions of Africans remained unrecorded for hundreds of years—in some cases until the nineteenth century and thereafter. During the tenth century, Arab scholars in Africa began to transcribe popular native tales and stories into Arabic. Over time, severßal of the traditional African languages have developed written forms and produced a liter ture of note. Even to this day, however, a highly prized oral tradition dominates African literature.

Ancient Africa's oral tradition was the province of ***griots***, a special class of professional poet–historians who preserved the legends of the past by chanting or singing them from memory. Like the *jongleurs* of the Early Middle Ages, *griots* transmitted the history of the people by way of stories that had been handed down from generation to generation. The most notable of these narratives is *Sundiata*, an epic describing the formative phase of Mali history. *Sundiata* originated around 1240, in the time of Mali's great empire, but it was not until the twentieth century that it was transcribed—first to written French and then to English. Recounted by a *griot*, who identifies himself in the opening passages, the epic immortalizes the adventures of Sundiata, the champion and founder of the Mali Empire. In the tradition of such Western heroes as Gilgamesh, Achilles, Alexander, and Roland, the "lion-child" Sundiata performs extraordinary deeds that bring honor and glory to himself and peace and prosperity to his people. The following excerpt includes the *griot's* introduction to the poem, the story of the Battle of Tabon, and a brief description of the lively festival that celebrates Sundiata's triumphs. In the final passages of the poem, Mali is pictured as a place of peace and prosperity; it is eternal in the memory of those who know its history.

READING 18.1 From *Sundiata: An Epic of Old Mali*

I am a griot. It is I, Djeli Mamoudou Kouyaté, son of Bintou Kouyaté and Djeli Kedian Kouyaté, master in the art of eloquence. Since time immemorial the Kouyatés have been in the service of the Keita[1] princes of Mali; we are vessels of speech, we are the repositories which harbor secrets many centuries old. The art of eloquence has no secrets for us; without us the names of kings would vanish into oblivion, we are the memory of mankind; by the spoken word we bring to life the deeds and exploits of kings for younger generations. 10

I derive my knowledge from my father Djeli Kedian, who also got it from his father; history holds no mystery for us; we teach to the vulgar just as much as we want to teach them, for it is we who keep the keys to the twelve doors of Mali.[2]

I know the list of all the sovereigns who succeeded to the throne of Mali. I know how the black people divided into tribes, for my father bequeathed to me all his learning; I know why such and such is called Kamara, another Keita, and yet another Sibibé or Traoré; every 20 name has a meaning, a secret import.

I teach kings the history of their ancestors so that the lives of the ancients might serve them as an example, for the world is old, but the future springs from the past.

My word is pure and free of all untruth; it is the word of my father; it is the word of my father's father. I will give you my father's words just as I received them; royal griots do not know what lying is. When a quarrel breaks out between tribes it is we who settle the difference, for we are the depositaries of oaths which the ancestors 30 swore.

Listen to my word, you who want to know; by my mouth you will learn the history of Mali.

By my mouth you will get to know the story of the ancestor of great Mali, the story of him who, by his exploits, surpassed even Alexander the Great; he who, from the East, shed his rays upon all the countries of the West.

Listen to the story of the son of the Buffalo, the son of the Lion.[3] I am going to tell you of Maghan Sundiata, of 40 Mari-Djata, of Sogolon Djata, of Naré Maghan Djata; the man of many names against whom sorcery could avail nothing.

. . . .

Kings have prescribed destinies just like men, and seers who probe the future know it. They have knowledge of the future, whereas we griots are depositaries of the knowledge of the past. But whoever knows the history of a country can read its future.

Other peoples use writing to record the past, but this invention has killed the faculty of memory among them. 50 They do not feel the past any more, for writing lacks the warmth of the human voice. With them everybody thinks he knows, whereas learning should be a secret. The

prophets did not write and their words have been all the more vivid as a result. What paltry learning is that which is congealed in dumb books!

I, Djeli Mamoudou Kouyaté, am the result of a long tradition. For generations we have passed on the history of kings from father to son. The narrative was passed on to me without alteration and I deliver it without 60 alteration, for I received it free from all untruth.

. . . .

Every man to his own land! If it is foretold that your destiny should be fulfilled in such and such a land, men can do nothing against it. Mansa Tounkara could not keep Sundiata back because the destiny of Sogolon's son was bound up with that of Mali. Neither the jealousy of a cruel stepmother, nor her wickedness, could alter for a moment the course of great destiny.

The snake, man's enemy, is not long-lived, yet the serpent that lives hidden will surely die old. Djata[4] was 70 strong enough now to face his enemies. At the age of eighteen, he had the stateliness of the lion and the strength of the buffalo. His voice carried authority, his eyes were live coals, his arm was iron, he was the husband of power.

Moussa Tounkara, king of Mema, gave Sundiata half of his army. The most valiant came forward of their own free will to follow Sundiata in the great adventure. The cavalry of Mema, which he had fashioned himself, formed his iron squadron. Sundiata, dressed in the 80 Muslim fashion of Mema, left the town at the head of his small but redoubtable army. The whole population sent their best wishes with him. He was surrounded by five messengers from Mali and Manding Bory rode proudly at the side of his brother. The horsemen of Mema formed behind Djata a bristling iron squadron. The troops took the direction of Wagadou, for Djata did not have enough troops to confront Soumaoro directly, and so the king of Mema advised him to go to Wagadou and take half of the men of the king, Soumaba Cissé. A swift messenger had 90 been sent there and so the king of Wagadou came out in person to meet Sundiata and his troops. He gave Sundiata half of his cavalry and blessed the weapons. Then Manding Bory said to his brother, "Djata, do you think yourself able to face Soumaoro now?"

"No matter how small a forest may be, you can always find there sufficient fibers to tie up a man. Numbers mean nothing; it is worth that counts. With my cavalry I shall clear myself a path to Mali."

Djata gave out his orders. They would head south, 100 skirting Soumaoro's kingdom. The first objective to be reached was Tabon, the iron-gated town in the midst of the mountains, for Sundiata had promised Fran Kamara that he would pass by Tabon before returning to Mali. He hoped to find that his childhood companion had become king. It was a forced march and during the halts the divines, Singbin Mara Cissé and Mandjan Bérété, related

---

[1] The ruling Muslim family, the Mali emperors identified themselves as descendants of the prophet Muhammad.

[2] The twelve provinces of which Mali was originally composed.

[3] According to tradition, the buffalo was the totem of Sundiata's mother, Sogolon, while the lion was the totem of his father.

[4] Sundiata.

to Sundiata the history of Alexander the Great[5] and several other heroes, but of all of them Sundiata preferred Alexander, the king of gold and silver, who crossed the world from west to east. He wanted to outdo his prototype both in the extent of his territory and the wealth of his treasury. . . .

In the evening, after a long day's march, Sundiata arrived at the head of the great valley which led to Tabon. The valley was quite black with men, for Sosso Balla had deployed his men everywhere in the valley, and some were positioned on the heights which dominated the way through. When Djata saw the layout of Sosso Balla's men he turned to his generals laughing.

"Why are you laughing, brother, you can see that the road is blocked."

"Yes, but no mere infantrymen can halt my course towards Mali," replied Sundiata.

The troops stopped. All the war chiefs were of the opinion that they should wait until the next day to give battle because, they said, the men were tired.

"The battle will not last long," said Sundiata, "and the men will have time to rest. We must not allow Soumaoro the time to attack Tabon."

Sundiata was immovable, so the orders were given and the war drums began to beat. On his proud horse Sundiata turned to right and left in front of his troops. He entrusted the rearguard, composed of a part of the Wagadou cavalry, to his younger brother, Manding Bory. Having drawn his sword, Sundiata led the charge, shouting his war cry.

The Sossos were surprised by this sudden attack for they all thought that the battle would be joined the next day. The lightning that flashes across the sky is slower, the thunderbolts less frightening and floodwaters less surprising than Sundiata swooping down on Sosso Balla and his smiths.[6] In a trice, Sundiata was in the middle of the Sossos like a lion in the sheepfold. The Sossos, trampled under the hooves of his fiery charger, cried out. When he turned to the right the smiths of Soumaoro fell in their tens, and when he turned to the left his sword made heads fall as when someone shakes a tree of ripe fruit. The horsemen of Mema wrought a frightful slaughter and their long lances pierced flesh like a knife sunk into a paw-paw.[7] Charging ever forwards, Sundiata looked for Sosso Balla; he caught sight of him and like a lion bounded towards the son of Soumaoro, his sword held aloft. His arm came sweeping down but at that moment a Sosso warrior came between Djata and Sosso Balla and was sliced like a calabash.[8] Sosso Balla did not wait and disappeared from amidst his smiths. Seeing their chief in flight, the Sossos gave way and fell into a terrible rout.

Before the sun disappeared behind the mountains there were only Djata and his men left in the valley.

. . . .

The festival began. The musicians of all the countries were there. Each people in turn came forward to the dais under Sundiata's impassive gaze. Then the war dances began. The sofas[9] of all the countries had lined themselves up in six ranks amid a great clatter of bows and spears knocking together. The war chiefs were on horseback. The warriors faced the enormous dais and at a signal from Balla Fasséké, the musicians, massed on the right of the dais, struck up. The heavy war drums thundered, the bolons[10] gave off muted notes while the griot's voice gave the throng the pitch for the "Hymn to the Bow."[11] The spearmen, advancing like hyenas in the night held their spears above their heads; the archers of Wagadou and Tabon,[12] walking with a noiseless tread, seemed to be lying in ambush behind bushes. They rose suddenly to their feet and let fly their arrows at imaginary enemies. In front of the great dais the Kéké-Tigui, or war chiefs, made their horses perform dance steps under the eyes of the Mansa.[13] The horses whinnied and reared, then, overmastered by the spurs, knelt, got up and cut little capers, or else scraped the ground with their hooves.

The rapturous people shouted the "Hymn to the Bow" and clapped their hands. The sweating bodies of the warriors glistened in the sun while the exhausting rhythm of the tam-tams[14] wrenched from them shrill cries. But presently they made way for the cavalry, beloved by Djata. The horsemen of Mema threw their swords in the air and caught them in flight, uttering mighty shouts. A smile of contentment took shape on Sundiata's lips, for he was happy to see his cavalry manoeuvre with so much skill. . . .

. . . .

After a year Sundiata held a new assembly at Niani, but this one was the assembly of dignitaries and kings of the empire. The kings and notables of all the tribes came to Niani. The kings spoke of their administration and the dignitaries talked of their kings. Fakoli, the nephew of Soumaoro, having proved himself too independent, had to flee to evade the Mansa's anger. His lands were confiscated and the taxes of Sosso were paid directly into the granaries of Niani. In this way, every year, Sundiata gathered about him all the kings and notables; so justice prevailed everywhere, for the kings were afraid of being denounced at Niani.

Djata's justice spared nobody. He followed the very word of God. He protected the weak against the strong and people would make journeys lasting several days to

[5] In Mali tradition, it is said that Alexander was the second great conqueror and Sundiata the seventh and last.

[6] Metalsmiths, within the clan, a powerful caste of men who were noted as makers of weapons and sorcerers or soothsayers.

[7] Papaya.

[8] The common bottle gourd.

[9] Sudanese infantrymen or soldiers.

[10] Large harps with three or four strings.

[11] A traditional song among the people of Mali.

[12] Kingdoms near Mali.

[13] Emperor.

[14] Large, circular gongs.

come and demand justice of him. Under his sun the upright man was rewarded and the wicked one punished.

In their new-found peace the villages knew prosperity again, for with Sundiata happiness had come into everyone's home. Vast fields of millet, rice, cotton, indigo and fonio[15] surrounded the villages. Whoever worked always had something to live on. Each year long caravans carried the taxes in kind[16] to Niani. You could go from village to village without fearing brigands. A thief would have his right hand chopped off and if he stole again he would be put to the sword.

New villages and new towns sprang up in Mali and elsewhere. "Dyulas," or traders, became numerous and during the reign of Sundiata the world knew happiness.

There are some kings who are powerful through their military strength. Everybody trembles before them, but when they die nothing but ill is spoken of them. Others do neither good nor ill and when they die they are forgotten. Others are feared because they have power, but they know how to use it and they are loved because they love justice. Sundiata belonged to this group. He was feared, but loved as well. He was the father of Mali and gave the world peace. After him the world has not seen a greater conqueror, for he was the seventh and last conqueror. He had made the capital of an empire out of his father's village, and Niani became the navel of the earth. In the most distant lands Niani was talked of and foreigners said, "Travelers from Mali can tell lies with impunity," for Mali was a remote country for many peoples.

The griots, fine talkers that they were, used to boast of Niani and Mali saying: "If you want salt, go to Niani, for Niani is the camping place of the Sahel[17] caravans. If you want gold, go to Niani, for Bouré, Dambougou and Wagadou work for Niani. If you want fine cloth, go to Niani, for the Mecca road passes by Niani. If you want fish, go to Niani, for it is there that the fishermen of Maouti and Djenné come to sell their catches. If you want meat, go to Niani, the country of the great hunters, and the land of the ox and the sheep. If you want to see an army, go to Niani, for it is there that the united forces of Mali are to be found. If you want to see a great king, go to Niani, for it is there that the son of Sogolon lives, the man with two names."

This is what the masters of the spoken word used to sing. . . .

How many piled-up ruins, how much buried splendour! But all the deeds I have spoken of took place long ago and they all had Mali as their background. Kings have succeeded kings, but Mali has always remained the same.

Mali keeps its secrets jealously. There are things which the uninitiated will never know, for the griots, their depositaries, will never betray them. Maghan Sundiata,

the last conqueror on earth, lies not far from Niani-Niani at Balandougou, the weir town.

After him many kings and many Mansas reigned over Mali and other towns sprang up and disappeared. Hajji Mansa Moussa, of illustrious memory, beloved of God, built houses at Mecca for pilgrims coming from Mali, but the towns which he founded have all disappeared, Karanina, Bouroun-Kouna—nothing more remains of these towns. Other kings carried Mali far beyond Djata's frontiers, for example Mansa Samanka and Fadima Moussa, but none of them came near Djata.

Maghan Sundiata was unique. In his own time no one equalled him and after him no one had the ambition to surpass him. He left his mark on Mali for all time and his taboos still guide men in their conduct.

Mali is eternal. To convince yourself of what I have said go to Mali.

. . . .

Men of today, how small you are beside your ancestors, and small in mind too, for you have trouble in grasping the meaning of my words. Sundiata rests near Niani-Niani, but his spirit lives on and today the Keitas still come and bow before the stone under which lies the father of Mali.

To acquire my knowledge I have journeyed all round Mali. At Kita I saw the mountain where the lake of holy water sleeps; at Segou, I learnt the history of the kings of Do and Kri; at Fadama, in Hamana, I heard the Kondé griots relate how the Keitas, Kondés and Kamaras conquered Wouroula. At Keyla, the village of the great masters, I learnt the origins of Mali and the art of speaking. Everywhere I was able to see and understand what my masters were teaching me, but between their hands I took an oath to teach only what is to be taught and to conceal what is to be kept concealed.

Q How does Sundiata compare with other epic heroes: Gilgamesh, Achilles, and Roland?

Q What does the griot mean by the statement, "the future springs from the past?"

As lines 161–191 of this excerpt suggest, in African ritual celebration, the arts of music, dance, poetry, and decorative display formed a synthesis that mirrored shared spiritual and communal values. Similarly, within the African community, the telling of stories was a group enterprise and an expression of social unity. Seated around the communal fire, the members of the tribe recited tales serially and from memory. Traditionally, such tales were told only after sundown, because, as favored entertainments, they might otherwise distract the group from daily labor.

African Myths and Proverbs

Among the many genres of African literature was the mythical tale that accounted for the origins of the universe, of the natural forces, and of the community. African

---

[15] A crabgrass with seeds that are used as a cereal.
[16] In produce or goods instead of money.
[17] A region of the Sudan bordering on the Sahara.

creation myths—like those of the Hebrews, Egyptians, and Mesopotamians—explained the beginnings of the world, the creation of human beings, and the workings of nature, while still other myths dealt with the origin of death. The following brief examples, which come from three different parts of Africa, represent only a sampling of the many African tales that explain how death came into the world.

READING 18.2 Three African Myths on the Origin of Death

1

In the beginning, Nzambi slid down to earth on a rainbow, and there created the animals and the trees. After this he also created a man and a woman, and he told them to marry and have children. Nzambi imposed only one prohibition upon men, that they should not sleep when the moon was up. If they disobeyed this command, they would be punished with death. When the first man had become old and had poor eyesight, it once happened that the moon was veiled behind the clouds, so that he could not see it shine. He went to sleep and died in his sleep. Since then all men have died, because they are unable to keep awake when the moon is up.

(Lunda)

2

One day God asked the first human couple who then lived in heaven what kind of death they wanted, that of the moon or that of the banana. Because the couple wondered in dismay about the implications of the two modes of death, God explained to them: the banana puts forth shoots which take its place, and the moon itself comes back to life. The couple considered for a long time before they made their choice. If they elected to be childless they would avoid death, but they would also be very lonely, would themselves be forced to carry out all the work, and would not have anybody to work and strive for. Therefore they prayed to God for children, well aware of the consequences of their choice. And their prayer was granted. Since that time man's sojourn is short on this earth.

(Madagascar)

3

Formerly men had no fire but ate all their food raw. At that time they did not need to die for when they became old God made them young again. One day they decided to beg God for fire. They sent a messenger to God to convey their request. God replied to the messenger that he would give him fire if he was prepared to die. The man took the fire from God, but ever since then all men must die.

(Darasa, Gada)

Q What aspects of ancient African culture do these myths reflect?

Q What do these myths have in common with those in Reading 0.1?

These myths offer valuable insights into ancient African culture. The directness with which the characters in these tales address the gods suggests the basic intimacy between Africans and the spirit world. Moreover, the tales stress human fallibility (as in the disastrous blunder of the nearly blind "first man"), rather than (as in most Christian literature) human sinfulness. They describe a gentle and casual, rather than a forbidding and patriarchal, relationship between divine and human realms. Finally, as the second myth suggests, Africans placed great value on their children; as was the case in most agricultural societies, children were prized as helpers and as perpetuators of tradition. One African proverb reads, "There is no wealth where there are no children." Another asserts, "Children are the wisdom of the nation."

Africans invented a huge and colorful literature of tales, proverbs, and riddles. The animal tale explains why certain creatures look and act as they do. In the trickster tale, a small animal, such as a hare or spider, outwits a larger one, such as a hyena or elephant. Explanatory tales treat such themes as "Why some people are good-looking" and "Why one never tells a woman the truth." African tales, proverbs, and riddles—often playfully swapped—functioned as sources of instruction and entertainment. Like most forms of African expression, they were characterized by animism: consider, for instance, the riddle "who goes down the street and passes the king's house without greeting the king?" The answer is "rainwater." Many proverbs call attention to the immutability of nature's laws. One states, "When it rains, the roof always drips in the same way." Africans used their riddles and proverbs to help teach moral values and even to litigate tribal disputes.

African Poetry

In ancient Africa, religious rituals and rites of passage featured various kinds of chant. Performed by shamans and priests, but also by nonprofessionals, and often integrated with mime and dance, the chant created a unified texture not unlike that of modern rap and Afro-pop music. Poets addressed the fragility of human life, celebrated the transition from one stage of growth to another, honored the links between the living and the dead, praised heroes and rulers, and recounted the experiences of everyday life. African poetry does not share the satiric thrust of Roman verse, the erotic mood of Indian poetry, the intimate tone of the Petrarchan or Shakespearean sonnet, or the reclusive spirit of Chinese verse; it is, rather, a frank and intensely personal form of vocal music.

African poetry is generally characterized by strong percussive qualities, by **anaphora** (the repetition of a word or words at the beginning of two or more lines), and by tonal patterns that—much like Chinese poetry—are based on voice inflections. Repetition of key phrases and call-and-response "conversations" between narrator and listeners add texture to oral performance. The rhythmic energy and raw vitality of African poetry set it apart from most other kinds of world poetry, including Chinese, which seems controlled and intellectualized by comparison. The poem of praise for the *oba* of Benin, reproduced in Reading 18.3, throbs with rhythms that invite accompanying drumbeats or hand-clapping of the kind familiar to us in gospel singing and contemporary rock music.

African poetry is also notable for its inventive similes and metaphors. In the Yoruba poem "The God of War," warfare is likened to a needle "that pricks at both ends," a vivid image of the perils of combat—compare the plain-spoken ode "On Civil War" by the Roman poet Horace (see chapter 6). And in the "Song for the Sun," the Hottentot poet invents the memorable image of God collecting the stars and piling them into a basket "like a woman who collects lizards and piles them into her pot."

READING 18.3 Selections from African Poetry

Song for the Sun that Disappeared behind the Rainclouds

The fire darkens, the wood turns black.   1
The flame extinguishes, misfortune upon us.
God sets out in search of the sun.
The rainbow sparkles in his hand,
the bow of the divine hunter.   5
He has heard the lamentations of his children.
He walks along the milky way, he collects the stars.
With quick arms he piles them into a basket
piles them up with quick arms
like a woman who collects lizards   10
and piles them into her pot, piles them up
until the basket overflows with light.

        (Hottentot)

Longing for Death

I have been singing, singing I have cried bitterly   1
I'm on my way.
How large this world!
Let the ferryman bring his boat
on the day of my death.   5
I'll wave with my left hand,
I'm on my way.
I'm on my way,
the boat of death is rocking near,
I'm on my way,   10
I who have sung you many songs.

        (Ewe)

The Oba of Benin

He who knows not the Oba   1
let me show him.
He has mounted the throne,
he has piled a throne upon a throne.
Plentiful as grains of sand on the earth   5
are those in front of him.
Plentiful as grains of sand on the earth
are those behind him.
There are two thousand people

to fan him.   10
He who owns you
is among you here.
He who owns you
has piled a throne upon a throne.
He has lived to do it this year;   15
even so he will live to do it again.

        (Bini)

The God of War

He kills on the right and destroys on the left.   1
He kills on the left and destroys on the right.
He kills suddenly in the house and suddenly in the field.
He kills the child with the iron with which it plays.
He kills in silence.   5
He kills the thief and the owner of the stolen goods.
He kills the owner of the slave—and the slave runs away.
He kills the owner of the house—and paints the hearth
   with his blood.
He is the needle that pricks at both ends.
He has water but he washes with blood.   10

        (Yoruba)

The Poor Man

The poor man knows not how to eat with the rich man.   1
When they eat fish, he eats the head.

Invite a poor man and he rushes in
licking his lips and upsetting the plates.

The poor man has no manners, he comes along   5
with the blood of lice under his nails.

The face of the poor man is lined
from the hunger and thirst in his belly.
Poverty is no state for any mortal man.
It makes him a beast to be fed on grass.   10

Poverty is unjust. If it befalls a man,
though he is nobly born, he has no power with God.

        (Swahili)

A Baby is a European

A baby is a European   1
he does not eat our food:
he drinks from his own water pot.

A baby is a European
he does not speak our tongue: 5
he is cross when the mother understands him not.

A baby is a European
he cares very little for others;
he forces his will upon his parents.

A baby is a European   10
he is always very sensitive:
the slightest scratch on his skin results in an ulcer.

        (Ewe)

The Moon

The moon lights the earth   1
it lights the earth but still
the night must remain the night.
The night cannot be like the day.
The moon cannot dry our washing.   5
Just like a woman cannot be a man
just like black can never be white.

(Soussou)

Q Based on these poems, how might
one describe the African's response
to nature? To the community?
To European culture?

African Music and Dance

African music shares the vigorous rhythms of poetry
and dance. In texture, it consists of a single line of melody
without harmony. As with most African dialects, where
pitch is important in conveying meaning, variations of
musical effect derive from tonal inflection and timbre. The
essentially communal spirit of African culture is reflected in
the use of **call-and-response** chants similar to those of
African poetry. The most distinctive characteristic of
African music however, is its polyrhythmic structure. A
single piece of music may simultaneously engage five to ten
different rhythms, many of which are repeated over and
over. African dance, also communally performed, shares
the distinctively dense polyrhythmic qualities of African
music. The practice of playing "against" or "off" the main
beat provided by the instruments is typical of much West
African music and is preserved in the "off-beat" patterns of
early modern jazz (see chapter 36).

See Music Listening Selections at end of chapter.

A wide variety of percussion instruments, including various types of drums and rattles, is used in the performance
of African ritual (Figure **18.7**). Also popular are the *balafo*
(a type of xylophone), the *bolon* or *kora* (a large harp), and
the *sansa* (an instrument consisting of a number of metal
tongues attached to a small wooden soundboard). The latter two of these instruments, used to accompany story-
telling, were believed to contain such potent supernatural
power that they were considered dangerous and were out-
lawed among some African tribes, except for use by *griots*.
Africa was the place of origin for the banjo, which may
have been the only musical instrument permitted on the
slave ships that traveled across the Atlantic in the sixteenth century (bells, drums, and other instruments were
forbidden). African culture is notably musical, and the
dynamic convergence of poetry, dance, and music gener-
ates a singularly dramatic experience.

The African Mask

African masks and headdresses were part of the amalgam of
poetry, music, and dance that served a ceremonial or ritual
event. The mask was usually part of a larger costume (made
of cloth or fiber) that covered the body (see Figure 18.7).
It functioned not simply to disguise the wearer's identity,
but to channel the spirit of an animal, god, or ancestor.
The masker embodied the spirit of the being he represented. By the transformative power of the mask, he became
the agent of the supernatural. Masked dancers took part in
rituals of exorcism, initiation, purification, and burial.
They functioned regularly in ceremonies that marked the
transition from one stage of being to another. Such ceremonies might feature a **totem**, the heraldic emblem of a
specific family or clan.

Figure 18.7 Bambara ritual Chi Wara dance, Mali.

MAKING CONNECTIONS

The Chi Wara headdress pictured in Figure **18.8** dates from the nineteenth century, but it belongs to a much older tradition honoring Mali's ancestral founders: its predecessors consisted of a wickerwork cap, antelope horns, and a leather face-mask. African sculpture had a major impact on European art of the early twentieth century, when numerous examples of this genre were introduced into Europe (see chapter 31). The Spanish artist Pablo Picasso was among the first to recognize the aesthetic power

Figure 18.8 Bambara antelope headpiece, from Mali, nineteenth century, based on earlier models. Wood, height 35¾ in., width 15¾ in.

of African masks, which he referred to as "magical objects." To this day, the African legacy continues to inspire the creative arts. In the sculpture entitled *Speedster Tji Wara* (Figure **18.9**), the African-American artist Willie Cole (b. 1955) gives the Chi Wara headdress a new, Postmodern identity. Assembling scavenged bicycle parts, Cole recasts the Mali totem as a symbol of popular urban culture.

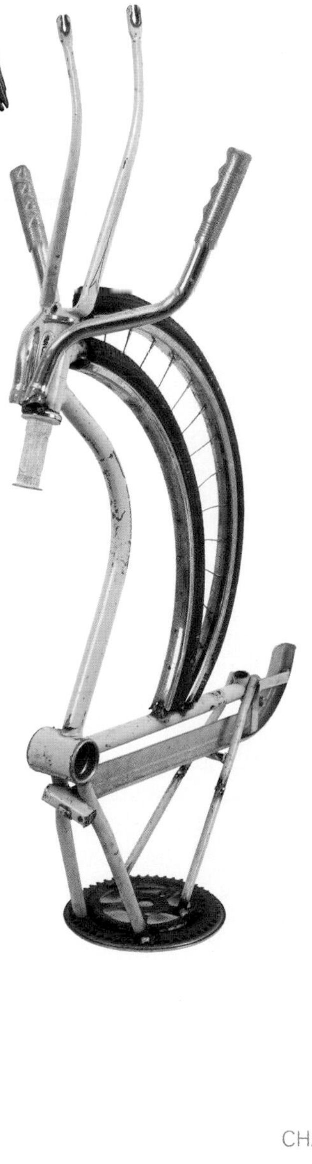

Figure 18.9 WILLIE COLE, *Speedster Tji Wara*, 2002. Bicycle parts, 3 ft. 10½ in. × 1 ft. 3 in.

The people of Mali have long regarded the antelope as their mythical ancestor, Chi Wara, who taught humankind how to cultivate the land. Chi Wara dance rituals incorporate movements that imitate those of the antelope (see Figure 18.7). The performers wear headdresses with huge crests that combine the features of the antelope, the anteater, and local birds (see Figure 18.8). In these magnificently carved headpieces, the triangular head of the antelope is repeated in the chevron patterns of the neck and the zigzags of the mane. The Chi Wara totem (which has become the logo for modern Mali's national airline) epitomizes the African taste for expressive simplification and geometric design.

While there exists a wide variety of mask types and styles, most African masks do not share the naturalism of the metal-cast and terracotta portraits from Ife and Benin; rather, they reflect a tradition of expressive abstraction. A case in point is the Songe mask from Zaire in Central Africa (Figure **18.10**). Worn at ceremonies for the death or installation of a king, its facial distortions and scarification seem to compress emotion and energy. A comparison of this mask with that of the portrait of an Ife *oba* (see Figure 18.5) reminds us that African artists developed a wide variety of styles ranging from idealized portraiture to stylized abstraction. The object that channeled spiritual energy clearly required a style more powerful than that which recreated the optical illusion of the natural world. Feathers, shells, teeth, beads, raffia, hair, and other materials were often added to a mask to enhance its vital powers. The color red

Figure 18.10 Songe mask, from Zaire, nineteenth century, based on earlier models. Wood and paint, height 17 in.

might be used to symbolize danger, blood, or power; black suggested chaos and evil; and white represented death.

Throughout world history, the religious rites and festivals of numerous cultures—from the Dionysian festivals of ancient Greece to the modern-day Catholic Mardi Gras—have involved the act of masking, usually as part of a larger ceremonial performance that includes music and dance. Among the African-American Mardi Gras "Indians" of New Orleans, such traditions prevail to this day.

African Sculpture

Over the course of centuries, African artisans mastered a wide variety of media. The techniques of terracotta modeling, ivory carving, and metal casting were well known to Africans before the end of the first millennium B.C.E. Works in these enduring media seem to have been produced mainly in the western and southern portions of Africa. The greater part of African sculpture was executed, however, in the less durable medium of wood. Using axes, knives, and chisels, professional sculptors—almost exclusively male—carved images from green or semidry timber. Unlike works in other media, few examples of Africa's wood sculpture survived the sixteenth century. Most were destroyed or damaged by Africa's corrosive climate, by termites, or by Muslims and Christians who deemed these objects sacrilegious or idolatrous. Among some African peoples, masks of soft wood seem to have been discarded after ritual use. Nevertheless, eleventh-century Arab chronicles confirm the existence of a rich native tradition of wood sculpture; this tradition is described as well by the Portuguese in the sixteenth century.

African figural sculpture served many functions: grave figures were designed to watch over the dead, fertility images were invoked to promote or assist in childbirth; still other sculptures served in rituals of divination and healing. In style, such objects range from realistic to abstract. The 4-foot-tall wooden sculpture of a mother and child was one of a group of sculptures displayed by the Bamana people at annual ceremonies associated with fertility and childbirth (Figure **18.11**). The woman's full breasts, which invert the shape of her conical cap, point downward toward the child she tenderly embraces.

Figure 18.11 Bamana people, Mother and Child, Bougouni-Dioila area, Mali, fifteenth to twentieth century. Wood, height 48⅞ in. Like the trunks of the trees from which they were carved, African sculptures like this one are rigid and tubular. Bamana figures often wear tokens of their physical powers, such as the knife strapped to this woman's left arm, and the amulets on her hat.

Figure 18.12 Standing male figure (*nkisi nkondi*, Mangaaka type), nineteenth century. Wood, iron, raffia, pigment, kaolin, and red camwood (tukula), 44 × 15⅝ × 1⅜ in. Condemned as pagan fetishes, such sculptures were destroyed by Christian missionaries following the colonial invasion of the Congo. An English trader in this area between 1607 and 1610 described similar figures; however, in that there is no mention of the use of nails, some scholars argue that this aspect of the genre was influenced by Christian representations of the Crucifixion.

Another type of African sculpture, the *nkisi*, describes a type of power object produced throughout the Congo basin in Central Africa (Figure **18.12**). Employed in rituals designed to channel spiritual energy, some *nkisi* were used to heal the sick, while others served functions ranging from sealing agreements to warding off evil spirits. On behalf of a client, a diviner or priest prepared "medicinal" ingredients (possibly hair or nail clippings) that were placed inside the *nkisi* or tied to it in packets. With ritual oversight, the client drove a nail or sharp

African Wood Sculpture: Text and Context

The fact that almost all surviving examples of African wood sculpture date from the nineteenth and twentieth centuries gives rise to some important questions. Should African art executed during the early Modern Era be considered in the context of modern Africa, or does such art, by its adherence to older traditions and practices, reflect the values of an earlier culture? How might we interpret the relationship of text (an African sculpture) to context (a specific culture or time period) if we are dealing with a modern object that perpetuates premodern traditions and practices?

The fact that the literature of both eleventh-century Muslims and sixteenth-century Portuguese describes Africa's amazing wood sculptures confirms the longevity of this tradition. Such records suggest that many types of nineteenth- and twentieth-century

African sculpture—such as the wooden mask and the *nkisi*—have histories that go back centuries before foreign intervention. More recently created, they nevertheless embody age-old traditions, both in their fabrication and in their function.

Little effort was made to preserve African sculptures as aesthetic objects prior to the development of **ethnography** in late nineteenth-century Europe (see chapter 30). In our own day, however, such objects have become commercialized. Attractive to art dealers and collectors, they are often produced and marketed by Africans who have long since discontinued the ritual practices to which their ancestors (and the sculptures themselves) were bound. Given these considerations, to what cultural context does "modern" African art belong?

object into the *nkisi* to activate its power. Such objects were among the first to be identified by sixteenth-century Europeans, who referred to them as "idols" and **"fetishes"** (a word derived from the Portuguese *"feiticoa,"* meaning "charm" or "spell").

African Architecture

As with the sculpture of pre-colonial Africa, little survives of its native architecture, and that which does suggests a wide diversity of structural forms. A survey of traditional African house forms lists almost three dozen different types of structure. Construction materials consist of mud, stones, and brushwood, or adobe brick—a sun-dried mixture of clay and straw. Outside of Benin and a few urban centers Africans seem to have had little need for monumental religious or administrative buildings. But at the ancient trade center of Zimbabwe (the name means "House of Stone"), in South Central Africa, where a powerful kingdom developed before the year 1000, the remains of huge stone walls and towers, constructed without mortar, indicate the presence of a royal residence or palace complex—the largest structures in Africa after the pyramids.

Africa's Muslim-dominated cities display some of the most visually striking structures in the history of world architecture. The adobe mosques of Mali, for instance, with their organic contours, bulbous towers, and conical finials (native symbols of fertility) resemble fantastic sand castles (see Figure 18.4). They have proved to be almost as impermanent: some have been rebuilt (and replastered) continuously since the twelfth century, hence their walls and towers bristle with sticks or wooden beams that provide a permanent scaffolding for restoration. African mosques are testimonials to the fusion of Muslim, Asian, and local ancestral traditions. Their domical contours, sim-

ilar to the temple-shrines and burial mounds of early cultures, recall the primordial mountain and the womb—sites of spiritual renewal. Africa's vernacular architecture calls to mind the sacred link between Mother Earth and the human community. Even the wooden pickets (see Figure 18.4) that serve as scaffolding have symbolic significance: used at Bambara initiation ceremonies and often buried with the dead, such tree branches are symbols of rebirth and regeneration.

Cross-Cultural Encounter

Ibn Battuta in West Africa

Islam was present in West Africa from at least the eighth century, and the religion increased in influence as Muslims came to dominate trans-Saharan trade. Occasional efforts to spread Islam by force were generally unsuccessful, yet the Islamization of the Sudan ultimately succeeded as the result of the peaceful and prosperous activities of Muslim merchants, administrators, and scholars. Mali's most famous ruler, Mansa ("King") Musa (1312–1337), came to symbolize the largesse of the African Muslim elite when, during his *hajj* of 1324, he and his retinue scattered large amounts of gold from Mali to Mecca. West African rulers like Musa patronized the arts, commissioned the construction of mosques, and encouraged conversion to Islam.

Nowhere in the literature of the age are the realities of cross-cultural encounter so well expressed as in the journal of the fourteenth-century Muslim traveler–scholar, Ibn Battuta (1304–1369). Born into an upper-class Muslim family in the North African city of Tangier, Battuta was educated in law and Arabic literature before he made the first of his seven pilgrimages in 1325. Over the course of his lifetime, this inveterate tourist journeyed on foot or by camel caravan some 75,000 miles, visiting parts of China, Indonesia, Persia, India, Burma, Spain, Arabia, Russia, Asia Minor, Egypt, and East and West Africa. Although his initial motives for travel were religious, he shared with other itinerant Muslim scholars an interest in Islamic law and a curiosity concerning the customs of Muslim communities throughout the world. In 1354, Battuta narrated the history of his travels, including his two-year trip from Morocco to Mali—his last recorded journey—to a professional scribe who recorded it in a *ribla* ("book of travels"). That portion of the *ribla* that recounts Battuta's visit to Mali is the only existing eyewitness account of the kingdom at the height of its power. It documents Battuta's keen powers of observation and reveals his efforts to evaluate social and cultural practices that differed sharply from his own.

READING 18.4 From Ibn Battuta's *Book of Travels* (1354)

We reached the city of Īwālātan[1] at the beginning   1
of the month of Rabi'I[2] after a journey of two full months
from Sijilmāsa. It is the first district of the country of the
Blacks. . . .

   When we arrived the merchants deposited their goods
in an open space and the Blacks took responsibility for
them. The merchants went to the Farbā who was sitting
on a rug under a shelter; his officials were in front of him
with spears and bows in their hands. The Massūfa[3]
notables were behind him. The merchants stood in front   10
of him and he spoke to them through an interpreter as a
sign of his contempt for them, although they were close
to him. At this I was sorry I had come to their country,
because of their bad manners and contempt for white
people. I made for the house of the Ibn Baddā', a kind
man of Salā to whom I had written asking him to let[4] a
house to me, which he did. . . .

   . . . I stayed in Īwālātan about fifty days. Its people
treated me with respect and gave me hospitality. Among
them were the qāḍī[5] of the town Muh·ammad b. 'Abdallāh   20
b. Yanūmar, and his brother the jurist and professor
Yahyā. The town of Īwālātan is extremely hot. There are a
few small palms and they sow melons in their shade.
Water comes from underground sources. Mutton is
plentiful. Their clothes are of fine quality and Egyptian
origin. Most of the inhabitants belong to the Massūfa.
The women are of outstanding beauty and are more
highly regarded than the men.

   Conditions among these people are remarkable and
their life style is strange. The men have no jealousy. No   30
one takes his name from his father, but from his maternal
uncle. Sons do not inherit, only sister's sons![6] This is

something I have seen nowhere in the world except
among the infidel Indians of al-Mulāibar. Nevertheless
these people are Muslims. They are strict in observing the
prayers, studying the religious law, and memorizing the
Qur'ān. Their women have no shame before men and do
not veil themselves, yet they are punctilious about their
prayers. Anyone who wants to take a wife among them
does so, but they do not travel with their husbands, and   40
even if one of them wished to, her family would prevent
her. Women there have friends and companions among
men outside the prohibited degrees for marriage, and in
the same way men have women friends in the same
category. A man goes into his house, finds his wife with
her man friend, and does not disapprove.

   One day I called upon the qāḍī at Īwālātan after he had
given permission for me to enter. I found him with a
young and exceptionally beautiful woman. When I saw her
I hesitated and was going to go back, but she laughed at   50
me and showed no embarrassment. The qāḍī said to me:
"Why are you turning back? She is my friend." I was
astonished at them, for he was a jurist and a Ḥājj.[7] I
learnt that he had asked the Sultan's permission to go on
pilgrimage that year with his female companion. I do not
know whether this was the one or not, but permission was
not given.

   One day I called on Abū Muh·ammad Yandakān al-
Massūfi, in whose company we had arrived, and found
him sitting on a rug. In the middle of the room was a   60
canopied couch and upon it was a woman with a man
sitting and talking together. I said to him: "Who is this
woman?" He said: "She is my wife." I said: "What about
the man who is with her?" He said: "He is her friend." I
said: "Are you happy about this, you who have lived in
our country and know the content of the religious law?"
He said: "The companionship of women and men among
us is a good thing and an agreeable practice, which
causes no suspicion; they are not like the women of your
country." I was astonished at his silliness. I left him and   70
did not visit him again. Afterwards he invited me a
number of times but I did not accept. . . .

   The Blacks are the most respectful of people to their
king and abase themselves most before him. . . . If he
summons one of them at his session in the cupola we
have mentioned, the man summoned removes his robe
and puts on a shabby one, takes off his turban, puts on a
dirty skull-cap and goes in with his robe and his trousers
lifted half way to his knees. He comes forward humbly
and abjectly, and strikes the ground hard with his   80
elbows. He stands as if he were prostrating himself in
prayer, and hears what the Sultan says like this. If one of
them speaks to the Sultan and he answers him, he takes
his robe off his back, and throws dust on his head and
back like someone making his ablutions with water. I was
astonished that they did not blind themselves.

---

[1] Near Timbuktu in Mali.
[2] April 1352.
[3] A Berber people of the western Sahara.
[4] Rent.
[5] Muslim judges.

[6] In the matrilineal sub-Saharan tribes, the mother's
   brother is considered the most important male
[7] One who has made the pilgrimage to Mecca.

When the Sultan makes a speech in his audience those present take off their turbans from their heads and listen in silence. Sometimes one of them stands before him, recounts what he has done for his service, and says: "On such and such a day I did such and such, and I killed so and so on such and such a day." Those who know vouch for the truth of that and he does it in this way. One of them draws the string of his bow, then lets it go as he would do if he were shooting. If the Sultan says to him: "You are right" or thanks him, he takes off his robe and pours dust on himself. That is good manners among them. . . .

Among their good practices are their avoidance of injustice; there is no people more averse to it, and their Sultan does not allow anyone to practice it in any measure; the universal security in their country, for neither the traveller nor the resident there has to fear thieves or bandits, they do not interfere with the property of white men who die in their country, even if it amounts to vast sums; they just leave it in the hands of a trustworthy white man until whoever is entitled to it takes possession of it; their punctiliousness in praying, their perseverance in joining the congregation, and in compelling their children to do so; if a man does not come early to the mosque he will not find a place to pray because of the dense crowd; it is customary for each man to send his servant with his prayer-mat to spread it out in a place reserved for him until he goes to the mosque himself; their prayer-mats are made of the leaves of a tree like the date-palm, but which has no fruit. They dress in clean white clothes on Fridays; if one of them has only a threadbare shirt he washes it and cleans it and wears it for prayer on Friday. They pay great attention to memorizing the Holy Qur'ān. If their children appear to be backward in learning it they put shackles on them and do not remove them till they learn it. I called on the qāḍī on the Feast Day. His children were in shackles. I said to him: "Are you not going to free them?" He said: "Not till they learn the Qur'ān by heart." One day I passed by a handsome youth, who was very well dressed, with a heavy shackle on his foot. I said to the person with me: "What has he done? Has he killed someone?" The youth understood what I said and laughed. I was told: "He has been shackled to make him memorize the Qur'ān."

Among their bad practices are that the women servants, slave-girls and young daughters appear naked before people, exposing their genitals. I used to see many like this in Ramaḍān,[8] for it is customary for the fararīs[9] to break the fast in the Sultan's palace, where their food is brought to them by twenty or more slave-girls, who are naked. Women who come before the Sultan are naked and unveiled, and so are his daughters. On the night of the twenty-seventh of Ramaḍān I have seen about a hundred naked slave-girls come out of his palace with food; with them were two daughters of the Sultan with full breasts and they too had no veil. They put dust and ashes on their heads as a matter of good manners. There is the clowning we have described when poets recite their works. Many of them eat carrion, dogs and donkeys.[10]

Q **What aspects of African life did Ibn Battuta find congenial? Which did he find most unusual?**

The Europeans in Africa

European commercial activity in Africa was the product of the quest for new sea routes to the East, and for control of the markets in gold, salt, and slaves. For thousands of years, slavery in Africa had been no different from that which had prevailed elsewhere in the ancient world: free people normally became slaves as captives of war, debtors, or convicted criminals. They made up a class of men and women used, for the most part, as laborers. Though some rose to high positions within society or were able to purchase their freedom, most were regarded as chattel, that is, property to be bought and sold. In the economies of ancient Mesopotamia, Greece, and Rome, as in Africa, slave-holding and slave-trading enhanced one's wealth and social status. With the arrival of Islam in North Africa, the slave trade expanded greatly. Scholars estimate the number of African slaves transported to foreign lands in the years between 750 and 1500 may have exceeded ten million.

During the sixteenth century, Portugal intruded upon the well-established Muslim-dominated trans-Saharan commercial slave trade. The Portuguese slave trade in West Africa, the Congo, and elsewhere developed according to the pattern that had already been established by Muslim traders: that is, in agreement with local African leaders who reaped profits from the sale of victims of war or raids on neighboring territories. The *obas* of Benin accommodated the Portuguese, establishing a royal monopoly over trade in ivory, cloth, and pepper. Benin prohibited the exportation of male slaves, while importing and reselling slaves purchased by Europeans elsewhere in West Africa.

By the year 1500, the Portuguese controlled the flow of both gold and slaves to Europe. Transatlantic slave trade commenced in 1551, when the Portuguese began to ship thousands of slaves from Africa to work in the sugar plantations of Brazil, a "New World" territory claimed by Portugal. European forms of slavery were more brutal and exploitative than any previously practiced in Africa: slaves shipped overseas were branded, shackled in chains like beasts, underfed, and—if they survived the ravages of dysentery and disease—conscripted into oppressive kinds of physical labor (see chapter 25).

In their relations with the African states, especially those in coastal areas, the Europeans were equally brutal. They often ignored the bonds of family and tribe, the local laws and religious customs; they pressured Africans to adopt European language and dress and fostered economic

---

[8] The Muslim month of fasting; the daily fast ends at sunset.
[9] Chiefs.

---

[10] The Qur'an forbids the eating of unclean meat.

rivalry. While in a spirit of missionary zeal and altruism they introduced Christianity and Western forms of education, they also brought ruin to some tribal kingdoms, and, in parts of Africa, they almost completely destroyed native cultural life. These activities were but a prelude to the more disastrous forms of exploitation that prevailed during the seventeenth and eighteenth centuries, when the transatlantic slave trade, now dominated by the Dutch, the French, and the English, reached massive proportions. By the mid-seventeenth century, a triangular trade route developed: European ships carried to Africa goods that were traded for African prisoners; the latter were transported to the Americas, where they were sold or traded for goods that were then brought to Europe. The notorious "Middle Passage" of this route (Africa to the Americas), came to describe the system of forced transportation (by some estimates fifteen to twenty million Africans) that flourished between 1450 and 1850 (see chapter 25).

Considering the repeated intrusion of outsiders over the centuries, it is remarkable that local traditions in the arts of Africa continued to flourish. Native traditions in literature and music remained intact. African metalworkers, enjoying an influx of European copper and brass, refined the techniques of metal casting that had brought them centuries of renown. Hundreds of bronze low-relief wall plaques decorated the royal palace at Benin. One shows a

Figure 18.13 Benin plaque showing a Portuguese warrior surrounded by *manillas* (horseshoe-shaped metal objects used as a medium of exchange), from Nigeria, sixteenth century. Bronze.

Figure 18.14 Mask, sixteenth century, Court of Benin, Nigeria. Ivory, height 9¾ in. While it is possible that the mask was used as a belt ornament, the lugs above the ears on either side of the head suggest that it was worn around the neck of the *oba*.

Portuguese warrior with a sword and trident, surrounded by *manillas*, the horseshoe-shaped metal objects that constituted a medium of exchange (Figure **18.13**). Sixteenth-century carved ivories reflect a high degree of expertise, and many individual ivories record the European presence. On the crown and collar of a small ivory mask, a row of bearded Portuguese heads alternates with symbolic mudfishes, emblematic of Benin royalty (Figure **18.14**). It is possible that the Benin regarded the foreigners as creatures who, like the mudfish, flourished on both land and sea. A skillfully executed blend of naturalism and stylization characterizes the portrait, whose eyes and forehead scarification were originally inlaid with iron. This commanding portrait, along with some 2000 other Benin artworks, were appropriated by the British in 1897 and transported to London.

The Americas

Native American Cultures

Native cultures in the territories of North, Central, and South America began to develop at least 20,000 years ago, following nomadic migrations across a land bridge that once linked Siberia and Alaska at the Bering Strait (see chapter 3). During the centuries prior to the first European contacts with the Americas, well over a thousand migrant groups established independent communities throughout North, South, and Middle (or Meso-) America (parts of present-day Mexico and South America (Map **18.3**). Like pre-colonial Africans, Native Americans were culturally and linguistically diverse. Individual societies shared deeply felt ethnic loyalties and an animistic view of the world as being infused with living spirits. The indigenous peoples of North America ranged culturally from the relative socioeconomic simplicity of some Pacific coast tribes to the complexity of the Iroquois town-dwellers.

Many Native American cultures produced illustrious histories, and several achieved the status of empire. In Middle America and on the western coast of South America, villages grew into states that conquered or absorbed their rivals. Settlers of essentially tropical areas, these agricultural peoples traded only regionally and made frequent war on each other. They fashioned their tools and weapons out of wood, stone, bone, and pieces of volcanic glass. They had no draft animals and no wheeled vehicles. Although after the ninth century copper came into use in Meso-America, iron was unknown until the arrival of the Spaniards in the fifteenth century. These facts make all the more remarkable the material achievements of the Maya, Inca, and Aztec civilizations, all three of which developed into empires of considerable authority in the pre-Columbian era.

Native North American Arts: The Northwest

There is no word for "art" in any Native American language; the aesthetically compelling objects produced among native Americans were either items of daily use or power-objects associated with ceremony and ritual. Moreover, the modern distinction between craft and fine art is non-existent among those who practice weaving, beadwork, ceramics, and jewelry-making. The Haida folk of the Queen Charlotte Islands, located near British

Columbia, continue the ancient practice of raising wooden poles carved and painted with totems—heraldic symbols of social status, spiritual authority, and ancestral pride. Other peoples of the Northwest Coast make portrait masks of spirits and ancestors whose powers help to cure the sick and predict events. Dance masks and clan helmets—which, like African masks, draw on the natural elements of wood, human hair and teeth, animal fur, seashell, and feathers—invoke the metamorphic powers of legendary creatures such as the raven (see Reading 18.6). Masks with hidden strings connected to moving parts that "become" different creatures or spirits are themselves vehicles of transformation (Figure **18.15**). Such "performance masks" are used in the orchestration of mythic cycles—often lasting many days—that enact the encounters of ancestors, totemic figures, and supernatural beings.

Native North American Arts: The Southwest

In various parts of the American Southwest, Native Americans raised communal villages, called "pueblos" by the Spanish. These communities consisted of flat-roofed structures built of stone or adobe arranged in terraces to accommodate a number of families. Among the most notable of the pueblo communities was that of the Anasazi (a Navajo word meaning "ancient ones"). Their settlements at Mesa Verde and Chaco Canyon in southwestern Colorado, which flourished between the eleventh and fourteenth centuries, consisted of elaborate multistoried living spaces with numerous rooms, storage areas, and circular underground ceremonial centers, known as **kivas**. Large enough to hold all of the male members of the community (women were not generally invited to attend

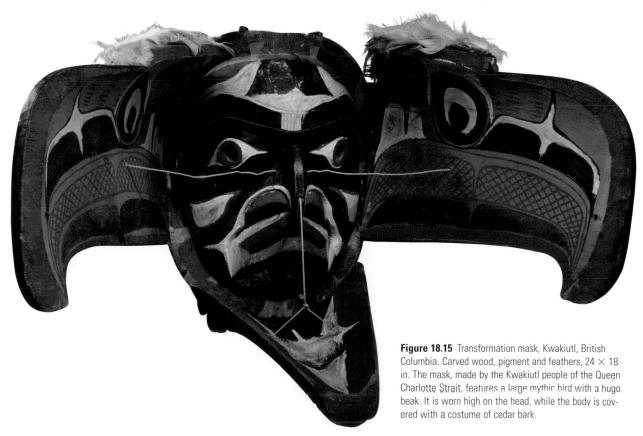

Figure 18.15 Transformation mask, Kwakiutl, British Columbia. Carved wood, pigment and feathers, 24 × 18 in. The mask, made by the Kwakiutl people of the Queen Charlotte Strait, features a large mythic bird with a hugo beak. It is worn high on the head, while the body is covered with a costume of cedar bark.

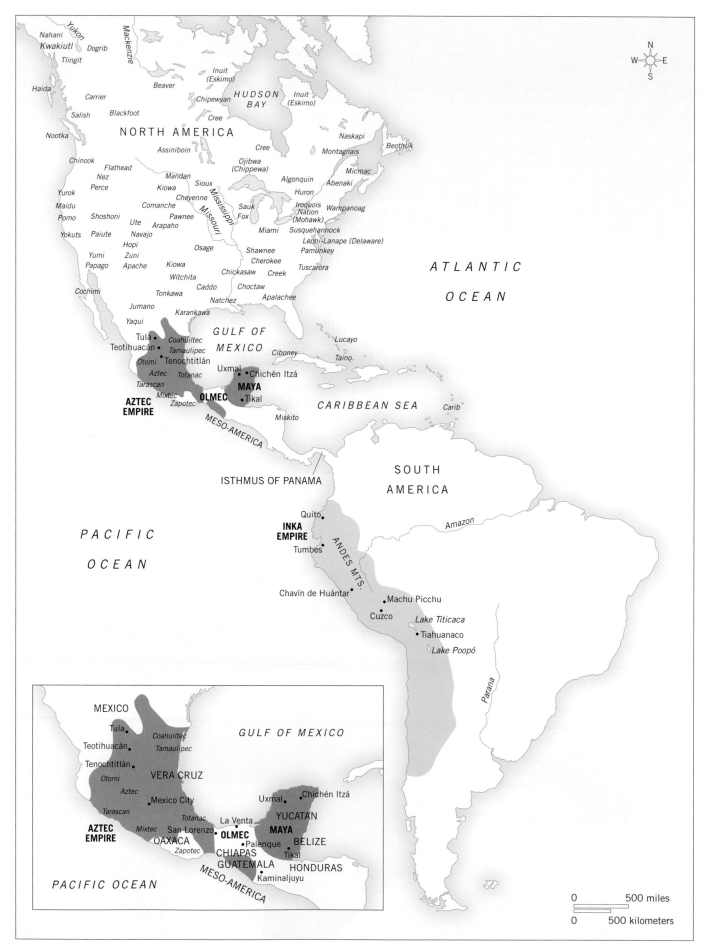

Map 18.3 The Americas Before 1500.

Figure 18.16 Cliff Palace, Mesa Verde, Colorado, inhabited 1073–1272.

Figure 18.17 Classic Mimbres bowl showing rabbit-man with burden basket, from Cameron Creek village, New Mexico, 1000–1150. Black-on-white pottery, height 4⅜ in., diameter 10¾ in.

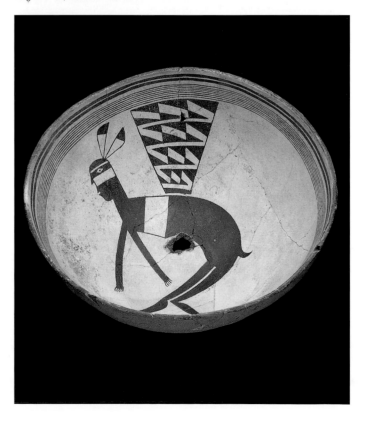

sacred ceremonies), *kivas* served as cosmic symbols of the underworld and as theaters for rites designed to maintain harmony with nature. The Cliff Palace at Mesa Verde, Colorado, positioned under an overhanging cliff canyon wall, whose horizontal configuration it echoes, is one of the largest cliff dwellings in America (Figure **18.16**). Its inhabitants—an estimated 250 people—engineered the tasks of quarrying sandstone, cutting logs (for beams and posts), and hauling water, sand, and clay (for the adobe core structure) entirely without the aid of wheeled vehicles, draft animals, or metal tools.

The pueblo tribes of the American Southwest produced some of the most elegant ceramic wares in the history of North American art. Lacking the potter's wheel, women handbuilt vessels for domestic and ceremonial uses. They embellished jars and bowls with designs that vary from a stark, geometric abstraction to stylized human, animal, and plant forms. One Mimbres bowl shows a rabbit-man carrying a basket on his back (Figure **18.17**): the shape of the creature, which subtly blends human and animal features, works harmoniously with the curves of the bowl and animates the negative space that surrounds the image. Mimbres pottery—usually pierced or ritually "killed" before being placed with its owner in the grave—testifies to the rich imagination and sophisticated artistry of pueblo culture.

For centuries, the Hopi people of Arizona and the Zuni of New Mexico, both of the pueblo culture, have fabricated the small wooden figures known as *kachinas* (Figure 18.18). Literally "life-bringers," *kachinas* are spirit-beings that embody ancestral spirits. They are presented to Hopi children during initiation ceremonies designed to familiarize them with the spirits that oversee agricultural productivity. Among the highly prized creations of the Hopi, Zuni, and Navajo peoples of the American Southwest are richly patterned textiles, hand-woven baskets, and silver jewelry, often embellished with turquoise and other semiprecious stones.

Native American religious rituals, like those of all ancient societies, integrated poetry, music, and dance. The sun dance was a principal part of the annual ceremony that celebrated seasonal renewal. In the Navajo tribal community of the American Southwest, the shaman still conducts the healing ceremony known as the Night Chant. Beginning at sunset and ending some nine days later at sunrise, the Night Chant calls for a series of meticulously executed sand paintings and the recitation of song cycles designed to remove evil and restore good. Characterized by monophonic melody and hypnotic repetition, the Night Chant is performed to the accompaniment of whistles and percussive instruments such as gourd rattles, drums, and rasps. Its compelling rhythms are evident in both the Music Listening Selection and in the "Prayer of the Night

Figure 18.18 Butterfly maiden, Hopi *Kachina*. Carved wood, pigment and feathers, height 13 in. During Hopi ceremonies, *kachina* maidens, representing the wives and sisters of the *kachinas*, are impersonated by male dancers, who wear painted wooden headdresses like the one seen on this doll.

♪ See Music Listening Selections at end of chapter.

Chant" reproduced below. Rituals like the Night Chant are not mere curiosities but, rather, living practices that remain sacred to the Navajo people.

READING 18.5 "A Prayer of the Night Chant" (Navajo)

Tségihi.	1
House made of dawn.	
House made of evening light.	
House made of the dark cloud.	
House made of male rain.	5
House made of dark mist.	
House made of female rain.	
House made of pollen.	
House made of grasshoppers.	
Dark cloud is at the door.	10
The trail out of it is dark cloud.	
The zigzag lightning stands high upon it.	
Male deity!	
Your offering I make.	
I have prepared a smoke for you.	15
Restore my feet for me.	
Restore my legs for me.	
Restore my body for me.	
Restore my mind for me.	
This very day take out your spell for me.	20
Your spell remove for me.	
You have taken it away for me.	
Far off it has gone.	
Happily I recover.	
Happily my interior becomes cool.	25
Happily I go forth.	
My interior feeling cool, may I walk.	
No longer sore, may I walk.	
Impervious to pain, may I walk.	
With lively feelings may I walk.	30
As it used to be long ago, may I walk.	
Happily may I walk.	
Happily, with abundant dark clouds, may I walk.	
Happily, with abundant showers, may I walk.	
Happily, with abundant plants, may I walk.	35
Happily, on a trail of pollen, may I walk.	
Happily may I walk.	
Being as it used to be long ago, may I walk.	
May it be beautiful before me.	
May it be beautiful behind me.	40
May it be beautiful below me.	
May it be beautiful above me.	
May it be beautiful all around me.	
In beauty it is finished.	

Q What is the purpose of repetition in the Night Chant?

Q What similarities do you detect between this chant (Music Listening Selection I-23), Gregorian Chant (MLS I-2), and Buddhist Chant (MLS I-3)?

Native American Literature

Myths and folktales, transmitted orally for generations (and only recorded since the seventeenth century), feature themes that call to mind those of Africa. Creation myths, myths of destruction (or death), and myths that describe the way things are served to provide explanations of the workings of nature (see Readings 0.1 and 18.2). Usually told by men who passed them down to boys, myths and tales often traveled vast distances, and, thus, may appear in many variant versions. As with African folklore, Native American myths feature heroes or heroines who work to transform nature; the heroes/tricksters may themselves be humans who are transformed into ravens, spiders, coyotes, wolves, or rabbits (see Figure 18.17). As with the African trickster tale, which usually points to a moral, the Native American trickster story means to teach or explain; nonetheless, heroes whose strategies involve deceit and cunning are often held in high regard.

READING 18.6 Two Native American Tales

How the Sun Came

There was no light anywhere, and the animal people
stumbled around in the darkness. Whenever one bumped
into another, he would say, "What we need in the world
is light." And the other would reply, "Yes, indeed, light is
what we badly need."

At last, the animals called a meeting, and gathered
together as well as they could in the dark. The red-
headed woodpecker said, "I have heard that over on the
other side of the world there are people who have light."

"Good, good!" said everyone.   10

"Perhaps if we go over there, they will give us some
light," the woodpecker suggested.

"If they have all the light there is," the fox said, "they
must be greedy people, who would not want to give any
of it up. Maybe we should just go there and take the
light from them."

"Who shall go?" cried everyone, and the animals all
began talking at once, arguing about who was strongest
and ran fastest, who was best able to go and get the light.

Finally, the 'possum said, "I can try. I have a fine big   20
bushy tail, and I can hide the light inside my fur."

"Good! Good!" said all the others, and the 'possum set
out.

As he traveled eastward, the light began to grow and
grow, until it dazzled his eyes, and the 'possum screwed
his eyes up to keep out the bright light. Even today, if you
notice, you will see that the 'possum's eyes are almost
shut, and that he comes out of his house only at night.

All the same, the 'possum kept going, clear to the
other side of the world, and there he found the sun. He   30
snatched a little piece of it and hid it in the fur of his
fine, bushy tail, but the sun was so hot it burned off all
the fur, and by the time the 'possum got home his tail
was as bare as it is today.

"Oh, dear!" everyone said. "Our brother has lost his
fine, bushy tail, and still we have no light."

"I'll go," said the buzzard. "I have better sense than to
put the sun on my tail. I'll put it on my head."

So the buzzard traveled eastward till he came to the
place where the sun was. And because the buzzard flies   40
so high, the sun-keeping people did not see him,
although now they were watching out for thieves. The
buzzard dived straight down out of the sky, the way he
does today, and caught a piece of the sun in his claws.
He set the sun on his head and started for home, but the
sun was so hot that it burned off all his head feathers,
and that is why the buzzard's head is bald today.

Now the people were in despair. "What shall we do?
What shall we do?" they cried. "Our brothers have tried
hard; they have done their best, everything a man can   50
do. What else shall we do so we can have light?"

"They have done the best a man can do," said a little
voice from the grass, "but perhaps this is something a
woman can do better than a man."

"Who are you?" everyone asked. "Who is that speaking
in a tiny voice and hidden in the grass?"

"I am your Grandmother Spider," she replied.
"Perhaps I was put in the world to bring you light. Who
knows? At least I can try, and if I am burned up it will
still not be as if you had lost one of your great warriors." 60

Then Grandmother Spider felt around her in the
darkness until she found some damp clay. She rolled it
in her hands, and molded a little clay bowl. She started
eastward, carrying her bowl, and spinning a thread
behind her so she could find her way back.

When Grandmother Spider came to the place of the
sun people, she was so little and so quiet no one noticed
her. She reached out gently, gently, and took a tiny bit of
the sun, and placed it in her clay bowl. Then she went
back along the thread that she had spun, with the sun's   70
light growing and spreading before her, as she moved
from east to west. And if you will notice, even today a
spider's web is shaped like the sun's disk and its rays,
and the spider will always spin her web in the morning,
very early, before the sun is fully up.

"Thank you, Grandmother," the people said when she
returned. "We will always honor you and we will always
remember you."

And from then on pottery making became woman's
work, and all pottery must be dried slowly in the shade   80
before it is put in the heat of the firing oven, just as
Grandmother Spider's bowl dried in her hand, slowly, in
the darkness, as she traveled toward the land of the sun.

(Cheyenne)

Raven and the Moon

One day Raven learnt that an old fisherman, living alone   1
with his daughter on an island far to the north, had a box
containing a bright light called the moon. He felt that he
must get hold of this wonderful thing, so he changed
himself into a leaf growing on a bush near to the old
fisherman's home. When the fisherman's daughter came
to pick berries from the wild fruit patch, she pulled at
the twig on which the leaf stood and it fell down and

entered into her body. In time a child was born, a dark-complexioned boy with a long, hooked nose, almost like a bird's bill. As soon as the child could crawl, he began to cry for the moon. He would knock at the box and keep calling, "Moon, moon, shining moon."

At first nobody paid any attention, but as the child became more vocal and knocked harder at the box, the old fisherman said to his daughter, "Well, perhaps we should give the boy the ball of light to play with." The girl opened the box and took out another box, and then another, from inside that. All the boxes were beautifully painted and carved, and inside the tenth there was a net of nettle thread. She loosened this and opened the lid of the innermost box. Suddenly light filled the lodge, and they saw the moon inside the box; bright, round like a ball, shining white. The mother threw it towards her baby son and he caught and held it so firmly they thought he was content. But after a few days he began to fuss and cry again. His grandfather felt sorry for him and asked the mother to explain what the child was trying to say. So his mother listened very carefully and explained that he wanted to look out at the sky and see the stars in the dark sky, but that the roof board over the smoke hole prevented him from doing so. So the old man said, "Open the smoke hole." No sooner had she opened the hole than the child changed himself back into the Raven. With the moon in his bill he flew off. After a moment he landed on a mountain top and then threw the moon into the sky where it remains, still circling in the heavens where Raven threw it.

(Northwest Coast)

Q What creatures assume importance in these tales?

The Arts of Meso- and South America

Until recently, scholars regarded the Olmecs as the largest and most advanced of early Meso-American cultures (see chapter 3). In the last ten years, however, archeologists have excavated sites near Peru's west coast that may have flourished as early as 3500 B.C.E. Clearly, the ancient history of the Americas is yet to be written. While it is difficult to generalize on the unique features of Middle and South American cultures before the fifteenth century, the abundance of objects created in a single medium—gold—suggests that this rare metal held great significance: The sheer number and quality of works produced in gold surpassed that of most world cultures. Over thousands of years, the techniques of metalwork, and especially gold-working, passed from generation to generation to attain remarkable levels of proficiency. Gold was associated with the sun, whose radiance gave life to the crops, and with the gods, whose blood (in the form of rain) was considered procreative and thus essential to community survival. The choice medium for the glorification of gods and their earthly representatives, gold was used to produce extraordinary artworks ranging from small items of jewelry to masks and weapons, especially those associated with rituals of blood sacrifice (Figure **18.19**).

In the sacrificial rites and royal ceremonies of pre-Columbian communities, human blood was shed to feed and appease the gods, thus saving the world from destruction. This fundamental sense of interdependence between earthly and spiritual realms is nowhere more clearly illustrated than in the civilization of the Maya.

Figure 18.19 Ceremonial knife, from the Lambayeque valley, Peru, ninth to eleventh centuries. Hammered gold with turquoise inlay, 13 × 5⅛ in.

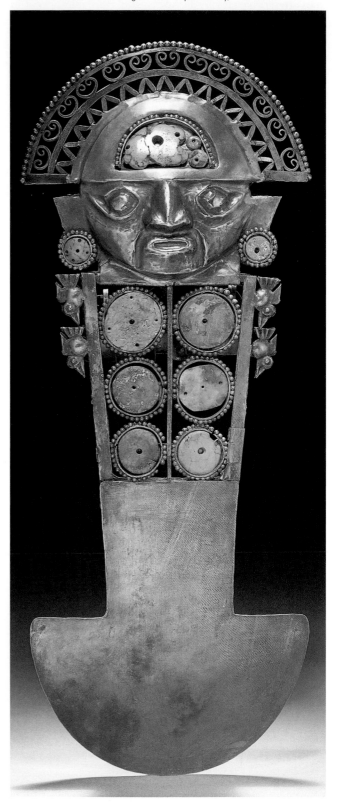

Figure 18.20 Reconstruction drawing of post-classic Maya fortress city of Chutixtiox, Quiche, Guatemala, ca. 1000, from Richard Adams, *Prehistoric Mesoamerica*.

Early Empires in the Americas

The Maya

Maya civilization reached its classic phase between 250 and 900 C.E. and survived with considerable political and economic vigor until roughly 1600. At sites in southern Mexico, Honduras, Guatemala, and the Yucatán Peninsula, the Maya constructed fortified cities consisting of elaborate palace complexes that are hauntingly reminiscent of those from ancient Mesopotamia (Figure **18.20**). These might include reclining stone figures known as "chacmools," which functioned as altars or bearers of sacrificial offerings. Like the Mesopotamian ziggurat (see chapter 1), the Maya temple was a terraced pyramid with a staircase ascending to a platform capped by a multiroomed superstructure (Figure

18.21). A shrine and sanctuary, it also served as a burial place for priests or rulers. On the limestone façades of such structures, the Maya carved and painted scenes of religious ceremonies and war, as well as images of their gods: Quetzalcoatl, the creator god—a hybrid of the Meso-American bird (*quetzal*) and the serpent (*coatl*)—hence, "Feathered Serpent" (see Figure 18.27); and Tlaloc, the long-snouted rain deity (see Figure 18.21, far left).

The Maya were the only known Native American culture to produce a written language. Their ancient script, comprised of hieroglyphs, was decoded during the second half of the twentieth century. Only since 1995 have the glyphs been recognized as a system of phonetic signs that operate like spoken syllables—a discovery made, in part, by studying the living language of modern-day descendants of

Figure 18.21 Castillo, with chacmool in the foreground, Chichén Itzá, Yucatán, Mexico. Maya, ninth to thirteenth centuries.

the Maya who inhabit the Guatemalan highlands and the Yucatán. Despite the survival of some codices and many stone inscriptions, nearly all of the literary evidence of this people was destroyed during the sixteenth century by Spanish missionaries and colonial settlers. Perhaps the most important source of Meso-American mythology, however, survives in the form of an oral narrative believed to date from the Maya classic period, transcribed into the Quiche language around 1500. This narrative, known as the *Popol Vuh* (see Reading 0.1), recounts the creation of the world. According to the Maya, the gods fashioned human beings out of maize—the principal Native American crop—but chose deliberately to deprive them of perfect understanding.

As if to challenge the gods, the Maya became accomplished mathematicians and astronomers. Carefully observing the earth's movements around the sun, they devised a calendar that was more accurate than any used in medieval Europe before the twelfth century. Having developed a mathematical system that recognized "zero," they computed planetary and celestial cycles with some accuracy, tracked the paths of Venus, Jupiter, and Saturn, and successfully predicted eclipses of the sun and moon. They recorded their findings in stone, on the limestone-covered bark pages of codices and on the façades of temples, some of which may have functioned as planetary observatories. At the principal pyramid at Chichén Itzá in the Yucatán (see Figure 18.21), the ninety-one steps on each of four sides, plus the platform on which the temple stands, correspond to the 365 days in the solar calendar. According to the Maya, the planets (and segments of time itself) were ruled by the gods, usually represented in Maya art as men and women carrying burdens on their shoulders. The Maya and the various Meso-American peoples who followed them believed in the cyclical creation and destruction of the world, and they prudently entrusted the sacred mission of timekeeping to their priests.

A key feature of almost all Meso-American sacred precincts was an I-shaped, high-walled stone court that served as a ballpark. It was used for the performance of ceremonial games played by two teams of nine to eleven men each. The ballgame was not exclusively a sport, but an age-old religious pageant whose symbolism was embedded in the mythic narrative of the *Popul Vuh*. It enacted a life-and-death ritual that maintained the regenerative power of the sun, thus securing cosmic order. The object of the game was to propel a 5-pound rubber ball, representing the sun, through the stone rings at either side of the court. Members of the losing team lost more than glory: they were sacrificed to the sun god, their hearts torn from their bodies on ritual altars adjacent to the court.

Blood sacrifice and bloodletting were ritual practices of the Maya nobility. A low-relief lintel from Yaxchilan in Chiapas, Mexico, shows a royal bloodletting ceremony that, according to hieroglyphs carved on the upper and left edges of the stone, took place in 709 C.E. (Figure **18.22**). It identifies King Shield Jaguar (the jaguar was a favorite symbol of military strength) and his queen, Lady Xoc. The

Figure 18.22 Lintel relief, Yaxchilan, Chiapas, Mexico, late classic period, 725 C.E. Limestone. Traces of red, green, and yellow pigments on this and other lintels from Yaxchilan confirm that many Maya sculptures were once brilliantly painted.

king, holding a staff and wearing a feathered headdress adorned with the shrunken head of a sacrificial victim, witnesses the ritual by which the queen pulls a thorn-lined rope through her tongue. The blood-soaked rope falls into a basket filled with slips of paper that absorb the royal blood. These would be burned in large sacrificial vessels, so that the smoke might lure the gods. Such ceremonies were performed on the accession of a new king, prior to waging war, and at ceremonies celebrating victory in battle. They served to honor the gods and confirm the political legitimacy of the ruler. A sophisticated blend of realistic detail and abstract design, the Yaxchilan lintel reveals the Maya genius for uniting representational and symbolic modes of expression.

Science and Technology

1500	Maya in the Yucatán utilize vegetable-based molds to treat wounds and infections
1568	Gerhard Kremen (Flemish) produces the first Mercator projection map
1596	Korean naval architects launch the first ironclad warship

The Inca

Until the fifteenth century, the Inca state was only one of many regional states that occupied the coastal areas of Andean South America. By way of a series of military campaigns that the Inca launched around 1438, it soon became an empire that, at its height at the end of the century, extended almost 3000 miles (from present-day Ecuador to Chile; see Map 18.3) to incorporate some sixteen million inhabitants. Ruling Peru's coastal plains and the mountains and valleys of the Andes, the Inca absorbed the traditions of earlier Peruvian cultures. Some of these, like Caral (discussed in chapter 3), flourished as early as 3500 B.C.E. in the coastal region northwest of Lima. Others, notable for their fine ceramics, rich textiles, and sophisticated goldwork (see Figure 18.19), had occupied the valleys of rivers that flowed from the Andes to the Pacific Ocean.

Like the ancient Romans, the Inca constructed thousands of miles of roads and bridges in order to expedite trade and communication. At Machu Picchu, they built a 3-square-mile city that straddled two mountain peaks some 9000 feet above sea level (Figure 18.23). With heavy stone and bronze tools (but without mortar), they constructed fortresslike walls and large ceremonial plazas filled with temples, terraces, and two-story buildings. While lacking the written word, they kept records by way of a system of knotted and colored cords known as *quipu*. The cult of the sun dominated religious festivals at which llamas or guinea pigs were daily sacrificed.

Associated with rain and fertility, the llama symbolized royal authority; it was also treasured for its wool and as a source of transportation in mountainous terrain. Images of the llama were hammered from sheets of gold and silver or cast by means of the lost-wax method (Figure 18.24). A

Figure 18.23 Machu Picchu, Peru, ca. 1500.

Figure 18.24 Silver long-haired Inca llama, ca. fifteenth century, 9⅛ × 8 in. The figure may represent the sacred white llama honored by Inca rulers. At ritual festivals, a white llama was dressed in a bright red tunic and wore gold ear ornaments.

sixteenth-century chronicler reported that life-sized gold and silver llamas guarded the Temple of the Sun, itself ornamented with hundreds of sheets of jewel-embedded gold.

The arts of feather ornamentation and textile weaving were also brought to remarkable heights by the Inca. Essential to the cold climate of the Andes, tunics and blankets were made of fibers spun, dyed with bright colors, and woven by highly skilled female weavers. Royal textiles often included complex geometric designs (see Figure 18.1).

The Aztecs

Small by comparison with the Inca civilization, that of the Aztecs—the last of the three great Meso-American empires—is estimated to have numbered between three and five million people. In their earliest history, the Aztecs (who called themselves *Mexica*) were an insignificant tribe of warriors who migrated to central Mexico in 1325. Driven by a will to conquer matched perhaps only by that of the ancient Romans, they created in less than a century an empire that encompassed all of central Mexico and Meso-America as far south as Guatemala. Their capital at Tenochtitlán ("Place of the Gods"), a city of some 250,000 people, was constructed on an island in the middle of Lake Texcoco. It was connected to the Mexican mainland by three great causeways and watered by artificial lakes and dams. The Aztecs were masterful engineers, whose roads, canals, and aqueducts astounded the Spaniards who arrived in Mexico in 1519. Upon encountering Tenochtitlán, with its huge temples and palaces connected by avenues and

ceremonial plazas, Spanish soldiers reported that it rivaled Venice and Constantinople—cities that were neither so orderly nor so clean.

Aztec civilization absorbed the cultural traditions of earlier Meso-Americans, including the Maya. They honored the pantheon of nature deities centering on the sun and extended the practice of blood sacrifice to the staggering numbers of victims captured in their incessant wars. They preserved native traditions of temple construction, ceramics, weaving, metalwork, and stone carving. During the fifteenth century, the Aztecs raised to new heights the art of monumental stone sculpture, carving great basalt statues that ranged from austere, realistic portraits to fantastic and terrifying icons of gods and goddesses such as Coatlique, Lady of the Skirt of Serpents and ancient earth mother of the gods (Figure **18.25**). Combining feline and human features, the over-life-sized "she-of-the-serpent-skirt" bears a head consisting of two snakes, clawed hands and feet, and a necklace of excised hearts and severed hands. Renaissance Europeans, whose idea of female divinity was shaped by Raphael's gentle Madonnas, found these blood-drenched "idols" outrageous; they destroyed as many as they could find.

Figure 18.25 *Coatlique, Mother of the Gods*, Aztec, 1487–1520. Andesite, height 8 ft. 3¼ in. According to Aztec mythology, the children of the pregnant mother goddess Coatlicue, jealous of the offspring she would produce, cut off her head. The two streams of blood took the form of snakes leaping from her severed neck, as seen here.

The Aztecs believed in the cyclical death and rebirth of the universe. They carried on the traditions of timekeeping begun by the Maya. Like the Maya, they devised a solar calendar of 365 days. The "Calendar Stone" functioned not as an actual calendar, but as a symbol of the Aztec cosmos (Figure **18.26**). Central to the stone is the face of the sun god, whose tongue is a sacrificial knife; his outstretched claws hold severed human heads. The four square panels that surround the face of the god represent the four previous creations of the world. Arranged around these panels are the twenty signs of the days of the month in the eighteen-month Aztec year, and embracing the entire cosmic configuration are two giant serpents that bear the sun on its daily journey. The stone is the pictographic counterpart of Aztec legends that bind human beings to the gods who govern the irreversible wheel of time.

Some of the most interesting records of Aztec culture are preserved in the form of codices, that is manuscripts—usually made of deer hide—with pictographic representations that recount tribal genealogy, history, and mythology. The most complex surviving Meso-American codex, which is housed today at the Vatican Library in Rome, illustrates the history of Quetzalcoatl in the underworld. The folio illustrated in Figure **18.27** recounts the life–death dualism that is fundamental to Aztec thought. Depicted on the left is the god of death, holding a blood-splattered skeleton; he is challenged by the creator god,

Figure 18.26 Sun disk, known as the "Calendar Stone," Aztec, fifteenth century. Diameter 13 ft., weight 24½ tons.

Quetzalcoatl, whom legend describes as having stolen the bones of older gods and returned them to earth in order to repopulate the land of the living. Pictographic signs representing twenty thirteen-day weeks are shown on either side of the scene.

Cross-Cultural Encounter

The Spanish in the Americas

Columbus made his initial landfall on one of the islands now called the Bahamas, and on successive voyages he explored the Caribbean islands and the coast of Central America. At every turn, he encountered people native to the area—people he called "Indians" in the mistaken belief that he had reached the "Indies," the territories of India and China. Other explorers soon followed and rectified Columbus' misconception. Spanish adventurers, called *conquistadores*, sought wealth and fortune in the New World. Although vastly outnumbered, the force of 600 soldiers under the command of Hernán Cortés (1485–1547), equipped with fewer than twenty horses and the superior technology of gunpowder and muskets, overcame the Aztec armies in 1521. Following a seventy-five-day siege, the Spanish completely demolished the island city of Tenochtitlán, from

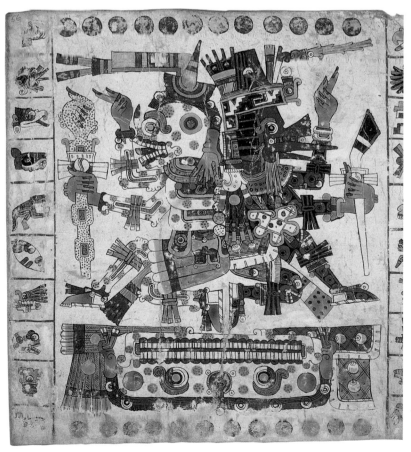

Figure 18.27 Aztec peoples, *Mictlantecuhtli and Quetzalcoatl.* Manuscript illumination. The inverted skull beneath the two gods may represent the land of the dead, or the bones that, according to legend, Quetzalcoatl dropped and scattered prior to his returning them to earth.

whose ruins Mexico City would eventually rise. While the technology of gunpowder and muskets had much to do with the Spanish victory, other factors contributed, such as religious prophecy (that Quetzalcoatl would return as a bearded white man), support from rebellious Aztec subjects, and an outbreak of smallpox among the Aztecs.

The Spanish destruction of Tenochtitlán and the melting down of most of the Aztec goldwork left little tangible evidence of the city's former glory. Consequently, the description that is the subject of Cortés' second letter to Spain is doubly important: not only does it offer a detailed picture of Aztec cultural achievement, but it serves as a touchstone by which to assess the conflicted reactions of Renaissance Europeans to their initial encounters with the inhabitants of strange and remote lands.

READING 18.7 From Cortés' Letters from Mexico (1520)

This great city of Temixtitan[1] is built on the salt lake, and no matter by what road you travel there are two leagues from the main body of the city to the mainland. There are four artificial causeways leading to it, and each is as wide as two cavalry lances. The city itself is as big as Seville or Córdoba. The main streets are very wide and very straight; some of these are on the land, but the rest and all the smaller ones are half on land, half canals where they paddle their canoes. All the streets have openings in places so that the water may pass from one canal to another. Over all these openings, and some of them are very wide, there are bridges made of long and wide beams joined together very firmly and so well made that on some of them ten horsemen may ride abreast.   10

Seeing that if the inhabitants of this city wished to betray us they were very well equipped for it by the design of the city, for once the bridges had been removed they could starve us to death without our being able to reach the mainland, as soon as I entered the city I made great haste to build four brigantines, and completed them in a very short time. They were such as could carry three hundred men to the land and transport the horses whenever we might need them.   20

This city has many squares where trading is done and markets are held continuously. There is also one square twice as big as that of Salamanca,[2] with arcades all around, where more than sixty thousand people come each day to buy and sell, and where every kind of merchandise produced in these lands is found; provisions as well as ornaments of gold and silver, lead,   30
brass, copper, tin, stones, shells, bones, and feathers. They also sell lime, hewn and unhewn stone, adobe bricks, tiles, and cut and uncut woods of various kinds. There is a street where they sell game and birds of every species found in this land: chickens, partridges and quails, wild ducks, flycatchers, widgeons, turtledoves, pigeons, cane birds, parrots, eagles and eagle owls, falcons, sparrow hawks and kestrels, and they sell the skins of some of these birds of prey with their feathers, heads and claws. They sell rabbits and hares, and stags   40
and small gelded dogs which they breed for eating.

There are streets of herbalists where all the medicinal herbs and roots found in the land are sold. There are shops like apothecaries', where they sell ready-made medicines as well as liquid ointments and plasters. There are shops like barbers' where they have their hair washed and shaved, and shops where they sell food and drink. There are also men like porters to carry loads. There is much firewood and charcoal, earthenware braziers and mats of various kinds like mattresses for   50
beds, and other, finer ones, for seats and for covering rooms and hallways. There is every sort of vegetable, especially onions, leeks, garlic, common cress and watercress, borage, sorrel, teasels and artichokes; and there are many sorts of fruit, among which are cherries and plums like those in Spain.

They sell honey, wax, and a syrup made from maize canes, which is as sweet and syrupy as that made from the sugar cane. They also make syrup from a plant which in the islands is called *maguey*,[3] which is much better than   60
most syrups, and from this plant they also make sugar and wine, which they likewise sell. There are many sorts of spun cotton, in hanks of every color, and it seems like the silk market at Granada, except here there is a much greater quantity. They sell as many colors for painters as may be found in Spain and all of excellent hues. They sell deerskins, with and without the hair, and some are dyed white or in various colors. They sell much earthenware, which for the most part is very good; there are both large and small pitchers, jugs, pots, tiles, and many other sorts   70
of vessel, all of good clay and most of them glazed and painted. They sell maize both as grain and as bread and it is better both in appearance and in taste than any found in the islands or on the mainland. They sell chicken and fish pies, and much fresh and salted fish, as well as raw and cooked fish. They sell hen and goose eggs, and eggs of all the other birds I have mentioned, in great number, and they sell *tortillas* made from eggs.

Finally, besides those things which I have already mentioned, they sell in the market everything else to be   80
found in this land, but they are so many and so varied that because of their great number and because I cannot remember many of them nor do I know what they are called I shall not mention them. Each kind of merchandise is sold in its own street without any mixture whatever; they are very particular in this. Everything is sold by number and size, and until now I have seen nothing sold by weight. There is in this great square a very large building like a courthouse, where ten or twelve

---

[1] Tenochtitlán.
[2] A Spanish university town.

[3] Fermented aloe or *pulque*, a powerful liquor still popular today in Mexico.

persons sit as judges. They preside over all that happens in the markets, and sentence criminals. There are in this square other persons who walk among the people to see what they are selling and the measures they are using; and they have been seen to break some that were false.

There are, in all districts of this great city, many temples or houses for their idols. They are all very beautiful buildings, and in the important ones there are priests of their sect who live there permanently; and, in addition to the houses for the idols, they also have very good lodgings. All these priests dress in black and never comb their hair from the time they enter the priesthood until they leave; and all the sons of the persons of high rank, both the lords and honored citizens also, enter the priesthood and wear the habit from the age of seven or eight years until they are taken away to be married; this occurs more among the first-born sons, who are to inherit, than among the others. They abstain from eating things, and more at some times of the year than at others; and no woman is granted entry nor permitted inside these places of worship.

Amongst these temples there is one, the principal one, whose great size and magnificence no human tongue could describe, for it is so large that within the precincts, which are surrounded by a very high wall, a town of some five hundred inhabitants could easily be built. All round inside this wall there are very elegant quarters with very large rooms and corridors where their priests live. There are as many as forty towers, all of which are so high that in the case of the largest there are fifty steps leading up to the main part of it; and the most important of these towers is higher than that of the cathedral of Seville. They are so well constructed in both their stone and woodwork that there can be none better in any place, for all the stonework inside the chapels where they keep their idols is in high relief, with figures and little houses, and the woodwork is likewise of relief and painted with monsters and other figures and designs. All these towers are burial places of chiefs, and the chapels therein are each dedicated to the idol which he venerated.

There are three rooms within this great temple for the principal idols, which are of remarkable size and stature and decorated with many designs and sculptures, both in stone and in wood. Within these rooms are other chapels, and the doors to them are very small. Inside there is no light whatsoever; there only some of the priests may enter, for inside are the sculptured figures of the idols, although, as I have said, there are also many outside.

The most important of these idols, and the ones in whom they have most faith, I had taken from their places and thrown down the steps; and I had those chapels where they were cleaned, for they were full of the blood of sacrifices; and I had images of Our Lady and of other saints put there, which caused Mutezuma[4] and the other natives some sorrow. First they asked me not to do it, for when the communities learnt of it they would rise against me, for they believed that those idols gave them all their worldly goods, and that if they were allowed to be ill treated, they would become angry and give them nothing and take the fruit from the earth leaving the people to die of hunger. I made them understand through the interpreters how deceived they were in placing their trust in those idols which they had made with their hands from unclean things. They must know that there was only one God, Lord of all things, who had created heaven and earth and all else and who made all of us; and He was without beginning or end, and they must adore and worship only Him, not any other creature or thing. And I told them all I knew about this to dissuade them from their idolatry and bring them to the knowledge of God our Saviour. All of them, especially Mutezuma, replied that they had already told me how they were not natives of this land, and that as it was many years since their forefathers had come here, they well knew that they might have erred somewhat in what they believed, for they had left their native land so long ago; and as I had only recently arrived from there, I would better know the things they should believe, and should explain to them and make them understand, for they would do as I said was best. Mutezuma and many of the chieftains of the city were with me until the idols were removed, the chapel cleaned and the images set up and I urged them not to sacrifice living creatures to the idols, as they were accustomed,[5] for, as well as being most abhorrent to God, Your Sacred Majesty's laws forbade it and ordered that he who kills shall be killed. And from then on they ceased to do it, and in all the time I stayed in that city I did not see a living creature killed or sacrificed.

The figures of the idols in which these people believe are very much larger than the body of a big man. They are made of dough from all the seeds and vegetables which they eat, ground and mixed together, and bound with the blood of human hearts which those priests tear out while still beating. And also after they are made they offer them more hearts and anoint their faces with the blood. Everything has an idol dedicated to it, in the same manner as the pagans who in antiquity honored their gods. So they have an idol whose favor they ask in war and another for agriculture; and likewise for each thing they wish to be done well they have an idol which they honor and serve.

There are in the city many large and beautiful houses, and the reason for this is that all the chiefs of the land, who are Mutezuma's vassals, have houses in the city and live there for part of the year;[6] and in addition there are many rich citizens who likewise have very good houses. All these houses have very large and very good rooms and also very pleasant gardens of various sorts of flowers both on the upper and lower floors.

Along one of the causeways to this great city run two

---

[4] Moctezuma II, the last Aztec monarch, who ruled from 1502 to 1520.

[5] In 1488, at the dedication of the Great Pyramid at Tenochtitlán, Aztec priests sacrificed more than 20,000 war captives.

[6] Provincial lords were required to spend part of each year at the capital.

When Ibn Battuta visited Mali, he was startled by the strange customs of its inhabitants, which differed from those of his own country. The same is true of Cortés, who, while marveling at the glories of the Aztec city of Tenochtitlán, found the religious practices of its inhabitants "barbarous" (see Reading 18.7). However, the European outreach took a different course from that of individual travelers. It also differed dramatically from the trading expeditions of the Chinese. Western expansion ultimately involved the colonization of foreign lands and, in some cases, the enslavement of foreign peoples.

In their exploration of Africa and the Americas, Europeans encountered people very different from themselves. Because these people differed from them in appearance, religious beliefs, and technological sophistication, they were regarded as "Other." Just as the ancient Greeks considered non-Greeks "barbarians," so

Renaissance Europeans perceived Africans and Native Americans as barbarous savages. Observing that despite many similarities to the way the Spanish lived, the Aztecs were "cut off from all civilized nations" (Reading 18.7), Cortés concluded that they were in need of enlightenment. This, in turn, became justification for the evangelical efforts of Catholic missionaries who worked to convert the "savages" to Christianity. It was, as well, sufficient justification for seeking dominion, or control, over them. The questions persist. Was the European colonization of Africa and the Americas rationalized by a belief in the inferiority of the "Other"? To what extent might such rationalization contribute to the age-old, imperialistic ambitions (still with us today) of powerful groups of people to dominate the less powerful—or, for that matter, simply those who are unlike themselves?

aqueducts made of mortar. Each one is two paces wide and some six feet deep, and along one of them a stream of very good fresh water, as wide as a man's body, flows into the heart of the city and from this they all drink. The other, which is empty, is used when they wish to clean the first channel. Where the aqueducts cross the bridges, the water passes along some channels which are as wide as an ox; and so they serve the whole city. 200

Canoes paddle through all the streets selling the water; they take it from the aqueduct by placing the canoes beneath the bridges where those channels are, and on top there are men who fill the canoes and are paid for their work. At all the gateways to the city and at the places where these canoes are unloaded, which is where the greater part of the provisions enter the city, there are guards in huts who receive a [percentage] of all that enters. I have not yet discovered whether this goes to the chief or to the city, but I think to the chief, because in other markets in other parts I have seen this tax paid to the ruler of the place. Every day, in all the markets and public places there are many workmen and craftsmen of every sort, waiting to be employed by the day. The people of this city are dressed with more elegance and are more courtly in their bearing than those of the other cities and provinces, and because Mutezuma and all those chieftains, his vassals, are always coming to the city, the people have more manners and politeness in all matters. Yet so as not to tire Your Highness with the description of the things of this city (although I would not complete it so briefly), I will say only that these people live almost like those in Spain, and in as much harmony and order as there, and considering that they are barbarous and so far from the knowledge of God and cut off from all 210 220 230

civilized nations, it is truly remarkable to see what they have achieved in all things.

Q What aspects of Aztec life and culture favorably impressed Cortés? Of what was he critical?

The Aftermath of Conquest

Mexican gold and (after Spain's conquest of the Incas) Peruvian silver were not the only sources of wealth for the conquerors; the Spanish soon turned to the ruthless exploitation of the native populations, enslaving them for use as miners and field laborers. During the sixteenth century, entire populations of Native Americans were destroyed as a result of the combined effects of such European diseases as smallpox and measles and decades of inhumane treatment. When Cortés arrived, for example, Mexico's population was approximately twenty-five million; in 1600, it had declined to one million. Disease traveled from America to Europe as well: European soldiers carried syphilis from the "New World" to the "Old." Guns and other weaponry came into the Americas, even as Christian missionaries brought a pacifistic Catholicism to the native populations. The impact of colonialism is described in the following eyewitness account from a *History of the New World* (1565) by the Italian Girolamo Benzoni (1519–1570), who spent fifteen years in the Americas:

> After the death of Columbus, other governors were sent to Hispaniola;* both clerical and secular, till the

---

* The name Columbus gave to the island in the West Indies that now comprises Haiti and the Dominican Republic.

natives, finding themselves intolerably oppressed and overworked, with no chance of regaining their liberty, with sighs and tears longed for death. Many went into the woods and having killed their children, hanged themselves, saying it was far better to die than to live so miserably serving such ferocious tyrants and villainous thieves. The women terminated their pregnancies with the juice of a certain herb in order not to produce children, and then following the example of their husbands, hanged themselves. Some threw themselves from high cliffs down precipices; others jumped into the sea and rivers; others starved themselves to death. Sometimes they killed themselves with their flint knives; others pierced their bosoms or sides with pointed stakes. Finally, out of two million inhabitants, through suicides and other deaths occasioned by the excessive labour and cruelties imposed by the Spaniards, there are not a hundred and fifty now to be found.

Such reports of Spanish imperialism in the Americas, brought to life by the illustrations of the Flemish engraver Theodore de Bry (1528–1598; Figure **18.28**), fueled the so-called "Black Legend" of Spanish cruelty toward the "Indians" and fed the heated debate that questioned the humanity of so-called "savage" populations. In this debate, the Spanish missionary-priest, Bartolomé de Las Casas (1474–1566), author of the infamous *Very Brief Account of the Destruction of the Indies* (1552), roundly denounced Spanish treatment of the "Indians." His humanitarian position prompted Pope Paul III to declare officially in 1537 that "the said Indians and all other people who may later be discovered by Christians, are by no means to be deprived of their liberty or . . . property." (The papal edict, it is worth noting, failed to extend such protection to Africans.) Las Casas, known as the "Apostle to the Indians," pleaded, ". . . all the peoples of the world are men, and the definition of all men collectively and severally, is one: that they are rational beings. All possess understanding and volition, being formed in the image and likeness of God. . . ."

Unlike the civilizations of India, China, and Africa, which have each enjoyed a continuous history from ancient times until the present, none of the empires that

Figure 18.28 THEODORE DE BRY, *Spanish Cruelties Cause the Indians to Despair*, from *Grands Voyages*. Frankfurt, 1594. Woodcut.

once flourished in ancient America has survived into modern times. The European invasion of the Americas severely arrested the cultural evolution of native tribal populations. Remnants of these populations, however, remain today among such groups as the Hopi and the Pueblo of the Southwestern United States, the Maya of the Yucatán, and the Inuit of the Pacific Northwest. Among these and other tribes, the ancient crafts of pottery, weaving, beadwork, and silverwork still reach a high degree of beauty and technical sophistication.

The Columbian Exchange

While the immediate effect of European expansion and cross-cultural encounter was a dramatic clash of traditions and values, the long-range effects were more positive, especially in the realms of commerce and culture. The so-called "Columbian Exchange" describes the interchange of hundreds of goods and products between Western Europe and the Americas. The Europeans introduced into the Americas horses, cattle, pigs, sheep, chickens, wheat, barley, oats, onions, lettuce, sugar cane, and various fruits, including peaches, pears, and citrus. From America, Western Europe came to enjoy corn, potatoes, tomatoes, peppers, chocolate, vanilla, tobacco, avocados, peanuts, pineapples, pumpkins, and a variety of beans. The most

important aspect of the Columbian Exchange, however, may be said to lie in the creation of vibrant new cultures and new peoples. The biological mix of Europeans, Native Americans, and Africans would alter the populations of the world to introduce the *mestizo* (a person of mixed European and Native American ancestry) and the various *creole* ("mixed") inhabitants of the Americas. Consequently, the Columbian Exchange generated new developments in all aspects of life, ranging from technology and industry to language, diet, and dance. On the threshold of modernity, the Euro-African and Euro-American exchanges opened the door to centuries of contact and diffusion that shaped the future of a brave new world.

Chronology

1404–1424	Zhu Di sponsors China's naval expeditions
1492	Columbus' first voyage
1498	Vasco da Gama reaches India
1519	Cortés enters Mexico
1531	Pizarro conquers Peru
1551	transatlantic slave trade begins
1571	Battle of Lepanto (defeat of Ottoman navy)

LOOKING BACK

Global Travel and Trade

- Ming China initiated a policy of global outreach that took some 300 wooden treasure ships to the shores of Africa, India, and Arabia.
- The period between 1400 and 1600 was the greatest age of trans-Eurasian travel since the days of the Roman Empire. European exploration was motivated by the fall of Constantinople in 1453 to the Ottoman Turks, who now dominated overland trade routes to the East.
- The technology of navigation was crucial to the success of European ventures. The Portuguese produced maps and charts that exceeded the accuracy of those drafted by Classical and Muslim cartographers. Renaissance Europeans improved such older Arab navigational devices as the compass and the astrolabe.
- By 1498, Vasco da Gama had navigated around Southern Africa to establish Portuguese trading posts in India.

- Christopher Columbus, an Italian in the employ of Spain, sailed west in search of an all-water route to China; his discovery of the Americas would change the course of world history.

The African Cultural Heritage

- Diversity characterizes all aspects of Africa's history and culture, from language to geography to political organization. Two features that distinguish the history of this vast continent are the dominance of a kinship system that forms the basis of social and communal organization, and an animistic view of nature.
- Even after the Muslim conquest of North Africa in the seventh century, many parts of Africa, such as the kingdom of Benin, remained independent of foreign domination. Nevertheless, the West African empires of Ghana, Mali, and Songhai all came under the influence of Muslim culture.

The Arts of Africa

- From the epic *Sundiata* to tales, proverbs, and poems of praise, the great body of African literature, emerges out of an oral tradition. Like African music and art, these works are characterized by strong rhythms and inventive imagery.
- African music, marked by a polyrhythmic structure and responsorial (call-and-response) patterns, reflects the communal spirit of African societies.
- African sculpture, including masks, royal portraits, and power-objects, manifests diverse styles, ranging from realistic representation to expressive abstraction. Inseparable from the rituals for which they were made, masks function as transformative objects that work to channel spiritual energy.

Cross-Cultural Encounter

- The fourteenth-century travels of the scholar Ibn Battuta document a cross-cultural encounter between peoples— Muslims and native North Africans—of vastly different customs and beliefs.
- European commercial activity in Africa was the product of the quest for new sea routes to the East, and for control of the markets in gold, salt, and slaves that had long made Africa a source of wealth for Muslim merchants.
- By the year 1500, the Portuguese controlled the flow of both gold and slaves to Europe. The transatlantic slave trade commenced in 1551, when the Portuguese began to ship thousands of slaves from Africa to work on the sugar plantations of Brazil.
- European forms of slavery were more brutal and exploitative than any previously practiced in Africa: slaves shipped overseas were conscripted into oppressive physical labor.

The Americas

- Similar to early African societies, Native Americans were culturally and linguistically diverse. Animistic and polytheistic, they maintained deep connections to nature and to the spirits associated with their kinship groups.
- Carved and painted wooden totems and masks are among the rich output of the native populations of the Northwest.
- Ceramics, textiles, baskets, metalwork, and *kachina* images, as well as the remains of pueblo architecture, testify to the vitality and originality of the native Southwest peoples.
- Orally transmitted, Native American folktales and myths explain natural phenomena and pass down moral truths. They often feature hero/trickster figures who work to transform nature.

Early Empires in the Americas

- The first of the great Meso-American empires, the Maya built civic centers with stone temples, palaces, and ballcourts. Ceremonies honoring the gods involved rituals of blood sacrifice. Accomplished mathematicians and astronomers, the Maya were the only Native American people to leave a system of writing.
- At their height in the late fifteenth century, the Inca ruled a Peruvian empire of some sixteen million people. They left monumental architecture, textiles, and ritual objects in silver and gold.
- The last of the Native American empires, that of the Aztecs, was centered in Mexico. Absorbing the cultural traditions and artistic practices of earlier native civilizations, they established a capital at Tenochitlán that is notable for its stone architecture and sculpture.

Cross-Cultural Encounter

- The Spanish destruction of Tenochtitlán left little tangible evidence of the city's former glory. When Cortés first arrived Mexico's population was approximately twenty-five million; in 1600 it had declined to one million.
- Mexican gold and Peruvian silver fueled foreign exploitation of native peoples. Unlike the civilizations of India, China, and Africa, which have enjoyed a continuous history from ancient times to the present, none of the empires that once flourished in ancient America has survived into modern times.
- The positive aspects of the European–American encounter lay in the exchange of goods and products, and in the biological mix of Africans, Native Americans, and Europeans that would produce the creolized cultures of the "New World."

Music Listening Selections

CD One Selection 21 Music of Africa, Senegal, "Greetings from Podor".
CD One Selection 22 Music of Africa, Angola, "Gangolo Song".
CD One Selection 23 Music of Native America, "Navajo Night Chant," male chorus with gourd rattles.

Glossary

anaphora the repetition of a word or words at the beginning of two or more lines of verse

call-and-response a vocal pattern in which the soloist raises a song and the chorus responds

ethnography the sociocultural study of human societies

fetish an object believed to have magical powers

griot a class of poet-historians who preserved the legends and lore of Africa by chanting or singing them from memory

kiva the underground ceremonial center of the Southwest Indian pueblo community

scarification the act or process of incising the flesh as a form of identification and rank, and/or for aesthetic purposes

totem an animal or other creature that serves as a heraldic emblem of a tribe, family, or clan

Chapter 19

Protest and Reform: The Waning of the Old Order

ca. 1400–1600

"Now what else is the whole life of mortals but a sort of comedy, in which the various actors, disguised by various costumes and masks, walk on and play each one his part, until the manager waves them off the stage?"
Erasmus

Figure 19.1 ALBRECHT DÜRER, *Knight, Death, and the Devil*, 1513. Engraving, 9⅝ × 7½ in. Dürer's engraving is remarkable for its wealth of microscopic detail. Objects in the real world—the horse, the dog, and the lizard—are depicted as precisely as those imagined: the devil and the horned demon.

LOOKING AHEAD

By the sixteenth century, the old medieval order was crumbling. Classical humanism and the influence of Italian Renaissance artist–scientists were spreading throughout Northern Europe (Map **19.1**). European exploration and expansion were promoting a broader world-view and new markets for trade. The rise of a global economy with vast opportunities for material wealth was inevitable. Europe's population grew from 69 million in 1500 to 188 million in 1600. As European nation-states tried to strengthen their international influence, political rivalry intensified. The "superpowers"—Spain, under the Hapsburg ruler Philip II (1527–1598) and England, under Elizabeth I (1533–1603)—contended for advantage in Atlantic shipping and trade. In order to resist the encroachment of Europe's stronger nation-states, the weaker ones formed balance-of-power alliances that often provoked war. The new order took Europe on an irreversibly modern course.

While political and commercial factors worked to transform the West, the event that most effectively destroyed the old medieval order was the Protestant Reformation. In the wake of Protestantism, the unity of European Christendom would disappear forever. Beginning in the fifteenth century, the Northern Renaissance, endorsed by middle-class patrons and Christian humanists, assumed a religious direction that set it apart from Italy's Classical revival. Its literary giants, from Erasmus to Shakespeare, and its visual artists, Flemish and German, shared little of the idealism of their Italian Renaissance counterparts. Their concern for the realities of human folly and for the fate of the Christian soul launched a message of protest and a plea for church reform expedited by way of the newly perfected printing press.

The Temper of Reform

The Impact of Technology

In the transition from medieval to early modern times, technology played a crucial role. Gunpowder, the light cannon, and other military devices made warfare more impersonal and ultimately more deadly. At the same time, Western advances in navigation, shipbuilding, and maritime instrumentation propelled Europe into a dominant position in the world.

Just as the musket and the cannon transformed the history of European warfare, so the technology of mechanical printing revolutionized learning and communication. Block printing originated in China in the ninth century and movable type in the eleventh, but print technology did not reach Western Europe until the fifteenth century. By

Figure 19.2 An early sixteenth-century woodcut of a printer at work.

1450, in the city of Mainz, the German goldsmith Johannes Gutenberg (ca. 1400–ca. 1468) perfected a printing press that made it possible to fabricate books more cheaply, more rapidly, and in greater numbers than ever before (Figure **19.2**). As information became a commodity for mass production, vast areas of knowledge—heretofore the exclusive domain of the monastery, the Church, and the university—became available to the public. The printing press facilitated the rise of popular education and encouraged individuals to form their own opinions by reading for themselves. It accelerated the growing interest in vernacular literature, which in turn enhanced national and individual self-consciousness. Print technology proved to be the single most important factor in the success of the Protestant Reformation, as it brought the complaints of Church reformers to the attention of all literate folk.

Science and Technology

1320	paper adopted for use in Europe (having long been in use in China)
1450	the Dutch devise the first firearm small enough to be carried by a single person
1451	Nicolas of Cusa (German) uses concave lenses to amend nearsightedness
1454	Johannes Gutenberg (German) prints the Bible with movable metal type

Map 19.1 Renaissance Europe, ca. 1500.

Christian Humanism and the Northern Renaissance

The new print technology broadcast an old message of religious protest and reform. For two centuries, critics had attacked the wealth, worldliness, and unchecked corruption of the Church of Rome. During the early fifteenth century, the rekindled sparks of lay piety and anticlericalism spread throughout the Netherlands, where religious leaders launched the movement known as the *devotio moderna* ("modern devotion"). Lay Brothers and Sisters of the Common Life, as they were called, organized houses in which they studied and taught Scripture. Living in the manner of Christian monks and nuns, but taking no monastic vows, these lay Christians cultivated a devotional lifestyle that fulfilled the ideals of the apostles and the church fathers. They followed the mandate of Thomas à Kempis (1380–1471), himself a Brother of the Common Life and author of the *Imitatio Christi* (*Imitation of Christ*), to put the message of Jesus into daily practice. After the Bible, the *Imitatio Christi* was the most frequently published book in the Christian West well into modern times.

The *devotio moderna* spread quickly throughout Northern Europe, harnessing the dominant strains of anticlericalism, lay piety, and mysticism, even as it coincided with the revival of Classical studies in the newly established universities of Germany. Although Northern humanists, like their Italian Renaissance counterparts, encouraged learning in Greek and Latin, they were more concerned with the study and translation of Early Christian manuscripts than with the Classical and largely secular texts that preoccupied the Italian humanists. This critical reappraisal of religious texts is known as Christian humanism. Christian humanists studied the Bible and the writings of the church fathers with the same intellectual fervor that the Italian humanists had brought to their examination of Plato and Cicero. The efforts of these Northern scholars gave rise to a rebirth (or renaissance) that focused on the late Classical world and, specifically, on the revival of church life and doctrine as gleaned from Early Christian literature. The Northern Renaissance put Christian humanism at the service of evangelical Christianity.

The leading Christian humanist of the sixteenth century—often called "the Prince of Humanists"—was Desiderius Erasmus of Rotterdam (1466–1536; Figure **19.3**). Schooled among the Brothers of the Common Life and learned in Latin, Greek, and Hebrew, Erasmus was a superb scholar and a prolific writer (see Reading 19.2). The first humanist to make extensive use of the printing press, he once dared a famous publisher to print his words as fast as he could write them. Erasmus was a fervent Neoclassicist— he held that almost everything worth knowing was set forth in Greek and Latin. He was also a devout Christian. Advocating a return to the basic teachings of Christ, he criticized the Church and all Christians whose faith had been jaded by slavish adherence to dogma and ritual. Using four different Greek manuscripts of the Gospels, he produced a critical edition of the New Testament that corrected Jerome's mistranslations of key passages. Erasmus' New Testament became the source of most sixteenth-century German and English vernacular translations of this central text of Christian humanism.

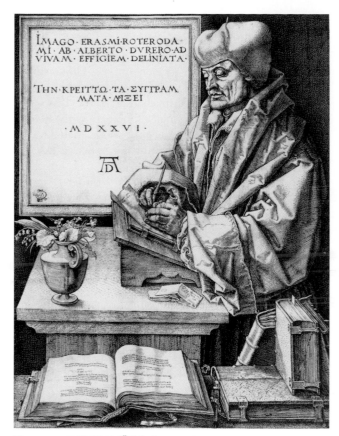

Figure 19.3 ALBRECHT DÜRER, *Erasmus of Rotterdam*, 1526. Engraving, 9¾ × 7½ in. The Latin inscription at the top of the engraving reports that Dürer executed the portrait from life. The Greek inscription below reads, "The better image [is found] in his writings." The artist wrote to his friend that he felt the portrait was not a striking likeness.

The Protestant Reformation

During the sixteenth century, papal extravagance and immorality reached new heights, and Church reform became an urgent public issue. In the territories of Germany, loosely united under the leadership of the Holy Roman emperor Charles V (1500–1558), the voices of protest were more strident than anywhere else in Europe. Across Germany, the sale of indulgences (see chapter 15) for the benefit of the Church of Rome—specifically for the rebuilding of Saint Peter's Cathedral—provoked harsh criticism, especially by those who saw the luxuries of the papacy as a betrayal of apostolic ideals. As with most movements of religious reform, it fell to one individual to galvanize popular sentiment. In 1505, Martin Luther (1483–1546), the son of a rural coal miner, abandoned his legal studies to become an Augustinian monk (Figure **19.4**). Thereafter, as a doctor of theology at the University of Wittenberg, he spoke out against the Church. His inflammatory sermons and essays offered radical remedies to what he called "the misery and wretchedness of Christendom."

Luther was convinced of the inherent sinfulness of humankind, but he took issue with the traditional medieval view—as promulgated, for instance, in *Everyman*—that salvation was earned through the performance of good works and grace mediated by the Church and its

priesthood. Inspired by the words of Saint Paul, "the just shall live by faith" (Romans 1:17), Luther argued that salvation could be attained only by faith in the validity of Christ's sacrifice: human beings were saved by the unearned gift of God's grace, not by their good works on earth. The purchase of indulgences, the veneration of relics, making pilgrimages, and seeking the intercession of the saints were useless, because only the grace of God could save the Christian soul. Justified by faith alone, Christians should assume full responsibility for their own actions and intentions.

In 1517, in pointed criticism of Church abuses, Luther posted on the door of the collegiate church at Wittenberg a list of ninety-five issues he intended for dispute with the leaders of the Church of Rome. The *Ninety-Five Theses*, which took the confrontational tone of the sample below, were put to press and circulated throughout Europe:

> 27 They are wrong who say that the soul flies out of Purgatory as soon as the money thrown into the chest rattles.
> 32 Those who believe that, through letters of pardon [indulgences], they are made sure of their own salvation will be eternally damned along with their teachers.
> 37 Every true Christian, whether living or dead, has a share in all the benefits of Christ and of the Church, given by God, even without letters of pardon.
> 43 Christians should be taught that he who gives to a poor man, or lends to a needy man, does better than if he bought pardons.
> 44 Because by works of charity, charity increases,

Figure 19.4 LUCAS CRANACH THE ELDER, *Portrait of Martin Luther*, 1533. Panel, 8 × 5¾ in.

and the man becomes better; while by means of pardons, he does not become better, but only freer from punishment.

45 Christians should be taught that he who sees any one in need, and, passing him by, gives money for pardons, is not purchasing for himself the indulgences of the Pope but the anger of God.

49 Christians should be taught that the Pope's pardons are useful if they do not put their trust in them, but most hurtful if through them they lose the fear of God.

50 Christians should be taught that if the Pope were acquainted with the exactions of the Preachers of pardons, he would prefer that the Basilica of St. Peter should be burnt to ashes rather than that it should be built up with the skin, flesh, and bones of his sheep.

54 Wrong is done to the Word of God when, in the same sermon, an equal or longer time is spent on pardons than on it.

62 The true treasure of the Church is the Holy Gospel of the glory and grace of God.

66 The treasures of indulgences are nets, wherewith they now fish for the riches of men.

67 Those indulgences which the preachers loudly proclaim to be the greatest graces, are seen to be truly such as regards the promotion of gain.

68 Yet they are in reality most insignificant when compared to the grace of God and the piety of the cross.

86 . . . why does not the Pope, whose riches are at this day more ample than those of the wealthiest of the wealthy, build the single Basilica of St. Peter with his own money rather than with that of poor believers? . . .

Luther did not set out to destroy Catholicism, but rather, to reform it. Gradually he extended his criticism of Church abuses to criticism of church doctrine. For instance, because he found justification in Scripture for only two Roman Catholic sacraments—baptism and Holy Communion—he rejected the other five. He attacked monasticism and clerical celibacy. (Luther himself married and fathered six children.) Luther's boldest challenge to the old medieval order, however, was his unwillingness to accept the pope as the ultimate source of religious authority. Denying that the pope was the spiritual heir to Saint Peter, he claimed that the head of the Church, like any other human being, was subject to error and correction. Christians, argued Luther, were collectively a priesthood of believers; they were "consecrated as priests by baptism." The ultimate source of authority in matters of faith and doctrine was Scripture, as interpreted by the individual Christian. To encourage the reading of the Bible among his followers, Luther translated the Old and New Testaments into German.

Luther's assertions were revolutionary because they defied both church dogma and the authority of the Church of Rome. In 1520, Pope Leo X issued an edict excommunicating the outspoken reformer. Luther promptly burned the edict in the presence of his students at the University of Wittenberg. The following year, he was summoned to the city of Worms in order to appear before the Diet—the German parliamentary council. Charged with heresy, Luther stubbornly refused to back down, concluding, "I cannot and will not recant anything, for to act against our conscience is neither safe for us, nor open to us. On this I take my stand. I can do no other. God help me. Amen." Luther's confrontational temperament and down-to-earth style are captured in this excerpt from his *Address to the German Nobility*, a call for religious reform written shortly before the Diet of Worms and circulated widely in a printed edition.

READING 19.1 From Luther's *Address to the German Nobility* (1520)

It has been devised that the Pope, bishops, priests, and   1
monks are called the *spiritual estate*; princes, lords,
artificers, and peasants are the *temporal estate*. This is
an artful lie and hypocritical device, but let no one be
made afraid by it, and that for this reason: that all
Christians are truly of the spiritual estate, and there is no
difference among them, save of office alone. As St. Paul
says (1 Cor.: 12), we are all one body, though each
member does its own work, to serve the others. This is
because we have one baptism, one Gospel, one faith, and   10
are all Christians alike; for baptism, Gospel, and faith,
these alone make spiritual and Christian people.

As for the unction by a pope or a bishop, tonsure,
ordination, consecration, and clothes differing from those
of laymen—all this may make a hypocrite or an anointed
puppet, but never a Christian or a spiritual man. Thus we
are all consecrated as priests by baptism. . . .

And to put the matter even more plainly, if a little
company of pious Christian laymen were taken prisoners
and carried away to a desert, and had not among them a   20
priest consecrated by a bishop, and were there to agree to
elect one of them, born in wedlock or not, and were to
order him to baptise, to celebrate the mass, to absolve,
and to preach, this man would as truly be a priest, as if
all the bishops and all the popes had consecrated him.
That is why in cases of necessity every man can baptise
and absolve, which would not be possible if we were not
all priests. . . .

[Members of the Church of Rome] alone pretend to be
considered masters of the Scriptures; although they learn   30
nothing of them all their life. They assume authority, and
juggle before us with impudent words, saying that the
Pope cannot err in matters of faith, whether he be evil or
good, albeit they cannot prove it by a single letter. That is
why the canon law contains so many heretical and
unchristian, nay unnatural, laws. . . .

And though they say that this authority was given
to St. Peter when the keys were given to him, it is plain
enough that the keys were not given to St. Peter alone,

but to the whole community. Besides, the keys were not ordained for doctrine or authority, but for sin, to bind or loose; and what they claim besides this from the keys is mere invention. . . .

Only consider the matter. They must needs acknowledge that there are pious Christians among us that have the true faith, spirit, understanding, word, and mind of Christ: why then should we reject their word and understanding, and follow a pope who has neither understanding nor spirit? Surely this were to deny our whole faith and the Christian Church. . . .

Therefore when need requires, and the Pope is a cause of offence to Christendom, in these cases whoever can best do so, as a faithful member of the whole body, must do what he can to procure a true free council. This no one can do so well as the temporal authorities, especially since they are fellow-Christians, fellow-priests, sharing one spirit and one power in all things, . . . Would it not be most unnatural, if a fire were to break out in a city, and every one were to keep still and let it burn on and on, whatever might be burnt, simply because they had not the mayor's authority, or because the fire perchance broke out at the mayor's house? Is not every citizen bound in this case to rouse and call in the rest? How much more should this be done in the spiritual city of Christ, if a fire of offence breaks out, either at the Pope's government or wherever it may! The like happens if an enemy attacks a town. The first to rouse up the rest earns glory and thanks. Why then should not he earn glory that decries the coming of our enemies from hell and rouses and summons all Christians?

But as for their boasts of their authority, that no one must oppose it, this is idle talk. No one in Christendom has any authority to do harm, or to forbid others to prevent harm being done. There is no authority in the Church but for reformation. Therefore if the Pope wished to use his power to prevent the calling of a free council, so as to prevent the reformation of the Church, we must not respect him or his power; and if he should begin to excommunicate and fulminate, we must despise this as the doings of a madman, and, trusting in God, excommunicate and repel him as best we may.

Q Which of Luther's assertions would the Church of Rome have found heretical? Why?

Q Which aspects of this selection might be called anti-authoritarian? Which might be called democratic?

The Spread of Protestantism

Luther's criticism constituted an open revolt against the institution that for centuries had governed the lives of Western Christians. With the aid of the printing press, his "protestant" sermons and letters circulated throughout Europe. His defense of Christian conscience worked to justify protest against all forms of dominion. In 1524, under the banner of Christian liberty, German commoners instigated a series of violent uprisings against the oppressive landholding aristocracy. The result was full-scale war, the so-called "Peasant Revolts," that resulted in the bloody defeat of thousands of peasants. Although Luther condemned the violence and brutality of the Peasant Revolts, social unrest and ideological warfare had only just begun. His denunciation of the lower-class rebels brought many of the German princes to his side; and some used their new religious allegiance as an excuse to seize and usurp church properties and revenues within their own domains. As the floodgates of dissent opened wide, civil wars broke out between German princes who were faithful to Rome and those who called themselves Lutheran. The wars lasted for some twenty-five years, until, under the terms of the Peace of Augsburg in 1555, it was agreed that each German prince should have the right to choose the religion to be practiced within his own domain. Nevertheless, religious wars resumed in the late sixteenth century and devastated German lands for almost a century.

Calvin

All of Europe was affected by Luther's break with the Church. The Lutheran insistence that enlightened Christians could arrive at truth by way of Scripture led reformers everywhere to interpret the Bible for themselves. The result was the birth of many new Protestant sects, each based on its own interpretation of Scripture. In the independent city of Geneva, Switzerland, the French theologian John Calvin (1509–1564) set up a government in which elected officials, using the Bible as the supreme law, ruled the community. Calvin held that Christians were predestined from birth for either salvation or damnation, a circumstance that made good works irrelevant. The "Doctrine of Predestination" encouraged Calvinists to glorify God by living an upright life, one that required abstention from dancing, gambling, swearing, drunkenness, and from all forms of public display. For, although one's status was known only by God, Christians might manifest that they were among the "elect" by a show of moral rectitude. Finally, since Calvin taught that wealth was a sign of God's favor, Calvinists extolled the "work ethic" as consistent with the divine will.

The Anabaptists

In nearby Zürich, a radical wing of Protestantism emerged: the Anabaptists (given this name by those who opposed their practice of "rebaptizing" adult Christians) rejected all seven of the sacraments (including infant baptism) as sources of God's grace. Placing total emphasis on Christian conscience and the voluntary acceptance of Christ, the Anabaptists called for the abolition of the Mass and the complete separation of Church and state: holding individual responsibility and personal liberty as fundamental ideals, they were among the first Westerners to offer religious sanction for political disobedience. Many Anabaptist reformers met death at the hands of local governments—the men were burned at the stake and the women were usually drowned. English offshoots of the Anabaptists—the Baptists and the Quakers—would come to follow

Anabaptist precepts, including the rejection of religious ritual (and imagery) and a fundamentalist approach to Scripture.

The Anglican Church

In England, the Tudor monarch Henry VIII (1491–1547) broke with the Roman Catholic Church and established a church under his own leadership. Political expediency colored the king's motives: Henry was determined to leave England with a male heir, but when eighteen years of marriage to Catherine of Aragon produced only one heir (a daughter), he attempted to annul the marriage and take a new wife. The pope refused, prompting the king—formerly a staunch supporter of the Catholic Church—to break with Rome. In 1526, Henry VIII declared himself head of the Church in England. In 1536, with the support of Parliament, he closed all Christian monasteries and sold church lands, accumulating vast revenues for the royal treasury. His actions led to years of dispute and hostility between Roman Catholics and Anglicans (members of the new English Church). By the mid-sixteenth century, the consequences of Luther's protests were evident: the religious unity of Western Christendom was shattered forever. Social and political upheaval had become the order of the day.

Music and the Reformation

Since the Reformation clearly dominated the religious and social history of the sixteenth century, it also touched, directly or indirectly, all forms of artistic endeavor, including music. Luther himself was a student of music, an active performer, and an admirer of Josquin des Prez (see chapter 17). Emphasizing music as a source of religious instruction, he encouraged the writing of hymnals and reorganized the German Mass to include both congregational and professional singing. Luther held that all religious texts should be sung in German, so that the faithful might understand their message. The text, according to Luther, should be both comprehensible and appealing.

Luther's favorite music was the **chorale**, a congregational hymn that served to enhance the spirit of Protestant worship. Chorales, written in German, drew on Latin hymns and German folk tunes. They were characterized by monophonic clarity and simplicity, features that encouraged performance by untrained congregations. The most famous Lutheran chorale (the melody of which may not have originated with Luther) is "Ein' feste Burg ist unser Gott" ("A Mighty Fortress Is Our God")—a hymn that has been called "the anthem of the Reformation." Luther's chorales had a major influence on religious music for centuries. And although in the hands of later composers the chorale became a complex polyphonic vehicle for voices and instruments, at its inception it was performed with all voices singing the same words at the same time. It was thus an ideal medium for the communal expression of Protestant piety.

Other Protestant sects, such as the Anabaptists and the Calvinists, regarded music as a potentially dangerous distraction to the faithful. In many sixteenth-century churches, the organ was dismantled and sung portions of the service edited or deleted. Calvin, however, who encouraged devotional recitation of psalms in the home, revised church services to include the congregational singing of psalms in the vernacular.

Northern Renaissance Art

Jan van Eyck

Prior to the Reformation, in the cities of Northern Europe, a growing middle class joined princely rulers and the Church to encourage the arts. In addition to traditional religious subjects, middle-class patrons commissioned portraits that—like those painted by Italian Renaissance artists (see chapter 17)—recorded their physical appearance and brought attention to their earthly achievements. Fifteenth-century Northern artists, unlike their Italian counterparts, were relatively unfamiliar with Greco-Roman culture; many of them moved in the direction of detailed Realism, already evident in the manuscript illuminations of the Limbourg brothers (see Figure 15.13).

The pioneer of Northern Realism was the Flemish artist Jan van Ecyk (ca. 1380–1441). Jan, whom we met in chapter 17, was reputed to have perfected the art of oil painting (see Figure 17.12). His application of thin glazes of colored pigments bound with linseed oil achieved the impression of dense, atmospheric space, and simulated the naturalistic effects of light reflecting off the surfaces of objects. Such effects were almost impossible to achieve in fresco or tempera. While Jan lacked any knowledge of the system of linear perspective popularized in Florence, he achieved an extraordinary level of realism both in the miniatures he executed for religious manuscripts and in his panel paintings.

Jan's full-length double portrait of 1434 was the first painting in Western art that portrayed a secular couple in a domestic interior (Figure **19.5**). The painting has long been the subject of debate among scholars who have questioned its original purpose, as well as the identity of the sitters. Most likely, however, it is a visual document recording the marriage of Giovanni Nicolas Arnolfini (an Italian merchant who represented the Medici bank in Bruges), and his Flemish bride, Jeanne Cenami. Clearly, the couple are in the process of making a vow, witness the raised right hand of the richly dressed Arnolfini; their hands are joined, a gesture traditionally associated with engagement or marriage. Behind the couple, an inscription on the back wall of the chamber reads "*Johannes de Eyck fuit hic*" ("Jan van Eyck was here"); this testimonial is reiterated by the presence of two figures, probably the artist himself and a second observer, whose painted reflections are seen in the convex mirror below the inscription.

This Lutheran chorale inspired Johann Sebastian Bach's Cantata No. 80, an excerpt from which may be heard on CD Two, as Music Listening Selection 4.

Figure 19.5 JAN VAN EYCK, *Marriage of Giovanni Arnolfini and His Bride*, 1434. Tempera and oil on panel, 32¼ × 23½ in.

Jan's consummate mastery of minute, realistic details—from the ruffles on the young woman's headcovering to the whiskers of the monkey-faced dog—demonstrate the artist's determination to capture the immediacy of the physical world. This love of physical detail, typical of Northern painting, sets it apart from that of most Italian Renaissance art. Also typical of the Northern sensibility is the way in which these details "speak" to the greater meaning of the painting: the burning candle (traditionally carried to the marriage ceremony by the bride) suggests the all-seeing presence of Christ; the ripening fruit lying on and near the window sill both symbolizes fecundity and alludes to the union of the First Couple in the Garden of Eden; the small dog represents fidelity; the carved image on the chairback near the bed represents Saint Margaret, the patron saint of childbirth. The physical objects in this domestic interior, recreated in loving detail, suggest a world of material comfort and pleasure; but they also make symbolic reference to a higher, spiritual order. In this effort to reconcile the world of the spirit with that of the flesh, Jan anticipated the unique character of Northern Renaissance art.

Bosch

The generation of Flemish artists that followed Jan van Eyck produced one of the most enigmatic figures of the Northern Renaissance: Hieronymus Bosch (1460–1516). Little is known about Bosch's life, and the exact meaning of some of his works is much disputed. His career spanned the decades of the High Renaissance in Italy, but comparison of his paintings with those of Raphael or Michelangelo underscores the enormous difference between Italian Renaissance art and that of the European North: whereas Raphael and Michelangelo elevated the natural nobility of the individual, Bosch detailed the fallibility of humankind, its moral struggle, and its apocalyptic destiny. Bosch's *Death and the Miser* (Figure **19.6**), for instance, belongs to the tradition of the *memento mori* (discussed in chapter 12), which works to warn the beholder of the inevitability of death. The painting also shows the influence of popular fifteenth-century handbooks on the art of dying (the *ars moriendi*), designed to remind Christians that they must choose between sinful pleasures and the way of Christ. As Death looms on the threshold, the miser, unable to resist worldly temptations even in his last minutes of life, reaches for the bag of gold offered to him by a demon. In the foreground, Bosch depicts the miser storing gold in his money chest while clutching his rosary. Symbols of worldly power—a helmet, sword, and shield—allude to earthly follies. The depiction of such still-life objects to symbolize vanity, transience, or decay would become a genre in itself among seventeenth-century Flemish artists.

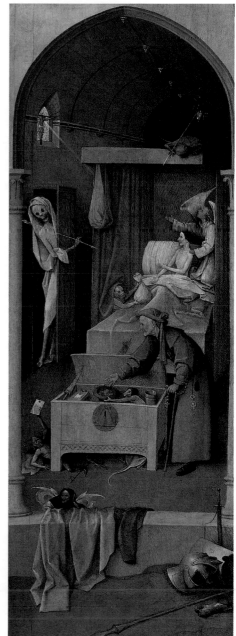

Figure 19.6 HIERONYMUS BOSCH, *Death and the Miser*, ca. 1485–1490. Oil on oak, 3 ft. ⅝in. × 12⅛ in.

Bosch's most famous work, *The Garden of Earthly Delights* (Figure **19.7**) was executed around 1510, the very time that Raphael was painting *The School of Athens*. In the central panel of the triptych, Bosch depicts a cosmic landscape in which youthful nudes cavort in a variety of erotic and playful pastimes. The terrain, filled with oversized flora, real and imagined animals and birds, and strangely shaped vessels, is similar to that of the panel on the left, where God is shown creating Adam and Eve. In the right wing of the triptych, Hell is pictured as a dark and sulfurous inferno where the damned are tormented by an assortment of terrifying creatures who inflict on sinners punishments appropriate to their sins—the greedy hoarder of gold (on the lower right) excretes coins into a pothole, while the nude nearby, fon-

dled by demons, is punished for the sin of lust. When the wings of the altarpiece are closed, one sees an image of God hovering above a huge transparent globe: the planet Earth in the process of creation.

The Garden of Earthly Delights has been described by some as an exposition on the decadent behavior of the descendants of Adam and Eve, but its distance from conventional religious iconography has made it the subject of endless scholarly interpretation. Bosch,

Figure 19.7 HIERONYMUS BOSCH, *The Creation of Eve: The Garden of Earthly Delights: Hell* (triptych), ca. 1510–1515. Oil on wood, 7 ft. 2⅝ in. × 6 ft. 4¾ in. Bosch probably painted this moralizing work for lay patrons. Many of its individual images would have been recognized as references to the Seven Deadly Sins, for instance: the bagpipe (a symbol of Lust) that sits on a disk crowning the Tree-Man (upper center) and the man who is forced to disgorge his food (symbolic of Gluttony) depicted beneath the enthroned frog (lower right).

a Roman Catholic, clearly drew his imagery from a variety of medieval and contemporary sources, including the Bible, popular proverbs, marginal grotesques in illuminated manuscripts, pilgrimage badges, and the popular pseudosciences of his time: astrology, the study of the influence of heavenly bodies on human affairs (the precursor of astronomy); and alchemy, the art of transmuting base metals into gold (the precursor of chemistry). The egg-shaped vessels, beakers, and transparent tubes that appear in all parts of the triptych were commonly used in alchemical transmutation. The process may have been familiar to Bosch as symbolic of creation and destruction, and, more specifically, as a metaphor for the biblical Creation and Fall.

Regardless of whether one interprets Bosch's "Garden" as a theater of perversity or a stage for innocent procreation, it is clear that the artist transformed standard Christian iconography to suit his imagination. Commissioned not by the Church, but by a private patron, he may have felt free to do so. The result is a moralizing commentary on the varieties of human folly afflicting creatures hopeful of Christian salvation.

Printmaking

The Protestant Reformation cast its long shadow upon the religious art of the North. Protestants rejected the traditional imagery of medieval piety, along with church relics

EXPLORING ISSUES

Humanism and Religious Fanaticism: The Persecution of Witches

The age of Christian humanism witnessed the rise of religious fanaticism, the most dramatic evidence of which is the witch hunts that infested Renaissance Europe and Reformation Germany. While belief in witches dates back to humankind's earliest societies, the practice of persecuting witches did not begin until the late fourteenth century. Based in the medieval practice of finding evidence of the supernatural in natural phenomena, and fueled by the popular Christian belief that the devil is actively engaged in human affairs, the first massive persecutions occurred at the end of the fifteenth century, reaching their peak approximately 100 years later. Among Northern European artists, witches and witchcraft became favorite subjects (Figure **19.8**).

In 1484, two German theologians published the *Malleus Maleficarum* (*The Witches' Hammer*), an encyclopedia that described the nature of witches, their collusion with the devil, and the ways in which they might be recognized and punished. Its authors reiterated the traditional claim that women—by nature more feeble than men—were dangerously susceptible to the devil's temptation. As a result, they became the primary victims of the mass hysteria that prevailed during the so-called "age of humanism." Women—particularly those who were single, old, or eccentric—constituted four-fifths of the roughly 70,000 witches put to death between the years 1400 and 1700. Females who served as midwives might be accused of causing infant deaths or deformities; others were condemned as witches at the onset of local drought or disease. One recent study suggests that witches were blamed for the sharp drops in temperature that devastated sixteenth-century crops and left many Europeans starving.

The persecution of witches may be seen as an instrument of post-Reformation religious oppression, or as the intensification of antifemale sentiment in an age when women had become more visible politically and commercially. Nevertheless, the witchcraft hysteria of the early Modern Era dramatizes the troubling gap between humanism and religious fanaticism.

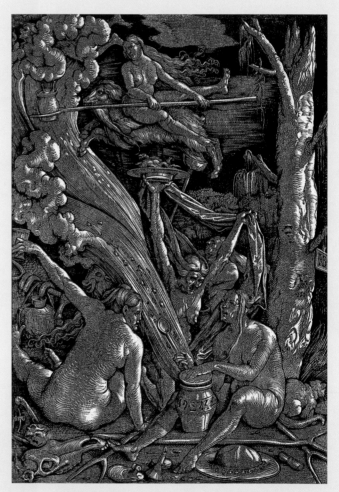

Figure 19.8 HANS BALDUNG ("Grien"), *Witches*, 1510. *Chiaroscuro* woodcut, 15⅞ × 10¼ in. Three witches, sitting under the branches of a dead tree, perform a black Mass. One lifts the chalice, while another mocks the Host by elevating the body of a dead toad. An airborne witch rides backward on a goat, a symbol of the devil.

and sacred images, which they associated with superstition and idolatry. Protestant iconoclasts stripped the stained glass from cathedral windows, shattered religious sculpture, whitewashed church frescoes, and destroyed altarpieces. At the same time, however, the voices of reform encouraged the proliferation of private devotional art, particularly that which illustrated biblical themes. In the production of portable, devotional images, the technology of printmaking played a major role. Just as movable type had facilitated the dissemination of the printed word, so the technology of the print made devotional subjects available more cheaply and in greater numbers than ever before.

The two new printmaking processes of the fifteenth century were **woodcut**, the technique of cutting away all parts of a design on a wood surface except those that will be inked and transferred to paper (Figure **19.9**), and **engraving** (Figure **19.10**), the process by which lines are incised on a metal (usually copper) plate that is inked and run through a printing press. Books with printed illustrations became cheap alternatives to the hand-illuminated manuscripts that were prohibitively expensive to all but wealthy patrons.

Dürer

The unassailed leader in Northern Renaissance printmaking and one of the finest graphic artists of all time was Albrecht Dürer of Nuremberg (1471–1528). Dürer earned international fame for his woodcuts and metal engravings. His mastery of the laws of linear perspective and human anatomy and his investigations into Classical principles of proportions (enhanced by two trips to Italy) equaled those of the best Italian Renaissance artist–scientists. In the genre of portraiture, Dürer was the match of Raphael but, unlike Raphael, he recorded the features of his sitters with little idealization. His portrait engraving of Erasmus (see Figure 19.3) captures the concentrated intelligence of the Prince of Humanists.

Figure 19.9 Woodcut. A relief printing process created by lines cut into the plank surface of wood. The raised portions of the block are inked and transferred by pressure to the paper by hand or with a printing press.

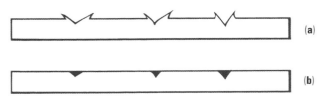

Figure 19.10 Engraving. An intaglio method of printing. The cutting tool, a *burin* or *graver*, is used to cut lines in the surface of metal plates. (**a**) A cross section of an engraved plate showing burrs (ridges) produced by scratching a burin into the surface of a metal plate; (**b**) the burrs are removed and ink is wiped over the surface and forced into the scratches. The plate is then wiped clean, leaving ink deposits in the scratches; the ink is forced from the plate onto paper under pressure in a special press.

Figure 19.11 ALBRECHT DÜRER, *The Four Horsemen of the Apocalypse*, ca. 1496. Woodcut, 15½ × 11 in.

Dürer brought to the art of his day a desire to convey the spiritual message of Scripture. His series of woodcuts illustrating the last book of the New Testament, The Revelation According to Saint John (also called the "Apocalypse"), reveals the extent to which he achieved his purpose. *The Four Horsemen of the Apocalypse*—one of fifteen woodcuts in the series—brings to life the terrifying events described in Revelation 6.1–8 (Figure **19.11**). Amidst billowing clouds, Death (in the foreground), Famine (carrying a pair of scales), War (brandishing a sword), and Pestilence (drawing his bow) sweep down upon humankind; their victims fall beneath the horses' hooves, or, as with the bishop in the lower left, are devoured by infernal monsters. Dürer's image seems a grim prophecy of the coming age, in which five million people would die in religious wars.

Dürer was a humanist in his own right and a great admirer of both the moderate Erasmus and the zealous Luther. In one of his most memorable engravings, *Knight, Death, and the Devil*, he depicted the Christian soul in the allegorical guise of a medieval knight (see Figure 19.1), a figure made famous in a treatise by Erasmus entitled *Handbook for the Militant Christian* (1504). The knight, the

Figure 19.12 ALBRECHT DÜRER, *Wire Drawing Mill*, undated. Watercolor, 11¼ × 16¾ in.

medieval symbol of fortitude and courage, advances against a dark and brooding landscape. Accompanied by his loyal dog, he marches forward, ignoring his fearsome companions: Death, who rides a pale horse and carries an hourglass, and the devil, a shaggy, cross-eyed, and horned demon. Here is the visual counterpart for Erasmus' message that the Christian must hold to the path of virtue, and in spite of "all of those spooks and phantoms" that come upon him, he must "look not behind." The knight's dignified bearing (probably inspired by heroic equestrian statues Dürer had seen in Italy) contrasts sharply with the bestial and cankerous features of his forbidding escorts. In the tradition of Jan van Eyck, but with a precision facilitated by the new medium of metal engraving, Dürer records every leaf and pebble, hair and wrinkle; and yet the final effect is not a mere piling up of minutiae but, like nature itself, an astonishing amalgam of organically related elements.

In addition to his numerous woodcuts and engravings, Dürer produced hundreds of paintings: portraits and large-scale religious subjects. His interest in the natural world inspired the first landscapes in Western art (Figure **19.12**). These detailed panoramic views of the countryside, executed in watercolor during his frequent travels to Italy and elsewhere, were independent works, not mere studies for larger, more formal subjects. To such landscapes, as well as

to his meticulously detailed renderings of plants, animals, and birds, Dürer brought the eye of a scientific naturalist and a spirit of curiosity not unlike that of his Italian contemporary, Leonardo da Vinci.

Grünewald

Dürer's German contemporary Matthias Gothardt Neithardt, better known as "Grünewald" (1460–1428) did not share his Classically inspired aesthetic ideals, nor his quest for realistic representation. The few paintings and drawings left by Grünewald (as compared with the hundreds of works left by Dürer) do not tell us whether the artist was Catholic or Protestant. In their spiritual intensity and emotional subjectivity, however, they are among the most striking devotional works of the Northern Renaissance.

Grünewald's landmark work, the Isenheim Altarpiece, was designed to provide solace to the victims of disease and especially plague at the Hospital of Saint Anthony in Isenheim, near Colmar, France (Figure **19.13**). Like the *Imitatio Christi*, which taught Christians to seek identification with Jesus, this multipaneled altarpiece reminded its beholders of their kinship with the suffering Jesus, depicted in the central panel. Following the tradition of the devotional German *Pietà* (see Figure 15.10), Grünewald

Figure 19.13 MATTHIAS GRÜNEWALD, Isenheim Altarpiece, ca. 1510–1515. Oil on panel, central panel 8 ft. × 10 ft. 1 in. The opened wings of the altarpiece show Saint Sebastian (left) and Saint Anthony (right), both protectors against disease and plague. Those afflicted with disease (including leprosy, syphilis, and poisoning caused by ergot, a cereal fungus), were able to contemplate the altarpiece daily in the hospital chapel.

made use of expressive exaggeration and painfully precise detail: the agonized body of Jesus is lengthened to emphasize its weight as it hangs from the bowed cross, the flesh putrefies with clotted blood and angry thorns, the fingers convulse and curl, while the feet—broken and bruised—contort in a spasm of pain. Grünewald reinforces the mood of lamentation by placing the scene in a darkened landscape. He exaggerates the gestures of the attending figures, including that of John the Baptist, whose oversized finger points to the prophetic Latin inscription that explains his mystical presence: "He must increase and I must decrease" (John 3:30).

Cranach and Holbein

The German cities of the sixteenth century produced some of the finest draftsmen in the history of Western art. Dürer's contemporary, Lucas Cranach the Elder (1472–1553), was a highly acclaimed court painter at Wittenberg and, like Dürer, a convert to the Protestant reform. In 1522 he produced the woodcuts for the first German edition of the New Testament. Although he also worked for Catholic patrons, he painted and engraved numerous portraits of Protestant leaders, the most notable of whom was his friend Martin Luther, whose likeness he recreated several times. In the portrait illustrated in Figure 19.4, Cranach exercised his skills as a master draftsman, capturing both the authoritative silhouette and the confident demeanor of the famous reformer.

Hans Holbein the Younger (1497–1543), celebrated as the greatest of the German portraitists, was born in Augsburg, but spent much of his life in Switzerland, France, and England. His woodcut series of the Dance of Death (see Figure 15.5) brought him renown as a draftsman and printmaker. With a letter of introduction from his friend Erasmus, Holbein traveled to England to paint the family of Sir Thomas More (see Figure 19.16)—Western Europe's first domestic group portrait (it survives only in drawings and copies). On a later trip to England, Holbein became the favorite of King Henry VIII, whose likeness he captured along with portraits of Henry's current and prospective wives. In common with Dürer and Cranach, Holbein was a master of line. All three artists manifested the integration of brilliant draftsmanship and precise, realistic detail that characterizes the art of the Northern

Renaissance. Holbein, however, was unique in his minimal use of line to evoke a penetrating sense of the sitter's personality. So lifelike are some of Holbein's portraits that modern scholars have suggested he made use of technical aids, such as the *camera lucida*, in their preparation (see chapter 17, Exploring Issues).

Brueghel

The career of the last great sixteenth-century Flemish painter, Pieter Brueghel the Elder (1525–1569), followed the careers of most other Northern Renaissance masters by a generation. Like Dürer, Brueghel had traveled to Italy and absorbed its Classical culture; his style, however, would remain relatively independent of Italian influence. Closer in temperament to Bosch, he was deeply concerned with human folly, especially as it was manifested in the everyday life of his Flemish neighbors. Among his early works were crowded panoramas depicting themes of human pride and religious strife. Brueghel's *Triumph of Death* may be read as an indictment of the brutal wars that plagued sixteenth-century Europe (Figure **19.14**). In a cosmic landscape that resembles the setting of a Last Judgment or a Boschlike underworld, Brueghel depicts throngs of skeletons relentlessly slaughtering all ranks of men and women. The armies of the dead are without mercy. In the left foreground, a cardinal collapses in the arms of a skeleton; in the left corner,

an emperor relinquishes his hoards of gold; on the right, death interrupts the pleasure of gamblers and lovers. Some of the living are crushed beneath the wheels of a death cart, others are hanged from scaffolds or subjected to torture. Brueghel's apocalyptic vision transforms the late medieval Dance of Death into a universal holocaust.

Many of Brueghel's best-known works were inspired by biblical parables or local proverbs, popular expressions of universal truths concerning human behavior. In his drawings, engravings, and paintings, Brueghel rendered these as visual narratives set in the Flemish countryside. His treatment of the details of rustic life, which earned him the title "Peasant Brueghel," and his landscapes illustrating the labors appropriate to each season, were the culmination of a tradition begun in the innovative miniatures of the Limbourg brothers (see Figure 15.13). However, Brueghel's **genre paintings** (representations of the everyday life of ordinary folk) were not small-scale illustrations, but monumental (and sometimes allegorical) transcriptions of rural activities. *The Wedding Dance* (Figure **19.15**) depicts peasant revelry in a country setting whose earthiness is reinforced by rich tones of russet, tan, and muddy green. At the very top of the panel the bride and groom sit before an improvised dais, while the villagers cavort to the music of the bagpipe (right foreground). Although Brueghel's figures are clumsy and often ill-proportioned,

Figure 19.14 PIETER BRUEGHEL THE ELDER, *Triumph of Death*, ca. 1562–1564. Oil on panel, 3 ft. 10 in. × 5 ft. 3¾ in.

Figure 19.15 PIETER BRUEGHEL THE ELDER, *The Wedding Dance*, 1566. Oil on panel, 3 ft. 11 in. × 5 ft. 2 in.

they share an ennobling vitality. In Brueghel's art, as in that of other Northern Renaissance painters, we discover an unvarnished perception of human beings in mundane and unheroic circumstances—a sharp contrast to the idealized conception of humankind found in the art of Renaissance Italy.

Sixteenth-Century Literature

Erasmus: *The Praise of Folly*

European literature of the sixteenth century was marked by heightened individualism and a progressive inclination to clear away the last remnants of medieval orthodoxy. It was, in many ways, a literature of protest and reform, and one whose dominant themes reflect the tension between medieval and modern ideas. European writers were especially concerned with the discrepancies between the noble ideals of Classical humanism and the ignoble realities of human behavior. Religious rivalries and the horrors of war, witch hunts, and religious persecution all seemed to contradict the optimistic view that the Renaissance had inaugurated a more enlightened phase of human self-consciousness. Satire, a literary genre that conveys the contradictions between real and ideal situations, was

especially popular during the sixteenth century. By means of satiric irony, Northern Renaissance writers held up prevailing abuses to ridicule, thus implying the need for reform.

The learned treatises and letters of Erasmus won him the respect of scholars throughout Europe; but his single most popular work was *The Praise of Folly*, a satiric oration attacking a wide variety of human foibles, including greed, intellectual pomposity, and pride. *The Praise of Folly* went through more than two dozen editions in Erasmus' lifetime, and influenced other humanists, including his lifelong

Science and Technology

1540	the Swiss physician Paracelsus (Philippus van Hohenheim) pioneers the use of chemistry for medical purposes
1543	Copernicus (Polish) publishes *On the Revolution of the Heavenly Spheres*, announcing his heliocentric theory
1553	Michael Servetus (Spanish) describes the pulmonary circulation of the blood

friend and colleague Thomas More, to whom it was dedicated (in Latin, *moria* means "folly").

A short excerpt from *The Praise of Folly* offers some idea of Erasmus' keen wit as applied to a typical Northern Renaissance theme: the vast gulf between human fallibility and human perfectibility. The reading opens with the image of the world as a stage, a favorite metaphor of sixteenth-century painters and poets—not the least of whom was William Shakespeare. Dame Folly, the allegorical figure who is the speaker in the piece, compares life to a comedy in which the players assume various roles: in the course of the drama (she observes), one may come to play the parts of both servant and king. She then describes each of a number of roles (or disciplines), such as medicine, law, and so on, in terms of its affinity with folly. Erasmus' most searing words were reserved for theologians and church dignitaries, but his insights expose more generally (and timelessly) the frailties of all human beings.

READING 19.2 From Erasmus' *The Praise of Folly* (1511)

Now what else is the whole life of mortals but a sort of   **1**
comedy, in which the various actors, disguised by various
costumes and masks, walk on and play each one his
part, until the manager waves them off the stage?
Moreover, this manager frequently bids the same actor
go back in a different costume, so that he who has but
lately played the king in scarlet now acts the flunkey in
patched clothes. Thus all things are presented by
shadows; yet this play is put on in no other way. . . .

[The disciplines] that approach nearest to common   **10**
sense, that is, to folly, are held in highest esteem.
Theologians are starved, naturalists find cold comfort,
astrologers are mocked, and logicians are slighted. . . .
Within the profession of medicine, furthermore, so far as
any member is eminently unlearned, impudent, or
careless, he is valued the more, even in the chambers of
belted earls. For medicine, especially as now practiced
by many, is but a subdivision of the art of flattery, no
less truly than is rhetoric. Lawyers have the next place
after doctors, and I do not know but that they should   **20**
have first place; with great unanimity the philosophers—
not that I would say such a thing myself—are wont to
ridicule the law as an ass. Yet great matters and little
matters alike are settled by the arbitrament of these
asses. They gather goodly freeholds with broad acres,
while the theologian, after poring over chestfuls of the
great corpus of divinity, gnaws on bitter beans, at the
same time manfully waging war against lice and fleas. As
those arts are more successful which have the greatest
affinity with folly, so those people are by far the happiest   **30**
who enjoy the privilege of avoiding all contact with the
learned disciplines, and who follow nature as their only
guide, since she is in no respect wanting, except as a
mortal wishes to transgress the limits set for his status.
Nature hates counterfeits; and that which is innocent of
art gets along far the more prosperously.

What need we say about practitioners in the arts? Self-
love is the hallmark of them all. You will find that they
would sooner give up their paternal acres than any piece
of their poor talents. Take particularly actors, singers,   **40**
orators, and poets; the more unskilled one of them is,
the more insolent he will be in his self-satisfaction, the
more he will blow himself up. . . . Thus the worst art
pleases the most people, for the simple reason that the
larger part of mankind, as I said before, is subject to
folly. If, therefore, the less skilled man is more pleasing
both in his own eyes and in the wondering gaze of the
many, what reason is there that he should prefer sound
discipline and true skill? In the first place, these will
cost him a great outlay; in the second place, they will   **50**
make him more affected and meticulous; and finally,
they will please far fewer of his audience. . . .

And now I see that it is not only in individual men that
nature has implanted self-love. She implants a kind of it as
a common possession in the various races, and even
cities. By this token the English claim, besides a few other
things, good looks, music, and the best eating as their
special properties. The Scots flatter themselves on the
score of high birth and royal blood, not to mention their
dialectical skill. Frenchmen have taken all politeness for   **60**
their province; though the Parisians, brushing all others
aside, also award themselves the prize for knowledge of
theology. The Italians usurp *belles lettres* and eloquence;
and they all flatter themselves upon the fact that they
alone, of all mortal men, are not barbarians. In this
particular point of happiness the Romans stand highest,
still dreaming pleasantly of ancient Rome. The Venetians
are blessed with a belief in their own nobility. The Greeks,
as well as being the founders of the learned disciplines,
vaunt themselves upon their titles to the famous heroes of   **70**
old. The Turks, and that whole rabble of the truly
barbarous, claim praise for their religion, laughing at
Christians as superstitious. . . .

[Next come] the scientists, reverenced for their beards
and the fur on their gowns, who teach that they alone are
wise while the rest of mortal men flit about as shadows.
How pleasantly they dote, indeed, while they construct
their numberless worlds, and measure the sun, moon,
stars, and spheres as with thumb and line. They assign
causes for lightning, winds, eclipses, and other   **80**
inexplicable things, never hesitating a whit, as if they
were privy to the secrets of nature, artificer of things, or
as if they visited us fresh from the council of the gods. Yet
all the while nature is laughing grandly at them and their
conjectures. For to prove that they have good intelligence
of nothing, this is a sufficient argument: they can never
explain why they disagree with each other on every
subject. Thus knowing nothing in general, they profess to
know all things in particular; though they are ignorant even
of themselves, and on occasion do not see the ditch or the   **90**
stone lying across their path, because many of them are
blear-eyed or absent-minded; yet they proclaim that they
perceive ideas, universals, forms without matter. . . .

Perhaps it were better to pass over the theologians in silence, [for] they may attack me with six hundred arguments, in squadrons, and drive me to make a recantation; which if I refuse, they will straightway proclaim me an heretic. By this thunderbolt they are wont to terrify any toward whom they are ill-disposed.

They are happy in their self-love, and as if they already inhabited the third heaven they look down from a height on all other mortal men as on creatures that crawl on the ground, and they come near to pitying them. They are protected by a wall of scholastic definitions, arguments, corollaries, implicit and explicit propositions; . . . they explain as pleases them the most arcane matters, such as by what method the world was founded and set in order, through what conduits original sin has been passed down along the generations, by what means, in what measure, and how long the perfect Christ was in the Virgin's womb, and how accidents subsist in the Eucharist without their subject.

But those are hackneyed. Here are questions worthy of the great and (as some call them) illuminated theologians, questions to make them prick up their ears—if ever they chance upon them. Whether divine generation took place at a particular time? Whether there are several sonships in Christ? Whether this is a possible proposition: God the Father hates the Son? Whether God could have taken upon Himself the likeness of a woman? Or of a devil? Of an ass? Of a gourd? Of a piece of flint? Then how would that gourd have preached, performed miracles, or been crucified?. . . .

Coming nearest to these in felicity are the men who generally call themselves "the religious" and "monks"—utterly false names both, since most of them keep as far away as they can from religion and no people are more in evidence in every sort of place. . . , For one thing, they reckon it the highest degree of piety to have no contact with literature, and hence they see to it that they do not know how to read. For another, when with asinine voices they bray out in church those psalms they have learned, by rote rather than by heart, they are convinced that they are anointing God's ears with the blandest of oil. Some of them make a good profit from their dirtiness and mendicancy, collecting their food from door to door with importunate bellowing; nay, there is not an inn, public conveyance, or ship where they do not intrude, to the great disadvantage of the other common beggars. Yet according to their account, by their very dirtiness, ignorance, these delightful fellows are representing to us the lives of the apostles.

Q **What disciplines does Dame Folly single out as having "the greatest affinity with folly"?**

Q **How does Erasmus attack the religious community of his day?**

Figure 19.16 HANS HOLBEIN THE YOUNGER, *Sir Thomas More*, ca. 1530. Oil on panel, 29½ × 23¼ in. In his attention to minute detail and textural contrast—fur collar, velvet sleeves, gold chain, and Tudor rose pendant—Holbein refined the tradition of realistic portraiture initiated by Jan van Eyck (compare Jan's self-portrait, Figure 17.12).

More's *Utopia*

In England Erasmus' friend, the scholar and statesman Sir Thomas More (1478–1535), served as chancellor to King Henry VIII at the time of Henry's break with the Catholic Church (Figure **19.16**). Like Erasmus, More was a Christian humanist and a man of conscience. He denounced the evils of acquisitive capitalism and religious fanaticism and championed religious tolerance and Christian charity. Unwilling to compromise his conviction as a Roman Catholic, he opposed the actions of the king and was executed for treason in 1535.

In 1516, More completed his classic political satire on European statecraft and society, a work entitled *Utopia* (the Greek word meaning both "no place" and "a good place"). More's *Utopia*, the first literary description of an ideal state since Plato's *Republic*, was inspired, in part, by accounts of wondrous lands reported by sailors returning from the "New World" across the Atlantic (see chapter 18). More's fictional island ("discovered" by a fictional explorer–narrator) is a socialistic state in which goods and property are shared, war and personal vanities are held in contempt, learning is available to all citizens (except slaves), and freedom of religion is absolute. Work, while essential to moral and communal well-being, is limited to six hours a day. In this ideal commonwealth, natural reason, benevolence, and scorn for material wealth ensure social harmony.

More's society differs from Plato's in that More gives to each individual, rather than to society's guardians, full responsibility for the establishment of social justice. Written as both a social critique and a satire, More draws the implicit contrast between his own corrupt Christian society and that of his ideal community. Although his Utopians are not Christians, they are guided by Christian principles of morality and charity. They have little use, for instance, for precious metals, jewels, and the "trifles" that drive men to war.

READING 19.3 From More's *Utopia* (1516)

[As] to their manner of living in society, the oldest man of every family . . . is its governor. Wives serve their husbands, and children their parents, and always the younger serves the elder. Every city is divided into four equal parts, and in the middle of each there is a marketplace: what is brought thither, and manufactured by the several families, is carried from thence to houses appointed for that purpose, in which all things of a sort are laid by themselves; and there every father goes and takes whatsoever he or his family stand in need of, **10** without either paying for it or leaving anything in exchange. There is no reason for giving a denial to any person, since there is such plenty of everything among them; and there is no danger of a man's asking for more than he needs; they have no inducements to do this, since they are sure that they shall always be supplied. It is the fear of want that makes any of the whole race of animals either greedy or ravenous; but besides fear, there is in man a pride that makes him fancy it a particular glory to excel others in pomp and excess. But by the **20** laws of the Utopians, there is no room for this. . . .

[Since the Utopians] have no use for money among themselves, but keep it as a provision against events which seldom happen, and between which there are generally long intervening intervals, they value it no farther than it deserves, that is, in proportion to its use. So that it is plain they must prefer iron either to gold or silver; for men can no more live without iron than without fire or water, but nature has marked out no use for the other metals so essential and not easily to be **30** dispensed with. The folly of men has enhanced the value of gold and silver, because of their scarcity. Whereas, on the contrary, it is their opinion that nature, as an indulgent parent, has freely given us all the best things in great abundance, such as water and earth, but has laid up and hid from us the things that are vain and useless. . . .

. . . They eat and drink out of vessels of earth, or glass, which make an agreeable appearance though formed of brittle materials: while they make their chamber-pots **40**

and close-stools[1] of gold and silver, and that not only in their public halls, but in their private houses: of the same metals they likewise make chains and fetters for their slaves; to some [slaves], as a badge of infamy, they hang an ear-ring of gold, and [they] make others wear a chain or coronet of the same metal; and thus they take care, by all possible means, to render gold and silver of no esteem. And from hence it is that while other nations part with their gold and silver as unwillingly as if one tore out their bowels, those of Utopia would look on **50** their giving in all they possess of those [metals] but as the parting with a trifle, or as we would esteem the loss of a penny. They find pearls on their coast, and diamonds and carbuncles on their rocks; they do not look after them, but, if they find them by chance, they polish them, and with them they adorn their children, who are delighted with them, and glory in them during their childhood; but when they grow to years, and see that none but children use such baubles, they of their own accord, without being bid by their parents, lay **60** them aside; and would be as much ashamed to use them afterward as children among us, when they come to years, are of their puppets and other toys. . . .

They detest war as a very brutal thing; and which, to the reproach of human nature, is more practiced by men than by any sort of beasts. They, in opposition to the sentiments of almost all other nations, think that there is nothing more inglorious than that glory that is gained by war. And therefore though they accustom themselves daily to military exercises and the discipline of war—in which not **70** only their men but their women likewise are trained up, that in cases of necessity they may not be quite useless— yet they do not rashly engage in war, unless it be either to defend themselves, or their friends, from any unjust aggressors; or out of good-nature or in compassion assist an oppressed nation in shaking off the yoke of tyranny. They indeed help their friends, not only in defensive, but also in offensive wars; but they never do that unless they had been consulted before the breach was made, and being satisfied with the grounds on which **80** they went, they had found that all demands of reparation were rejected, so that a war was unavoidable. . . .

If they agree to a truce, they observe it so religiously that no provocations will make them break it. They never lay their enemies' country waste nor burn their corn, and even in their marches they take all possible care that neither horse nor foot may tread it down, for they do not know but that they may have for it themselves. They hurt no man whom they find disarmed, unless he is a spy. When a town is surrendered to them, they take it into their protection; **90** and when they carry a place by storm, they never plunder it, but put those only to the sword that opposed the rendering of it up, and make the rest of the garrison slaves, but for the other inhabitants, they do them no hurt; and if

[1] A covered chamber pot set in a stool.

any of them had advised a surrender, they give them good rewards out of the estates of those that they condemn, and distribute the rest among their auxiliary troops, but they themselves take no share of the spoil.

Q What sort of social organization does More set forth in his Utopia?

Q How would you describe More's views on precious metals and on war?

Cervantes: *Don Quixote*

While Erasmus and More wrote primarily in Latin—*Utopia* was not translated into English until 1551—other European writers preferred the vernacular. The language of everyday speech was favored for such literary genres as the medieval romance (see chapter 11) and the more realistic and satiric **picaresque novel**, which emerged as a popular form of literary entertainment in sixteenth-century Spain. Narrated by the hero, the picaresque novel recounted the comic misadventures of a *picaro* ("rogue"). Its structure—a series of episodes converging on a single theme—anticipated the emergence of the novel in Western literature.

As a genre, the novel, a large-scale prose narrative, had its origins in eleventh-century Japan, with Murasaki Shikibu's *Tale of Genji*. However, in the West, the first such work in this genre was *Don Quixote*, written in two volumes (over a decade apart) by Miguel de Cervantes (1547–1616). *Don Quixote* resembles the picaresque novel in its episodic structure and in its satiric treatment of Spanish society, but the psychological complexity of its hero and the profundity of its underlying theme—the conflict between reality and the ideal—set it apart from the picaresque.

The fifty-year-old Alonso Quixado, who assumes the title of a nobleman, Don Quixote de la Mancha, sets out to roam the world as a knight errant, defending the ideals glorified in medieval books of chivalry. (Cervantes himself had fought in the last of the crusades against the Muslim Turks.) Seeking to bring honor to himself and his imaginary ladylove, he pursues a long series of adventures in which he repeatedly misperceives the ordinary for the sublime: he attacks a flock of sheep as a hostile army, advances on a group of windmills that he mistakes for giants. (The expression "tilting at windmills" has come to represent the futility of self-deluding action.) The hero's eternal optimism is measured against the practical realism of his potbellied sidekick, Sancho Panza, who tries to expose the Don's illusions of grandeur. In the end, the don laments in self-reflection that the world "is nothing but schemes and plots."

Cervantes' masterpiece, *Don Quixote* attacks outworn medieval values, especially as they reflect sixteenth-century Spanish society. In Spain, on the eve of the early Modern Era, New World wealth was transforming the relationship between peasants and aristocrats; the tribunal of Catholic orthodoxy known as the Inquisition worked to expel the large populations of Jews and Muslims that had powerfully influenced earlier Iberian culture. While the novel emerged from this context of transformation and (often misguided) reform, it left a timeless, universal message, captured in the English word "quixotic," which means "foolishly idealistic" or "impractical."

READING 19.4 From Cervantes' *Don Quixote* (1605–1615)

The great success won by our brave Don Quijote[1] in his dreadful, unimaginable encounter with two windmills, plus other honorable events well worth remembering

Just then, they came upon thirty or forty windmills, which (as it happens) stand in the fields of Montiel, and as soon as Don Quijote saw them he said to his squire:

"Destiny guides our fortunes more favorably than we could have expected. Look there, Sancho Panza, my friend, and see those thirty or so wild giants, with whom I intend to do battle and to kill each and all of them, so with their stolen booty we can begin to enrich ourselves. This is noble, righteous warfare, for it is wonderfully useful to God to have such an evil race wiped from the **10** face of the earth."

"What giants?" asked Sancho Panza.

"The ones you can see over there," answered his master, "with the huge arms, some of which are very nearly two leagues long."

"Now look, your grace," said Sancho, "what you see over there aren't giants, but windmills, and what seem to be arms are just their sails, that go around in the wind and turn the millstone."

"Obviously," replied Don Quijote, "you don't know **20** much about adventures. Those are giants—and if you're frightened, take yourself away from here and say your prayers, while I go charging into savage and unequal combat with them."

Saying which, he spurred his horse, Rocinante, paying no attention to the shouts of Sancho Panza, his squire, warning him that without any question it was windmills and not giants he was going to attack. So utterly convinced was he they were giants, indeed, that he neither heard Sancho's cries nor noticed, close as he **30** was, what they really were, but charged on, crying:

"Flee not, oh cowards and dastardly creatures, for he who attacks you is a knight alone and unaccompanied."

Just then the wind blew up a bit, and the great sails began to stir, which Don Quijote saw and cried out:

"Even should you shake more arms than the giant Briareus himself, you'll still have to deal with me."

As he said this, he entrusted himself with all his heart to his lady Dulcinea, imploring her to help and sustain him at such a critical moment, and then, with his shield **40** held high and his spear braced in its socket, and Rocinante at a full gallop, he charged directly at the first windmill he came to, just as a sudden swift gust of wind sent its sail swinging hard around, smashing the spear to bits and sweeping up the knight and his horse, tumbling

[1] A variant spelling of Quixote is Quijote, as in this excerpt.

them all battered and bruised to the ground. Sancho Panza came rushing to his aid, as fast as his donkey could run, but when he got to his master found him unable to move, such a blow had he been given by the falling horse.   50

"God help me!" said Sancho. "Didn't I tell your grace to be careful what you did, that these were just windmills, and anyone who could ignore that had to have windmills in his head?"

"Silence, Sancho, my friend," answered Don Quijote. "Even more than other things, war is subject to perpetual change. What's more, I think the truth is that the same Frestón the magician, who stole away my room and my books, transformed these giants into windmills, in order to deprive me of the glory of vanquishing them, so bitter   60 is his hatred of me. But in the end, his evil tricks will have little power against my good sword."

"God's will be done," answered Sancho Panza.

Then, helping his master to his feet, he got him back up on Rocinante, whose shoulder was half dislocated. After which, discussing the adventure they'd just experienced, they followed the road toward Lápice Pass, for there, said Don Quijote, they couldn't fail to find adventures of all kinds, it being a well-traveled highway. But having lost his lance, he went along very sorrowfully,   70 as he admitted to his squire, saying:

"I remember having read that a certain Spanish knight named Diego Pérez de Vargas, having lost his sword while fighting in a lost cause, pulled a thick bough, or a stem, off an oak tree, and did such things with it, that day, clubbing down so many Moors that ever afterwards they nicknamed him Machuca [Clubber], and indeed from that day on he and all his descendants bore the name Vargas y Machuca. I tell you this because, the first oak tree I come to, I plan to pull off a branch like that,   80 one every bit as good as the huge stick I can see in my mind, and I propose to perform such deeds with it that you'll be thinking yourself blessed, having the opportunity to witness them, and being a living witness to events that might otherwise be unbelievable."

"It's in God's hands," said Sancho. "I believe everything is exactly the way your grace says it is. But maybe you could sit a little straighter, because you seem to be leaning to one side, which must be because of the great fall you took."   90

"True," answered Don Quijote, "and if I don't say anything about the pain it's because knights errant are never supposed to complain about a wound, even if their guts are leaking through it."

"If that's how it's supposed to be," replied Sancho, "I've got nothing to say. But Lord knows I'd rather your grace told me, any time something hurts you. Me, I've got to groan, even if it's the smallest little pain, unless that rule about knights errant not complaining includes squires, too."   100

Don Quijote couldn't help laughing at his squire's simplicity, and cheerfully assured him he could certainly complain any time he felt like it, voluntarily or

involuntarily, since in all his reading about knighthood and chivalry he'd never once come across anything to the contrary. Sancho said he thought it was dinner-time. His master replied that, for the moment, he himself had no need of food, but Sancho should eat whenever he wanted to. Granted this permission, Sancho made himself as comfortable as he could while jogging along on his   110 donkey and, taking out of his saddlebags what he had put in them, began eating as he rode, falling back a good bit behind his master, and from time to time tilting up his wineskin with a pleasure so intense that the fanciest barman in Málaga might have envied him. And as he rode along like this, gulping quietly away, none of the promises his master had made were on his mind, nor did he feel in the least troubled or afflicted—in fact, he was thoroughly relaxed about this adventure-hunting business, no matter how dangerous it was supposed   120 to be.

In the end, they spent that night sleeping in a wood, and Don Quijote pulled a dry branch from one of the trees, to serve him, more or less, as a lance, fitting onto it the spearhead he'd taken off the broken one. Nor did Don Quijote sleep, that whole night long, meditating on his lady Dulcinea—in order to fulfill what he'd read in his books, namely, that knights always spent long nights out in the woods and other uninhabited places, not sleeping, but happily mulling over memories of their   130 ladies. Which wasn't the case for Sancho Panza: with his stomach full, and not just with chicory water, his dreams swept him away, nor would he have bothered waking up, for all the sunlight shining full on his face, or the birds singing—brightly, loudly greeting the coming of the new day—if his master hadn't called to him. He got up and, patting his wineskin, found it a lot flatter than it had been the night before, which grieved his heart, since it didn't look as if they'd be making up the shortage any time soon. Don Quijote had no interest in breakfast,   140 since, as we have said, he had been sustaining himself with delightful memories. They returned to the road leading to Lápice Pass, which they could see by about three that afternoon.

"Here," said Don Quijote as soon as he saw it, "here, brother Sancho Panza, we can get our hands up to the elbows in adventures. But let me warn you: even if you see me experiencing the greatest dangers in the world, never draw your sword to defend me, unless of course you see that those who insult me are mere rabble, people   150 of low birth, in which case you may be permitted to help me. But if they're knights, the laws of knighthood make it absolutely illegal, without exception, for you to help me, unless you yourself have been ordained a knight."

"Don't worry, your grace," answered Sancho Panza. "You'll find me completely obedient about this, especially since I'm a very peaceful man—I don't like getting myself into quarrels and fights. On the other hand, when it comes to someone laying a hand on me, I won't pay much attention to those laws, because whether   160 they're divine or human they permit any man to defend himself when anyone hurts him."

"To be sure," answered Don Quijote. "But when it comes to helping me against other knights, you must restrain your natural vigor."

"And that's what I'll do," replied Sancho. "I'll observe this rule just as carefully as I keep the Sabbath."

Q What rules of chivalry forbid Sancho's assisting his master in battle, and with what exception?

Rabelais and Montaigne

Another master of vernacular prose, the French humanist François Rabelais (1495–1553), mocked the obsolete values of European society. Rabelais drew upon his experiences as a monk, a student of law, a physician, and a specialist in human affairs to produce *Gargantua and Pantagruel*, an irreverent satire filled with biting allusions to contemporary institutions and customs. The world of the two imaginary giants, Gargantua and Pantagruel, is one of fraud and folly drawn to fantastic dimensions. It is blighted by the absurdities of war, the evils of law and medicine, and the failure of Scholastic education. To remedy the last, Rabelais advocates education based on experience and action, rather than rote memorization. In the imaginary abbey of Thélème, the modern version of a medieval monastery, he pictures a coeducational commune in which well-bred men and women are encouraged to live as they please. *Gargantua and Pantagruel* proclaims Rabelais' faith in the ability of educated individuals to follow their best instincts for establishing a society free from religious prejudice, petty abuse, and selfish desire.

The French humanist Michel de Montaigne (1533–1592) was neither a satirist nor a reformer, but an educated aristocrat who believed in the paramount importance of cultivating good judgment. Trained in Latin, Montaigne was one of the leading proponents of Classical learning in Renaissance France. He earned universal acclaim as the "father" of the personal **essay**, a short piece of expository prose that examines a single subject or idea. The essay—the word comes from the French *essayer* ("to try")—is a vehicle for probing or "trying out" ideas.

Montaigne regarded his ninety-four vernacular French essays as studies in autobiographical reflection—in them, he confessed, he portrayed himself. Addressing such subjects as virtue, friendship, old age, education, and idleness, he examined certain fundamentally humanistic ideas: that contradiction is a characteristically human trait, that self-examination is the essence of true education, that education should enable us to live more harmoniously, and that skepticism and open-mindedness are sound alternatives to dogmatic opinion. Like Rabelais, Montaigne defended a kind of teaching that posed questions rather than provided answers. In his essay on the education of children, he criticized teachers who might pour information into students' ears "as though they were pouring water into a funnel" and then demand that students repeat that information instead of exercising original thought.

Science and Technology

1556	Georg Agricola (German) publishes *On the Principles of Mining*
1571	Ambroise Paré (French) publishes five treatises on surgery
1587	Conrad Gesner (Swiss) completes his *Historiae Animalum*, the first zoological encyclopedia
1596	Sir John Harington (English) invents the "water closet," providing indoor toilet facilities

Reflecting on the European response to overseas expansion (see chapter 18), Montaigne examined the ways in which behavior and belief vary from culture to culture. In his essay *On Cannibals*, a portion of which appears below, he weighted the reports of "New World" barbarism and savagery against the morals and manners of "cultured" Europeans. War, which he calls the "human disease," he finds less vile among "barbarians" than among Europeans, whose warfare is motivated by colonial expansion. Balancing his own views with those of Classical Latin writers, whom he quotes freely throughout his essays, Montaigne questions the superiority of any one culture over another. Montaigne's essays, an expression of reasoned inquiry into human values, constitute the literary high-water mark of the French Renaissance.

READING 19.5 From Montaigne's *On Cannibals* (1580)

I had with me for a long time a man who had lived for ten or twelve years in that other world which has been discovered in our century, in the place where Villegaignon landed, and which he called Antarctic France.[1] This discovery of a boundless country seems worthy of consideration. I don't know if I can guarantee that some other such discovery will not be made in the future, so many personages greater than ourselves having been mistaken about this one. I am afraid we have eyes bigger than our stomachs, and more curiosity than capacity. We embrace everything, but we clasp only wind. . . .

This man I had was a simple, crude fellow—a character fit to bear true witness; for clever people observe more things and more curiously, but they interpret them; and to lend weight and conviction to their interpretation, they cannot help altering history a little. They never show you things as they are, but bend and disguise them according to the way they have seen them; and to give credence to their judgment and attract you to it, they are prone to add

[1] *La France antartique* was the French term for South America. In 1555, Nicolaus Durard de Villegaignon founded a colony on an island in the Bay of Rio de Janeiro, Brazil. The colony collapsed some years later, and many of those who had lived there returned to France.

something to their matter, to stretch it out and amplify it. We need a man either very honest, or so simple that he has not the stuff to build up false inventions and give them plausibility; and wedded to no theory. Such was my man; and besides this, he at various times brought sailors and merchants, whom he had known on that trip, to see me. So I content myself with his information, without inquiring what the cosmographers say about it.

We ought to have topographers who would give us an exact account of the places where they have been. But because they have over us the advantage of having seen Palestine, they want to enjoy the privilege of telling us news about all the rest of the world. I would like everyone to write what he knows, and as much as he knows, not only in this, but in all other subjects; for a man may have some special knowledge and experience of the nature of a river or a fountain, who in other matters knows only what everybody knows. However, to circulate this little scrap of knowledge, he will undertake to write the whole of physics. From this vice spring many great abuses.

Now to return to my subject, I think there is nothing barbarous and savage in that nation, from what I have been told, except that each man calls barbarism whatever is not his own practice; for indeed it seems we have no other test of truth and reason than the example and pattern of the opinions and customs of the country we live in. *There* is always the perfect religion, perfect government, the perfect and accomplished manners in all things. Those people are wild, just as we call wild the fruits that Nature has produced by herself and in her normal course; whereas really it is those that we have changed artificially and led astray from the common order, that we should rather call wild. The former retain alive and vigorous their genuine, their most useful and natural, virtues and properties, which we have debased in the latter in adapting them to gratify our corrupted taste. And yet for all that, the savor and delicacy of some uncultivated fruits of those countries is quite as excellent, even to our taste, as that of our own. It is not reasonable that art should win the place of honor over our great and powerful mother Nature. We have so overloaded the beauty and richness of her works by our inventions that we have quite smothered her. Yet wherever her purity shines forth, she wonderfully puts to shame our vain and frivolous attempts

> *Ivy comes readier without our care;*
> *In lonely caves the arbutus grows more fair;*
> *No art with artless bird song can compare.*
> Propertius

All our efforts cannot even succeed in reproducing the nest of the tiniest little bird, its contexture, its beauty and convenience; or even the web of the puny spider. All things, say Plato, are produced by nature, by fortune, or by art; the greatest and most beautiful by one or the other of the first two, the least and most imperfect by the last.

These nations, then, seem to me barbarous in this sense, that they have been fashioned very little by the human mind, and are still very close to their original naturalness. The laws of nature still rule them, very little corrupted by ours, and they are in such a state of purity that I am sometimes vexed that they were unknown earlier, in the days when there were men able to judge them better than we. I am sorry that Lycurgus[2] and Plato did not know of them; for it seems to me that what we actually see in these nations surpasses not only all the pictures in which poets have idealized the golden age and all their inventions in imagining a happy state of man, but also the conceptions and the very desire of philosophy. They could not imagine a naturalness so pure and simple as we see by experience; nor could they believe that our society could be maintained with so little artifice and human solder. This is a nation, I should say to Plato, in which there is no sort of traffic, no knowledge of letters, no science of numbers, no name for a magistrate or for political superiority, no custom of servitude, no riches or poverty, no contracts, no successions, no partitions, no occupations but leisure ones, no care for any but common kinship, no clothes, no agriculture, no metal, no use of wine or wheat. The very words that signify lying, treachery, dissimulation, avarice, envy, belittling, pardon—unheard of. How far from this perfection would he find the republic that he imagined:

> *Men fresh sprung from the gods*
> Seneca

. . . .

They have their wars with the nations beyond the mountains, further inland, to which they go quite naked, with no other arms than bows or wooden swords ending in a sharp point, in the manner of the tongues of our boar spears. It is astonishing what firmness they show in their combats, which never end but in slaughter and bloodshed; for as to routs and terror, they know nothing of either.

Each man brings back as his trophy the head of the enemy he has killed, and sets it up at the entrance to his dwelling. After they have treated their prisoners well for a long time with all the hospitality they can think of, each man who has a prisoner calls a great assembly of his acquaintances. He ties a rope to one of the prisoner's arms, by the end of which he holds him, a few steps away, for fear of being hurt, and gives his dearest friend the other arm to hold in the same way; and these two, in the presence of the whole assembly, kill him with their swords. This done, they roast him and eat him in common and send some pieces to the absent friends. This is not, as people think, for nourishment, as of old the Scythians used to do; it is to betoken an extreme revenge.[3] And the proof of this came when they saw the Portuguese, who had joined forces with their adversaries, inflict a different kind of death on them when they took them prisoner, which was to bury them up to the waist, shoot the rest of their body full of arrows, and

---

[2] The legendary lawgiver of ancient Sparta.
[3] Montaigne overlooks the fact that ritual cannibalism might also involve the will to consume the power of the opponent, especially if he were a formidable opponent.

afterward hang them. They thought that these people from the other world, being men who had sown the knowledge of many vices among their neighbors and were much greater masters than themselves in every sort of wickedness, did not adopt this sort of vengeance without some reason, and that it must be more painful than their own; so they began to give up their old method and to follow this one.

I am not sorry that we notice the barbarous horror of such acts, but I am heartily sorry that, judging their faults rightly, we should be so blind as to our own. I think there is more barbarity in eating a man alive than in eating him dead; and in tearing by tortures and the rack a body still full of feeling, in roasting a man bit by bit, in having him bitten and mangled by dogs and swine (as we have not only read but seen within fresh memory, not among ancient enemies, but among neighbors and fellow citizens, and what is worse, on the pretext of piety and religion), than in roasting and eating him after he is dead.

Indeed, Chrysippus and Zeno, heads of the Stoic sect, thought there was nothing wrong in using our carcasses for any purpose in case of need, and getting nourishment from them; just as our ancestors, when besieged by Caesar in the city of Alésia, resolved to relieve their famine by eating old men, women, and other people useless for fighting.

The Gascons once, 'tis said, their life renewed
By eating of such food.

Juvenal

And physicians do not fear to use human flesh in all sorts of ways for our health, applying it either inwardly or outwardly. But there never was any opinion so disordered as to excuse treachery, disloyalty, tyranny, and cruelty, which are our ordinary vices.

So we may well call these people barbarians, in respect of the rules of reason, but not in respect of ourselves, who surpass them in every kind of barbarity.

Their warfare is wholly noble and generous, and as excusable and beautiful as this human disease can be; its only basis among them is their rivalry in valor. They are not fighting for the conquest of new lands, for they still enjoy that natural abundance that provides them without toil and trouble with all necessary things in such profusion that they have no wish to enlarge their boundaries. They are still in that happy state of desiring only as much as their natural needs demand; any thing beyond that is superfluous to them.

Q "Each man calls barbarism whatever is not his own practice," writes Montaigne. What illustrations does he offer? Does this claim hold true in our own day and age?

Figure 19.17 DROESHOUT, first Folio edition portrait of William Shakespeare, 1623.

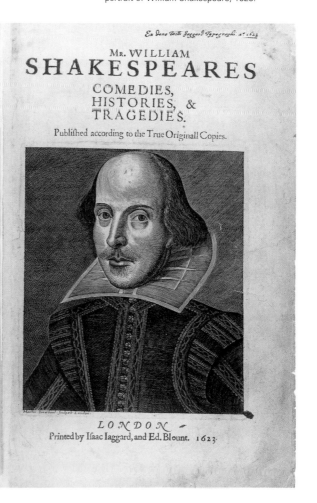

To the Reader.

This Figure, that thou here seest put,
    It was for gentle Shakespeare cut;
Wherein the Grauer had a strife
    with Nature, to out-doo the life :
O, could he but haue drawne his wit
    As well in brasse, as he hath hit
His face ; the Print would then surpasse
    All, that was euer writ in brasse.
But, since he cannot, Reader, looke
    Not on his Picture, but his Booke.

B. I.

MR. WILLIAM
SHAKESPEARES
COMEDIES,
HISTORIES, &
TRAGEDIES.
Published according to the True Originall Copies.

LONDON
Printed by Isaac Iaggard, and Ed. Blount. 1623.

Shakespeare

No assessment of the early Modern Era would be complete without some consideration of the literary giant of the age: William Shakespeare (1564–1616; Figure **19.17**). A poet of unparalleled genius, Shakespeare emerged during the golden age of England under the rule of Elizabeth I (1533–1603). He produced thirty-seven plays—comedies, tragedies, romances, and histories—as well as 154 sonnets and other poems. These works, generally considered to be the greatest examples of English literature, have exercised an enormous influence on the evolution of the English language and the development of the Western literary tradition.*

Little is known about Shakespeare's early life and formal education. He grew up in Stratford-upon-Avon in the English Midlands, married Anne Hathaway (eight years his senior), with whom he had three children, and moved to London sometime before 1585. In London, a city of some 80,000 inhabitants, he formed an acting company, the Lord Chamberlain's Company (also called "the King's Men"), in which he was shareholder, actor, and playwright. Like fifteenth-century Florence, sixteenth-century London (and especially the queen's court) supported a galaxy of artists, musicians, and writers who enjoyed a mutually stimulating interchange of ideas. Shakespeare's theater company performed at the court of Elizabeth I and that of her successor James I (1566–1625). But its main activities took place in the Globe, one of a handful of playhouses built just outside London's city limits—along with brothels and taverns, theaters were generally relegated to the suburbs.

Shakespeare's Sonnets

While Shakespeare is best known for his plays, he also wrote some of the most beautiful sonnets ever produced in the English language. Indebted to Petrarch, Shakespeare nevertheless devised most of his own sonnets in a form that would come to be called "the English sonnet": **quatrains** (four-line stanzas) with alternate rhymes, followed by a concluding **couplet**. Shakespeare's sonnets employ—and occasionally mock—such traditional Petrarchan themes as the blind devotion of the unfortunate lover, the value of friendship, and love's enslaving power. Some, like Sonnet 18, reflect the typically Renaissance (and Classical) concern for immortality achieved through art and love. In Sonnet 18, Shakespeare contrives an extended metaphor: like the summer day, his beloved will fade and die. But, exclaims the poet, she will remain eternal in and through the sonnet; for, so long as the poem survives, so will the object of its inspiration remain alive. Stripped of sentiment, Sonnet 116 states the unchanging nature of love; Shakespeare exalts the "marriage of true minds" that most Renaissance humanists perceived as only possible among men. Sonnet 130, on the other hand, pokes fun at the literary conventions of the Petrarchan love sonnet. Satirizing

* The complete works of Shakespeare are available at the following website: http://shakespeare.mit.edu/works.html

the fair-haired, red-lipped heroine as object of desire, Shakespeare celebrates the real—though somewhat ordinary—features of his beloved.

READING 19.6 From Shakespeare's Sonnets (1609)

Sonnet 18

Shall I compare thee to a summer's day?	1
Thou art more lovely and more temperate.	
Rough winds do shake the darling buds of May,	
And summer's lease[1] hath all too short a date.	
Sometime too hot the eye[2] of heaven shines,	5
And often is his gold complexion dimm'd;	
And every fair from fair sometime declines,[3]	
By chance or nature's changing course untrimm'd;[4]	
But thy eternal summer shall not fade	
Nor lose possession of that fair thou ow'st,	10
Nor shall Death brag thou wand'rest in his shade,	
When in eternal lines to time thou grow'st.[5]	
So long as men can breathe or eyes can see,	
So long lives this[6] and this gives life to thee.	

Sonnet 116

Let me not to the marriage of true minds	1
Admit impediments. Love is not love	
Which alters when it alteration finds,	
Nor bends with the remover to remove.[7]	
O, no, it is an ever-fixed mark,[8]	5
That looks on tempests and is never shaken;	
It is the star to every wand'ring bark,	
Whose worth's unknown, although his height be taken.[9]	
Love's not Time's fool, though rose lips and cheeks	
Within his bending sickle's compass come;	10
Love alters not with his brief hours and weeks,	
But bears it out even to the edge of doom.[10]	
If this be error, and upon me proved,	
I never writ, nor no man ever loved.	

Sonnet 130

My mistress' eyes are nothing like the sun;	1
Coral is far more red than her lips' red:	
If snow be white, why then her breasts are dun;	
If hairs be wires, black wires grow on her head.	
I have seen roses damasked, red and white,	5
But no such roses see I in her cheeks;	
And in some perfumes is there more delight	

[1] Allotted time.
[2] The sun.
[3] Beautiful thing from beauty.
[4] Stripped of beauty.
[5] Your fame will grow as time elapses.
[6] The sonnet itself.
[7] Changes as the beloved changes.
[8] Sea mark, an aid to navigation.
[9] Whose value is beyond estimation.
[10] Endures to the very Day of Judgment.

Figure 19.18 GEORGE GOWER, *"Armada" Portrait of Elizabeth I*, ca. 1588. Oil on panel, 3 ft 6 in × 4 ft 5 in. Bedecked with jewels, the queen rests her hand on the globe, an allusion to its circumnavigation by her vice-admiral, Sir Francis Drake. In the background at the right, the Spanish Armada sinks into the Atlantic amidst the "Protestant winds" of a fierce storm.

> Than in the breath that from my mistress reeks.
> I love to hear her speak, yet well I know
> That music hath a far more pleasing sound: **10**
> I grant I never saw a goddess go,—
> My mistress, when she walks, treads on the ground:
>   And yet, by heaven, I think my love as rare
>   As any she belied with false compare.

Q **What does each of these sonnets convey about the nature of love?**

The Elizabethan Stage

In the centuries following the fall of Rome, the Church condemned all forms of pagan display, including the performance of comedies and tragedies. Tragedy, in the sense that it was defined by Aristotle ("the imitation of an action" involving "some great error" made by an extraordinary man), was philosophically incompatible with the medieval world-view, which held that all events were pre-determined by God. If redemption was the goal of Christian life, there was no place for literary tragedy in the Christian cosmos. (Hence Dante's famous journey, though far from humorous, was called a "comedy" in acknowledgment of its "happy" ending in Paradise.) Elizabethan poets revived secular drama, adapting Classical and medieval texts to the writing of contemporary plays. While the context and the characters of such plays might be Christian, the plot and the dramatic action were secular in focus and in spirit.

The rebirth of secular drama, Renaissance England's most original contribution to the humanistic tradition, unfolded during an era of high confidence. In 1588, the English navy defeated a Spanish fleet of 130 ships known as the "Invincible Armada." The victory gave clear advantage to England as the dominant commercial power in the Atlantic. The routing of the Spanish Armada was a victory as well for the partisans of Protestantism over Catholicism. It encouraged a sense of national pride that found its counterpart in a revival of interest in English history and its theatrical recreation. It also contributed to a renewed spirit of confidence in the ambitious policies of the "Protestant Queen," Elizabeth I (Figure **19.18**). In its wake followed a period of high prosperity, commercial expansion, and cultural vitality, all of which converged in London.

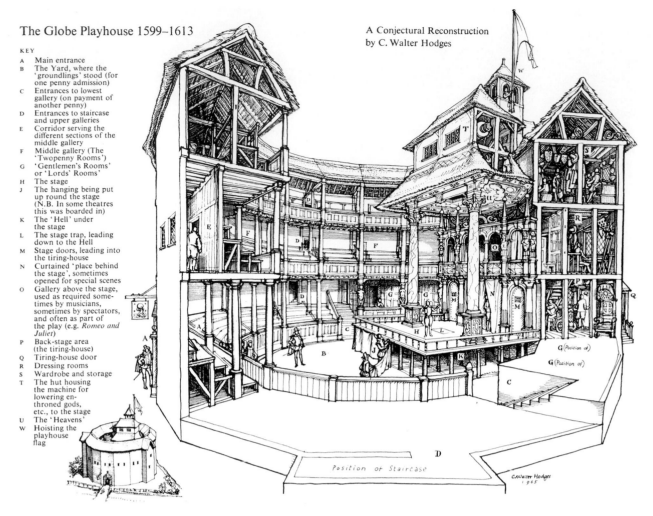

The Globe Playhouse 1599–1613

A Conjectural Reconstruction
by C. Walter Hodges

KEY

A Main entrance
B The Yard, where the 'groundlings' stood (for one penny admission)
C Entrances to lowest gallery (on payment of another penny)
D Entrances to staircase and upper galleries
E Corridor serving the different sections of the middle gallery
F Middle gallery (The 'Twopenny Rooms')
G 'Gentlemen's Rooms' or 'Lords' Rooms'
H The stage
J The hanging being put up round the stage (N.B. In some theatres this was boarded in)
K The 'Hell' under the stage
L The stage trap, leading down to the Hell
M Stage doors, leading into the tiring-house
N Curtained 'place behind the stage', sometimes opened for special scenes
O Gallery above the stage, used as required sometimes by musicians, sometimes by spectators, and often as part of the play (e.g. Romeo and Juliet)
P Back-stage area (the tiring-house)
Q Tiring-house door
R Dressing rooms
S Wardrobe and storage
T The hut housing the machine for lowering enthroned gods, etc., to the stage
U The 'Heavens'
W Hoisting the playhouse flag

Figure 19.19 Globe playhouse, London, 1599–1613. Architectural reconstruction by **C. WALTER HODGES**, 1948.

Elizabethan London played host to groups of traveling actors (or "strolling players") who performed in public spaces or for generous patrons. In the late sixteenth century, a number of playhouses were built along the Thames River across from the city of London. Begun in 1599, the Globe, which held between 2,000 and 3,000 spectators, offered all levels of society access to professional theater (Figure **19.19**). The open-air structure consisted of three tiers of galleries and standing room for commoners (known as "groundlings") at the cost of only a penny—one-sixth of the price of a seat in the covered gallery. The projecting, rectangular stage, some 40 feet wide, included balconies (for musicians and special scenes such as required in *Romeo and Juliet*), exits to dressing areas, and a trapdoor (used for rising spirits and for burial scenes, such as required in *Hamlet*). Stage props were basic, but costumes were favored, and essential for the male actors who played the female roles—women were not permitted on the public stage. Performances were held in the afternoon and advertised by flying a flag above the theater roof. A globe, the signature logo, embellished the theater, along with a sign that read "*Totus mundus agit histrionem*" (loosely, "All the World's a Stage"). The bustling crowd that attended the theater—some of whom stood through two or more hours of performance—often ate and drank as they enjoyed the most cosmopolitan entertainment of their time. A reconstruction of the Globe playhouse, located on the south bank of the Thames River, opened in 1997.

Shakespeare's Plays

In Shakespeare's time, theater ranked below poetry as a literary genre. As popular entertainment, however, Shakespeare's plays earned high acclaim in London's theatrical community. Thanks to the availability of printed editions, the Bard of Stratford was familiar with the tragedies of Seneca and the comedies of Plautus and Terence. He knew the popular medieval morality plays that addressed the contest between good and evil, as well as the popular improvisational form of Italian comic theater known as the *commedia dell'arte*, which made use of stock or stereotypical characters. All of these resources came to shape the texture of his plays. For his plots, Shakespeare drew largely on Classical history, medieval chronicles, and contemporary romances.

Like Machiavelli, Shakespeare was an avid reader of ancient and medieval history, as well as a keen observer of his own complex age; but the stories his sources provided became mere springboards for the exploration of human nature. His history plays, such as *Henry V* and *Richard III*, celebrate England's medieval past and its rise to power under the Tudors. The concerns of these plays, however, are not exclusively historical; rather, they explore the ways in which individuals behave under pressure: the weight of kingly responsibilities on mere humans and the difficulties of reconciling royal obligations and human aspirations.

Shakespeare's comedies, which constitute about one-half of his plays, deal with such popular themes as the battle of the sexes, rivalry among lovers, and mistaken identities. But here too, in such plays as *Much Ado About Nothing*, *All's Well That Ends Well*, and *The Taming of the Shrew*, it is Shakespeare's characters—their motivations exposed, their weaknesses and strengths laid bare—that command our attention.

It is in the tragedies, and especially the tragedies of his mature career—*Hamlet*, *Macbeth*, *Othello*, and *King Lear*—that Shakespeare achieved the concentration of thought and language that have made him the greatest English playwright of all time. Human flaws and failings—jealousy, greed, ambition, insecurity, and self-deception—give substance to most of Shakespeare's plays, but in these last tragedies they become definitive: they drive the action of the play. They are, in short, immediate evidence of the playwright's efforts to probe the psychological forces that motivate human action.

No discussion of Shakespeare's plays can substitute for the experience of live performance. Yet, in focusing on two of the late tragedies, *Hamlet* and *Othello*, it is possible to isolate Shakespeare's principal contributions to the humanistic tradition. These lie in the areas of character development and in the brilliance of the language with which characters are brought to life. Despite occasional passages in prose and rhymed verse, Shakespeare's plays were written in **blank verse**. This verse form was popular among Renaissance writers because, like Classical poetry, it was unrhymed, and it closely approximated the rhythms of vernacular speech. In Shakespeare's hands, the English language took on a breadth of expression and a majesty of eloquence that has rarely been matched to this day.

Shakespeare's *Hamlet*

Hamlet, the world's most quoted play, belongs to the popular Renaissance genre of revenge tragedy; the story itself came to Shakespeare from the history of medieval Denmark. Hamlet, the young heir to the Danish throne, learns that his uncle has murdered his father and married his mother in order to assume the throne; the burden of avenging his father falls squarely on his shoulders. The arc of the play follows Hamlet's inability to take action—his melancholic lack of resolve that, in due course, results in the deaths of his mother (Gertrude), his betrothed (Ophelia), her father (Polonius), the king (Claudius), and, finally, Hamlet himself.

Shakespeare's protagonist differs from the heroes of ancient and medieval times: Hamlet lacks the sense of obligation to country and community, the religious loyalties, and the clearly defined spiritual values that impassioned Gilgamesh, Achilles, and Roland. He represents a new, more modern personality, afflicted by a self-questioning and

brooding skepticism. Though sunk in melancholy, he shares Pico della Mirandola's view (see Reading 16.4) that human nature is freely self-formed by human beings themselves. Hamlet marvels, "What a piece of work is a man! How noble in reason! How infinite in faculty! In form and moving how express and admirable! In action how like an angel! In apprehension how like a god! The beauty of the world! The paragon of animals." Nevertheless he concludes on a note of utter skepticism, "And yet, to me, what is this quintessence of dust?" (Act II, ii, ll. 303–309). It is in the oral examination of his innermost thoughts—the *soliloquy*—that Hamlet most fully reveals himself. He questions the motives for meaningful action and the impulses that prevent him from action; at the same time, he contemplates the futility of all human action.

READING 19.7 From Shakespeare's *Hamlet* (1602)

***Hamlet*, Act III, Scene 1**
Enter King, Queen, Polonius, Ophelia, Rosencrantz, Guildenstern, lords.

King: And can you by no drift of conference   1
    Get from him why he puts on this confusion,
    Grating so harshly all his days of quiet
    With turbulent and dangerous lunacy?
Rosencrantz: He does confess he feels himself distracted,
    But from what cause 'a will by no means speak.
Guildenstern: Nor do we find him forward to be sounded,
    But with a crafty madness keeps aloof
    When we would bring him on to some confession
    Of his true state.
Queen: Did he receive you well?   10
Rosencrantz: Most like a gentleman.
Guildenstern: But with much forcing of his disposition.
Rosencrantz: Niggard of question, but of our demands
    Most free in his reply.
Queen: Did you assay him
    To any pastime?
Rosencrantz: Madam, it so fell out that certain players
    We o'erraught on the way. Of these we told him,
    And there did seem in him a kind of joy
    To hear of it. They are here about the court,
    And, as I think, they have already order   20
    This night to play before him.
Polonius: 'Tis most true,
    And he beseeched me to entreat Your Majesties
    To hear and see the matter.
King: With all my heart, and it doth much content me
    To hear him so inclined.
    Good gentlemen, give him a further edge

III.1. Location: The castle.
1 drift of conference directing of conversation **7 forward** willing
Sounded questioned **12 disposition** inclination **13 Niggard** stingy
question conversation **14 assay** try to win **17 o'erraught** overtook
26 edge incitement

And drive his purpose into these delights.

Rosencrantz: We shall, my lord.

Exeunt Rosencrantz and Guildenstern.

King: Sweet Gertrude, leave us too,
For we have closely sent for Hamlet hither,
That he, as 'twere by accident, may here   30
Affront Ophelia.
Her father and myself, lawful espials,
Will so bestow ourselves that seeing, unseen,
We may of their encounter frankly judge,
And gather by him, as he is behaved,
If 't be th' affliction of his love or no
That thus he suffers for.

Queen: I shall obey you.
And for your part, Ophelia, I do wish
That your good beauties be the happy cause
Of Hamlet's wildness. So shall I hope your virtues   40
Will bring him to his wonted way again,
To both your honors.

Ophelia: Madam, I wish it may.

[Exit Queen.]

Polonius: Ophelia, walk you here.—Gracious, so please you,
We will bestow ourselves. [*To Ophelia.*] Read on this
   book,   [*giving her a book*]
That show of such an exercise may color
Your loneliness. We are oft to blame in this—
'Tis too much proved—that with devotion's visage
And pious action we do sugar o'er
The devil himself.

King [*aside*]:   O, 'tis too true!   50
How smart a lash that speech doth give my conscience!
The harlot's cheek, beautied with plastering art,
Is not more ugly to the thing that helps it
Than is my deed to my most painted word.
O heavy burden!

Polonius: I hear him coming. Let's withdraw, my lord.

[The King and Polonius withdraw.]

Enter Hamlet. [*Ophelia pretends to read a book.*]

Hamlet: To be, or not to be, that is the question:
Whether 'tis nobler in the mind to suffer
The slings and arrows of outrageous fortune,
Or to take arms against a sea of troubles   60
And by opposing end them. To die, to sleep—
No more—and by a sleep to say we end
The heartache and the thousand natural shocks
That flesh is heir to. 'Tis a consummation
Devoutly to be wished. To die, to sleep;
To sleep, perchance to dream. Ay, there's the rub,

For in that sleep of death what dreams may come,
When we have shuffled off this mortal coil,
Must give us pause. There's the respect
That makes calamity of so long life.   70
For who would bear the whips and scorns of time,
Th' oppressor's wrong, the proud man's contumely,
The pangs of disprized love, the law's delay,
The insolence of office, and the spurns
That patient merit of th' unworthy takes,
When he himself might his quietus make
With a bare bodkin? Who would fardels bear,
To grunt and sweat under a weary life,
But that the dread of something after death,
The undiscovered country from whose bourn   80
No traveler returns, puzzles the will,
And makes us rather bear those ills we have
Than fly to others that we know not of?
Thus conscience does make cowards of us all;
And thus the native hue of resolution
Is sicklied o'er with the pale cast of thought,
And enterprises of great pitch and moment
With this regard their currents turn awry
And lose the name of action.—Soft you now,
The fair Ophelia. Nymph, in thy orisons   90
Be all my sins remembered.

Ophelia: Good my lord,
How does your honor for this many a day?

Hamlet: I humbly thank you; well, well, well.

Ophelia: My lord, I have remembrances of yours,
That I have longèd long to redeliver.
I pray you, now receive them.   [*She offers tokens.*]

Hamlet: No, not I, I never gave you aught.

Ophelia: My honored lord, you know right well you did,
And with them words of so sweet breath composed
As made the things more rich. Their perfume lost,   100
Take these again, for to the noble mind
Rich gifts wax poor when givers prove unkind.
There, my lord.   [*She gives tokens.*]

Hamlet: Ha, ha! Are you honest?

Ophelia: My lord?

Hamlet: Are you fair?

Ophelia: What means your lordship?

Hamlet: That if you be honest and fair, your honesty
   should admit no discourse to your beauty.

---

29 closely privately **31 Affront** confront, meet **32 espials** spies **41 wonted** accustomed **43 Gracious** Your Grace (i.e., the king) **44 bestow** conceal **45 exercise** religious exercise (The book she reads is one of devotion) **color** give a plausible appearance to **46 loneliness** being alone **47 too much proved** too often shown to be true, too often practiced **53 to** compared to **the thing** i.e., the cosmetic **56 s.d. withdraw** (The king and Polonius may retire behind an arras. The stage directions specify that they "enter" again near the end of the scene.) **59 slings** missiles **66 rub** (Literally, an obstacle in the game of bowls)

---

68 shuffled sloughed, cast **Coil** turmoil **69 respect** consideration **70 of . . . life** so long-lived, something we willingly endure for so long (alsosuggesting that long life is itself a calamity) **72 contumely** insolent abuse **73 disprized** unvalued **74 office** officialdom **spurns** insults **75 of . . . takes** receives from unworthy persons **76 quietus** acquittance; here, death **77 a bare bodkin** a mere dagger, unsheathed **fardels** burdens **80 bourn** frontier, boundary-Pic credit **85 native hue** natural color, complexion **86 cast** tinge, shade of color **87 pitch** height (as of a falcon's flight) **moment** importance **88 regard** respect, consideration **currents** courses **89 Soft you** i.e., wait a minute, gently **90 orisons** prayers **104 honest** (1) truthful (2) chaste **106 fair** (1) beautiful (2) just, honorable **108 your honesty** your chastity **109 discourse to** familiar dealings with

Ophelia: Could beauty, my lord, have better commerce 110
than with honesty?

Hamlet: Ay, truly, for the power of beauty will sooner
transform honesty from what it is to a bawd than the
force of honesty can translate beauty into his likeness.
This was sometime a paradox, but now the time gives
if proof. I did love you once.

Ophelia: Indeed, my lord, you made me believe so.

Hamlet: You should not have believed me, for virtue
cannot so inoculate our old stock but we shall relish of
it. I loved you not. 120

Ophelia: I was the more deceived.

Hamlet: Get thee to a nunnery. Why wouldst thou be a
breeder of sinners? I am myself indifferent honest, but
yet I could accuse me of such things that it were better
my mother had not borne me: I am very proud,
revengeful, ambitious, with more offenses at my beck
than I have thoughts to put them in, imagination to
give them shape, or time to act them in. What should
such fellows as I do crawling between earth and
heaven? We are arrant knaves all; believe none of us. 130
Go thy ways to a nunnery. Where's your father?

Ophelia: At home, my lord.

Hamlet: Let the doors be shut upon him, that he may
play the fool nowhere but in 's own house. Farewell.

Ophelia: O, help him, you sweet heavens!

Hamlet: If thou dost marry, I'll give thee this plague for
thy dowry: be thou as chaste as ice, as pure as snow,
thou shalt not escape calumny. Get thee to a nunnery,
farewell. Or, if thou wilt needs marry, marry a fool, for
wise men know well enough what monsters you 140
make of them. To a nunnery, go, and quickly too.
Farewell.

Ophelia: Heavenly powers, restore him!

Hamlet: I have heard of your paintings too, well
enough. God hath given you one face, and you make
yourselves another. You jig, you amble, and you
lisp, you nickname God's creatures, and make your
wantonness your ignorance. Go to, I'll no more on 't;
it hath made me mad. I say we will have no more
marriage. Those that are married already—all but 150
one—shall live. The rest shall keep as they are. To a
nunnery, go.   *Exit.*

Ophelia: O, what a noble mind is here o'erthrown!
The courtier's, soldier's, scholar's, eye, tongue,
sword,

Th' expectancy and rose of the fair state,
The glass of fashion and the mold of form,
Th' observed of all observers, quite, quite down!
And I, of ladies most deject and wretched,
That sucked the honey of his music vows,
Now see that noble and most sovereign reason 160
Like sweet bells jangled out of tune and harsh,
That unmatched form and feature of blown youth
Blasted with ecstasy. O, woe is me,
T' have seen what I have seen, see what I see!

Enter King and Polonius.

King: Love? His affections do not that way tend;
Nor what he spake, though it lacked form a little,
Was not like madness. There's something in his soul
O'er which his melancholy sits on brood,
And I do doubt the hatch and the disclose
Will be some danger; which for to prevent, 170
I have in quick determination
Thus set it down: he shall with speed to England
For the demand of our neglected tribute.
Haply the seas and countries different
With variable objects shall expel
This something-settled matter in his heart,
Whereon his brains still beating puts him thus
From fashion of himself. What think you on 't?

Polonius: It shall do well. But yet do I believe
The origin and commencement of his grief 180
Sprung from neglected love.—How now, Ophelia?
You need not tell us what Lord Hamlet said;
We heard it all.—My lord, do as you please,
But, if you hold it fit, after the play
Let his queen-mother all alone entreat him
To show his grief. Let her be round with him;
And I'll be placed, so please you, in the ear
Of all their conference. If she find him not,
To England send him, or confine him where
Your wisdom best shall think.

King: It shall be so. 190
Madness in great ones must not unwatched go. *Exeunt.*

— **Q.** **What profound question does Hamlet
address in his soliloquy?**

— **Q.** **What conclusion does Ophelia reach at
the end of her conversation with Hamlet?**

110–111 commerce dealings, intercourse **114 his** its **115 sometime**
formerly **a paradox** a view opposite to commonly held opinion **the
time** the present age **119 inoculate** graft, be engrafted to **119–120
but . . . it** that we do not still have about us a taste of the old stock,
i.e., retain our sinfulness **122 nunnery** convent (with possibly an
awareness that the word was also used derisively to denote a brothel)
123 indifferent honest reasonably virtuous **126 beck** command **140
monsters** (An illusion to the horns of a cuckold) **you** i.e., you women
146 jig dance **amble** move coyly **147 you nickname . . .creatures**
i.e., you give trendy names to things in place of their God-given names
147–148 make . . . ignorance i.e., excuse your affectation on the
grounds of pretended ignorance **148 on 't** of it

155 expectancy hope   **rose** ornament **156 The glass . . . form** the
mirror of true self-fashioning and the pattern of courtly behavior **157
Th' observed . . . observers** i.e., the center of attention and honorin
the court **159 music** musical, sweetly uttered **162 blown** blooming
163 Blasted withered **ecstasy** madness **165 affections** emotions,
feelings **168 sits on brood** sits like a bird on a nest, about to *hatch*
mischief (line 169) **169 doubt** fear **disclose** disclosure, hatching **172
set it down** resolved **173 For . . . of** to demand **175 variable objects**
various sights and surroundings to divert him **176 This something . . .
heart** the strange matter settled in his heart **177 still** continually **178
From . . . himself** out of his matural manner **185 queen-mother**
queen and mother **186 round** blunt **188 find him not** fails to discover
what is troubling him

Shakespeare's *Othello*

The Tragedy of Othello, the Moor of Venice was based on a story from a collection of tales published in Italy in the sixteenth century. The life of the handsome and distinguished Othello, an African soldier whose leadership in the Venetian wars against the Turks has brought him heroic esteem, takes a tragic turn when his ensign Iago beguiles him into thinking that his beautiful wife Desdemona has betrayed him with another man. Enraged with jealousy, Othello destroys the person he loves most in the world, his wife; and, in the unbearable grief of his error, he takes his own life as well. While Othello's jealousy is the flaw that brings about his doom, it is Iago whose unmitigated evil drives the action of the plot. Conniving Iago is the Machiavellian villain, "a demi-devil," as he is called in the play. In contrast, Desdemona is the paragon of virtue and beauty. Such characters hark back to the allegorical figures in medieval morality plays, but Shakespeare transforms these figures into complex personalities, allowing them full freedom to falter and fail through their own actions.

That Shakespeare made a black man the hero of one of his tragedies is significant, since his treatment of the character seems to have challenged Elizabethan stereotypes. Medieval and Renaissance literature described anyone who was black as vengeful, hot-blooded, and evil, black being the color traditionally associated with the devil. But in Shakespeare's play, the Moor (the Elizabethan name for any African) is unwitting, ingenuous, and pure, while Iago, the white man who confounds him, is the personification of evil. Perhaps more significant than this irony is Shakespeare's implication that underlying the most untainted acts of heroism and the purest emotions of love is the dark possibility of misguided action that leads to self-defeat. Shakespeare's plays generally preach no explicit moral; rather, they suggest that, in a universe in which order and disorder coexist, human choices play a vital and potentially destructive part. The nihilism that darkens *The Tragedy of Othello*, *Macbeth*, and *Hamlet* was unthinkable before the Modern Era.

READING 19.8 From Shakespeare's *Othello* (1604)

***Othello*, Act IV, Scene III**
Enter Othello, Lodovico, Desdemona, Emilia, and Attendants.

Lodovico: I do beseech you, sir, trouble yourself no further.   1
Othello: O, pardon me; 'twill do me good to walk.
Lodovico: Madam, good night. I humbly thank your
   ladyship.
Desdemona: Your honor is most welcome.
Othello: Will you walk, sir?
   O, Desdemona!
Desdemona: My lord?
Othello: Get you to bed on th' instant; I will be return'd
   forthwith. Dismiss your attendant there. Look 't be done.

---

19 stubbornness roughness   **checks** rebukes

IV.iii **Location:** The citadel.
11 incontinent immediately

Desdemona: I will, my lord.
                 Exit [Othello, with Lodovico and Attendants].
Emilia: How goes it now? He looks gentler than he did.   10
Desdemona: He says he will return incontinent,
   And hath commanded me to go to bed,
   And bade me to dismiss you.
Emilia: Dismiss me?
Desdemona: It was his bidding; therefore, good Emilia,
   Give me my nightly wearing, and adieu.
   We must not now displease him.
Emilia: I would you had never seen him!
Desdemona: So would not I. My love doth so approve him,
   That even his stubbornness, his checks, his frowns—
   Prithee unpin me—have grace and favor in them.   20
                 [Emilia prepares Desdemona for bed.]
Emilia: I have laid those sheets you bade me on the bed.
Desdemona: All's one. Good faith, how foolish are our
   minds!
   If I do die before thee, prithee shroud me
   In one of those same sheets.
Emilia: Come, come, you talk.
Desdemona: My mother had a maid call'd Barbary.
   She was in love, and he she lov'd prov'd mad
   And did forsake her. She had a song of "Willow,"
   An old thing 'twas, but it express'd her fortune,
   And she died singing it. That song tonight
   Will not go from my mind; I have much to do   30
   But to go hang my head all at one side
   And sing it like poor Barbary. Prithee, dispatch.
Emilia: Shall I go fetch your nightgown?
Desdemona: No, unpin me here.
   This Lodovico is a proper man.
Emilia: A very handsome man.
Desdemona: He speaks well.
Emilia: I know a lady in Venice would have walk'd barefoot
   to Palestine for a touch of his nether lip.
Desdemona [*Singing*]:
   "The poor soul sat sighing by a sycamore tree,
      Sing all a green willow;   40
   Her hand on her bosom, her head on her knee,
      Sing willow, willow, willow.
   The fresh streams ran by her, and murmur'd her moans;
      Sing willow, willow, willow;
   Her salt tears fell from her, and soft'ned the stones"—
   Lay by these.
[*Singing*]: "Sing willow, willow, willow"—
   Prithee, hie thee; he'll come anon.
[*Singing*] "Sing all a green willow must be my garland.
      Let nobody blame him; his scorn I approve"—   50
   Nay, that's not next.—Hark! Who is 't that knocks?
Emilia: It's the wind.
Desdemona [*Singing*]
   "I call'd my love false love; but what said he then?
      Sing willow, willow, willow;

---

26 mad wild, i.e., faithless   **30–31 I . . . hang** I can scarcely keep myself from hanging   **48 hie thee** hurry

If I court moe women, you'll couch with moe men"—
So, get thee gone; good night. Mine eyes do itch;
Doth that bode weeping?

Emilia: 'Tis neither here nor there.

Desdemona: I have heard it said so. O, these men, these
    men!
    Dost thou in conscience think—tell me, Emilia—
    That there be women do abuse their husbands   60
    In such gross kind?

Emilia: There be some such, no question.

Desdemona: Wouldst thou do such a deed for all the world?

Emilia: Why, would not you?

Desdemona: No, by this heavenly light!

Emilia: Nor I neither by this heavenly light; I might do
    't as well i' th' dark.

Desdemona: Wouldst thou do such a deed for all the
    world?

Emilia: The world's a huge thing. It is a great price
    For a small vice.

Desdemona: Good troth, I think thou wouldst not.

Emilia: By my troth, I think I should; and undo 't when I
    had done. Marry, I would not do such a thing for a joint-   70
    ring, nor for measures of lawn, nor for gowns, petticoats,
    nor caps, nor any petty exhibition; but, for all the whole
    world—'ud's pity, who would not make her husband a
    cuckold to make him a monarch? I should venture
    purgatory for 't.

Desdemona: Beshrew me if I would do such a wrong for the
    whole world.

Emilia: Why, the wrong is but a wrong i' th' world; and

having the world for your labor, 'tis a wrong in your own
world, and you might quickly make it right.   80

Desdemona: I do not think there is any such woman.

Emilia: Yes, a dozen; and as many to th' vantage as
    would store the world they play'd for.
    But I do think it is their husbands' faults
    If wives do fall. Say that they slack their duties,
    And pour our treasures into foreign laps,
    Or else break out in peevish jealousies,
    Throwing restraint upon us? Or say they strike us,
    Or scant our former having in despite?
    Why, we have galls, and though we have some grace,
    Yet have we some revenge. Let husbands know   90
    Their wives have sense like them. They see, and smell,
    And have their palates both for sweet and sour,
    As husbands have. What is it that they do
    When they change us for others? Is it sport?
    I think it is. And doth affection breed it?
    I think it doth. Is 't frailty that thus errs?
    It is so too. And have not we affections,
    Desires for sport, and frailty, as men have?
    Then let them use us well; else let them know,
    The ills we do, their ills instruct us so.   100

Desdemona: Good night, good night. God me such uses
    send,
    Not to pick bad from bad, but by bad mend!   *Exeunt.*

Q. **How do Emilia's views on women as wives compare with those of Desdemona?**

70–71 joint-ring a ring made in separate halves **71 lawn** fine linen **72 exhibition** gift **73 'ud's** i.o., God's **82 to th' vantage** in addition, to boot **store** populate **85 pour . . . laps** i.e., are unfaithful, give what is rightfully ours (semen) to other women **88 scant . . . despite** reduce our allowance to spite us **89 have galls** i.e., are capable of resenting injury and insult **91 sense** physical sense **101 uses** habit, practice **102 Not . . . mend** i.e., not to learn bad conduct from others' badness (as Emilia has suggested women learn from men), but to mend my ways by perceiving what badness is, making spiritual benefit out of evil and adversity

Chronology

1450   Gutenberg perfects the printing press
1517   Luther posts the *Ninety-Five Theses*
1524   German Peasant Revolts
1526   Henry VIII establishes the Anglican Church
1588   England defeats the Spanish Armada

Glossary

blank verse unrhymed lines of iambic pentameter, that is, lines consisting of ten syllables each with accents on every second syllable

chorale a congregational hymn, first sung in the Lutheran church

couplet two successive lines of verse with similar end-rhymes

engraving the process by which lines are incised on a metal plate, then inked and printed; see Figure 19.10

essay a short piece of expository prose that examines a single subject

genre painting art depicting scenes from everyday life; not to be confused with "genre," a term used to designate a particular category in literature or art, such as the essay (in literature) and portraiture (in painting)

picaresque novel a prose genre that narrates the comic misadventures of a roguish hero

quatrain a four-line stanza

woodcut a relief printing process by which all parts of a design are cut away except those that will be inked and printed; see Figure 19.9

LOOKING BACK

The Temper of Reform

- The printing press facilitated the rise of popular education and encouraged individuals to form their own opinions by reading for themselves. The new print technology would be essential to the success of the Protestant Reformation.
- The Netherlandish religious movement known as the *devotio moderna* harnessed the dominant strains of anticlericalism, lay piety, and mysticism, even as it coincided with the revival of Classical studies in Northern Europe.
- Erasmus, the leading Christian humanist, led the critical study of the Bible and writings of the church fathers. Northern humanists brought to their efforts the same intellectual fervor that the Italian humanists had applied to their examination of Plato and Cicero.

The Protestant Reformation

- Across Germany, the sale of indulgences to benefit of the Church of Rome provoked harsh criticism, especially by those who saw the luxuries of the papacy as a betrayal of apostolic ideals.
- Martin Luther was the voice of the Protestant Reformation. In his sermons and essays he criticized the worldliness of the Church and bemoaned "the misery and wretchedness of Christendom."
- Luther's greatest attempt at reforming the Catholic Church came in the form of his *Ninety-Five Theses* (1517), which listed his grievances against the Church and called for reform based on scriptural precedent.
- Luther's teachings, with the aid of the printing press, circulated throughout Europe, giving rise to other Protestant sects, including Calvinism and Anabaptism, and, in England, the Anglican Church.
- The Lutheran chorale became the vehicle of Protestant piety.

Northern Renaissance Art

- Even before the North felt the impact of the Italian Renaissance, Netherlandish artists initiated a painting style rich in realistic detail. Jan van Eyck's pioneering use of thin oil glazes captured the naturalistic effects of light on objects that, while tangible, also functioned as sacred symbols.
- The paintings of Hieronymus Bosch infused traditional religious subjects with a unique combination of moralizing motifs drawn

from illuminated manuscripts, pilgrimage badges, and the popular pseudo-sciences: astrology and alchemy.
- The Protestant Reformation, which rejected relics and sacred images as reflections of superstition and idolatry, favored devotional, and especially biblical, subjects. The two new graphic techniques, woodcutting and engraving, facilitated the mass production of devotional images that functioned as book illustrations and individual prints.
- A growing middle class provided patronage for portraiture, landscapes, and scenes of everyday life, subjects that were pursued by Albrecht Dürer, Lucas Cranach, Hans Holbein, and Pieter Brueghel. Nevertheless, deeply felt religious sentiment persisted in many Northern artworks, such as Matthias Grünewald's rivetingly expressive Isenheim Altarpiece.

Sixteenth-Century Literature

- Northern Renaissance writers took a generally skeptical and pessimistic view of human nature. Erasmus, More, and Rabelais lampooned individual and societal failings and described the ruling influence of folly in all aspects of human conduct.
- In France, Montaigne devised the essay as an intimate form of rational reflection, while in Spain Cervantes' novel, *Don Quixote*, wittily attacked feudal values and outmoded ideals.
- Northern Renaissance literature was, in many ways, a literature of protest and reform, and one whose dominant themes reflect the tension between medieval and modern ideas.

Shakespeare

- Shakespeare emerged during the golden age of England, which flourished under the rule of Elizabeth I. He produced thirty-seven plays—comedies, tragedies, romances, and histories—as well as 154 sonnets and other poems. His work, along with that of other Northern artists and writers, brought the West to the threshold of modernity.
- The most powerful form of literary expression to evolve in the late sixteenth century was secular drama. In the hands of William Shakespeare, Elizabethan drama became the ideal vehicle for exposing the psychological forces that motivate human behavior.

Picture Credits

The author and publishers wish to thank the following for permission to use copyright material. Every effort has been made to trace or contact copyright holders, but if notified of any omissions, Laurence King Publishing would be pleased to insert the appropriate acknowledgement in any subsequent edition of this publication.

Chapter 15

Figure:

15.1 © Photo Scala, Florence.
15.2 By permission of the British Library, London. MS Roy.14.E.IV, f.281v.
15.3 Musée Dobrée, Nantes, France. MS 17, f. 176. Photo: Bridgeman Art Library.
15.4 Bibliothèque Royale, Brussels. MS13076–77, f.24v.
15.5 Library of Congress, Washington, D.C. Lessing J. Rosenwald Collection.
15.6 Bibliothèque Nationale Paris.
15.7 Uffizi Gallery, Florence. © Studio Fotografico Quattrone, Florence.
15.8 Uffizi Gallery, Florence. © 1991 Photo Scala, Florence—courtesy of the Ministero Beni e Att. Culturali.
15.9 © Quattrone, Florence.
15.10 Rheinisches Landesmuseum, Bonn.
15.11 Carthusian Monastery of Champmol, Dijon, France. Photo: Erich Lessing/Art Resource, NY.
15.12 The Metropolitan Museum of Art, New York. The Cloisters Collection, 1954 (54.1.2. ff.15v and 16r).
15.13 Musée Condé, Chantilly, France. Giraudon/Bridgeman Art Library, London.
15.14 San Francesco, Siena, Italy. © 1990, Photo Scala, Florence.
15.15 Louvre, Paris. © Photo Josse, Paris.

Chapter 16

16.1 © Studio Fotografico Quattrone, Florence.
16.2 Sala della Pace, Palazzo Pubblico, Siena, Italy. © Quattrone, Florence.
16.3 © 2009 Board of Trustees, National Gallery of Art, Washington, D.C. Samuel H. Kress Collection.
16.4 Archivi Alinari, Florence.
16.5 and 16.6 Galleria degli Uffizi, Florence. © 1992, Photo Scala, Florence—courtesy of the Ministero Beni e Att. Culturali.
16.7 Scala, Florence.
16.8 © 2009 Board of Trustees, National Gallery of Art, Washington, D.C. Samuel H. Kress Collection.
16.9 Louvre, Paris. © R.M.N.
16.10 The National Museum of Women in the Arts, Washington, DC. Gift of Wallace and Wilhelmina Holladay.

Chapter 17

17.1 Museo dell'Opera del Duomo, Florence. © 1990, Photo Scala, Florence.
17.2 Museo Nazionale del Bargello, Florence. © Studio Fotografico Quattrone, Florence.
17.3 Museo Nazionale del Bargello, Florence. © 1990 Photo Scala, Florence—courtesy of the Ministero Beni e Att. Culturali.

17.4 Uffizi Gallery, Florence. © 1991, Photo Scala, Florence—courtesy of the Ministero Beni e Att. Culturali.
17.5 Uffizi Gallery, Florence. Alinari, Florence.
17.6 AKG Images/A. F. Kersting.
17.8 © 1990, Photo Scala, Florence.
17.9 © Studio Fotografico Quattrone, Florence.
17.10 © 1990, Photo Scala, Florence.
17.11 © Studio Fotografico Quattrone, Florence.
17.12 National Gallery, London.
17.13 Louvre, Paris. Photo: © Studio Fotografico Quattrone, Florence.
17.14 Campo Santi Giovanni e Paolo, Venice. (left image) Angelo Hornak, London.
17.16 © Quattrone, Florence.
17.18 Brancacci Chapel, Santa Maria del Carmine, Florence. Photo: © Studio Fotografico Quattrone, Florence.
17.19 Santa Maria del Carmine, Florence. Photo: © Studio Fotografico Quattrone, Florence.
17.20 Canali Photobank, Capriolo, Italy.
17.21 Museo dell'Opera del Duomo, Florence. © Quattrone, Florence.
17.22 The Royal Collection, Royal Library, Windsor Castle. © 2005 Her Majesty Queen Elizabeth II.
17.23 Biblioteca Ambrosiana, Milan. Codex Atlanticus, f.309v–a.
17.24 Galleria dell'Accademia, Venice.
17.25 Refectory, Santa Maria delle Grazie, Milan. AKG Images, London.
17.26 © Quattrone, Florence.
17.27 © 2009 Board of Trustees, National Gallery of Art, Washington, D.C. Andrew W. Mellon Collection.
17.28 © Photo Vatican Museums.
17.29 Photo: © Vincenzo Pirozzi, Rome.
17.30 Photo: Bridgeman Art Library, London.
17.32 St. Peter's, Rome. © 1990, Photo Scala, Florence.
17.33 © Quattrone, Florence.
17.34 Monumenti Musei e Gallerie Pontificie, Vatican, Rome, Italy. Photo Vatican Museums; A. Bracchetti - P. Zigrossie, March 1992.
17.36 Vatican Museums, Rome.
17.38 Photo: © James Morris, London.
17.39 Galleria dell'Accademia, Venice. © Cameraphoto Arte, Venice.
17.40 Louvre, Paris. Photo: © R.M.N., Paris.
17.41 Uffizi Gallery, Florence. © 1996, Photo Scala, Florence—courtesy of the Ministero Beni e Att. Culturali.
17.42 National Gallery, London.
17.43 The J. Pierpont Morgan Library, New York. © 1990. Art Resource, NY.

Chapter 18

18.1 Dumbarton Oaks Research Library and Collections, Washington, D.C.
18.2 Alcazar, Seville. Photo: Institut Amatller D'Art Hispanic, Barcelona.
18.3 © V&A Images, Victoria and Albert Museum.
18.4 Gavin Hellier/JAI/Corbis.
18.5 © The Trustees of the British Museum.
18.6 © The Trustees of the British Museum.
18.7 Photographic Archives, National Museum of African Art, Smithsonian Institution, Washington, D.C. (neg. no. VIII–58, 4A). Photo: Eliot Elisofon.
18.8 The Metropolitan Museum of Art, New York. The Michael C. Rockefeller Memorial Collection of Primitive Art. Gift of Nelson A. Rockefeller, 1964 (1978.412.435.436).

18.9 Albright-Knox Art Gallery, Buffalo, New York. Sarah Norton Goodyear Fund, 2002.
18.10 The Metropolitan Museum of Art, New York. The Michael C. Rockefeller Memorial Collection of Primitive Art. Bequest of Nelson A. Rockefeller, 1979 (1979.206.83).
18.11 The Metropolitan Museum of Art, New York. The Michael Rockefeller Memorial Collection. Bequest of Nelson A. Rockefeller, 1979. no. 79.206.121.
18.12 Foundation for the Arts Collection 1996.184.FA Dallas Museum of Art.
18.13 Museum für Volkerkunde, Vienna.
18.14 Metropolitan Museum of Art, New York. The Michael C. Rockefeller Memorial Collection of Primitive Art. Gift of Nelson A. Rockefeller.
18.15 American Museum of Natural History, New York. Neg/Transparency No: 4811, courtesy the Library, American Museum of Natural History.
18.16 Photo: Werner Forman Archive, London.
18.17 Museum of Indian Arts and Culture/Laboratory of Anthropology, Santa Fe, New Mexico. Cat. 20420/11. Photo: Blair Clark.
18.18 Courtesy Museum of Northern Arizona, photo archives.
18.19 The Metropolitan Museum of Art, New York. The Jan Mitchell Treasury for Precolumbian works of art in gold (1991.419.58).
18.20 Boston: Little Brown, 1977.
18.21 © Lee Boltin Picture Library, Crotin-on-Hudson, New York.
18.22 © The Trustees of the British Museum.
18.23 © South American Pictures/Tony Morrison, Woodbridge, U.K.
18.24 American Museum of Natural History. Photographer: John Bigelow Taylor.
18.25 National Anthropological Museum, Mexico. Dagli Orti, Paris/Art Archive, London.
18.26 National Anthropological Museum, Mexico.
18.27 Vatican Library, Rome. Codex Borgia, f.56.
18.28 The John Carter Brown Library, Providence, Rhode Island. Photo: AKG, London.

Chapter 19

19.1 Musée de la Ville de Paris, Musée du Petit-Palais, France/ Giraudon/ The Bridgeman Art Library.
19.2 Victoria and Albert Museum.
19.3 © The Trustees of the British Museum.
19.4 City of Bristol Museum and Art Gallery.
19.5 National Gallery, London.
19.6 Image courtesy of the Board of Trustees, National Gallery of Art, Washington.
19.7 © Museo del Prado, Madrid.
19.8 Louvre, Paris. Collection Rothschild. Photo: © R.M.N., Paris.
19.11 Photograph © 2009 Museum of Fine Arts, Boston. Bequest of Francis Bullard, M24884.
19.12 State Museums, Berlin. Photo: B. P. K.
19.13 Musée d'Unterlinden, Colmar, France. Photo: O. Zimmerman.
19.14 © Museo del Prado, Madrid.
19.15 Photo: © 2009 The Detroit Institute of Arts. City of Detroit Purchase. 30.374.
19.16 © The Frick Collection, New York.
19.17 By permission of the Folger Shakespeare Library, Washington, D.C.
19.18 By kind permission of His Grace the Duke of Bedford and the Trustees of the Bedford Estates.
19.19 © Yann Arthus-Bertrand/CORBIS.

Literary Credits

The author and publishers wish to thank the following for permission to use copyright material. Every effort has been made to trace or contact copyright holders, but if notified of any omissions or errors, Laurence King Publishing would be pleased to insert the appropriate acknowledgement in any subsequent edition of this publication.

Chapter 15
READING
15.3 (p. 9): Christine de Pisan, from *The Book of the City of Ladies,* translated by Earl Jeffrey Richards (Persea Books, 1982), © 1982, 1998, by Persea Books Inc. (New York).

15.4 (p. 12): Geoffrey Chaucer, from "Prologue" and "The Miller's Tale" from *The Canterbury Tales of Geoffrey Chaucer*, translated by R. M. Lumiansky (Rinehart, 1954), © 1948 by Simon & Schuster, © renewed by Simon & Schuster.

Chapter 16
16.3 (p. 26): Leon Battista Alberti, from "On the Family" from *The Albertis of Florence*, translated by Guido A. Guarino (Associated University Press, 1971), © Associated University Presses, 1971. Reprinted by permission of the publisher.

(p. 35): Laura Cereta, from "Defense of Liberal Instruction of Women" from *Her Immaculate Hand: Selected Words by and About the Humanists of Quattrocento Italy*, edited by Margaret L. King and Albert Rabil (Pegasus Press, 1997).

16.6 (p. 36): Lucrezia Marinella, from *The Nobility and Excellence of Women, and the Defects and Vices of Men*, edited and translated by Anne Dunhill (University of Chicago Press, 1999). Reprinted by permission of the publisher.

Chapter 17
17.2 (p. 62): Giorgio Vasari, from *The Lives of the Most Excellent Painters, Architects, and Sculptors*, edited by Betty Burroughs (Simon and Schuster, 1946).

(p. 71): Robert J. Clements, *The Poetry of Michelangelo* (New York University Press, 1966).

(p. 76): Roland de Lassus, "My lady, my beloved" , translated by Susan Peach, © Calmann & King, 1998.

Chapter 18
18.1 (p. 86): From *Sundiata: An Epic of Old Mali* (Presence Africaine, 1960). Reprinted by permission of the publisher

18.3 (p. 91): From *African Poetry: An Anthology of Traditional African Poems*, compiled and edited by Ulli Beier (Cambridge University Press, 1966).

18.4 (p. 96): Ibn Battuta, from "Book of Travels" from *The Travels of Ibn Battuta A.D. 1325-1354*, volume IV, translated by H. A. R. Gibb (The Hakluyt Society, 1994). Reprinted by permission of David Higham Associates.

18.7 (p. 110): Hernan Cortés, from *Hernan Cortés: Letters from Mexico*, edited by Anthony Pagden (Yale University Press, 1986).

Chapter 19
19.2 (p. 132): Desiderius Erasmus, from *The Praise of Folly*, translated by Hoyt Hopewell Hudson (Princeton University Press, 1941), © 1941 Princeton University Press, 1969 renewed. Reprinted by permission of the publisher.

19.4 (p. 135): Miguel de Cervantes Saavedra, from *Don Quixote*, translated by Burton Raffel (W.W. Norton, 1996).

19.5 (p. 137): Michel de Montaigne, "On Cannibals" from *The Complete Works of Montaigne: Essays, Travel Journal, Letters*, edited by Donald Frame (Stanford University Press, 1958), copyright 1943 by Donald Frame, copyright 1948, 1957 by the Board of Trustees of the Leland Stanford Junior University. Reprinted by permission of the publisher, www.sup.org.

19.7 (p. 143), and **19.8** (p. 146): William Shakespeare, Footnotes for "Hamlet" and "The Tragedy of Othello" from *The Complete Works of Shakespeare*, Third Edition, edited by David M. Bevington (Scott, Foresman & Company, 1980).

Index

Numbers in **bold** refer to figure numbers. Text excerpts are indicated by (quoted).